The Separation of Heaven and Earth

The Advent of Social Hierarchy and Its Implications

Harold W. Montzka

Order this book online at www.trafford.com
or email orders@trafford.com

Most Trafford titles are also available at major online book retailers.

Printed in North America.

ISBN: 978-1-4269-2516-0 (sc)
ISBN: 978-1-4269-2517-7 (dj)
ISBN: 978-1-4269-4126-9 (e)

Library of Congress Control Number: 2009913767

*Our mission is to efficiently provide the world's finest, most comprehensive
book publishing service, enabling every author to experience success.
To find out how to publish your book, your way, and have it available
worldwide, visit us online at www.trafford.com*

Trafford rev. 8/10/2010

www.trafford.com

North America & international
toll-free: 1 888 232 4444 (USA & Canada)
phone: 250 383 6864 ♦ fax: 812 355 4082

Origin and Development of Religion Revisited

Some time after I took a religion course in a university affiliated with a liberal Christian denomination, I came to a personal faith in Jesus Christ. I remembered very well many of the "intellectual problems" identified in that religion course as obstacles to such a commitment. And while the business of living detained me for quite a while, looking for solutions to those "problems" eventually led me to more than thirty years of study, first independently and then under the influence of several university courses.

The specific questions raised in that religion course were not that difficult to unravel. However, my curiosity always led to a little more reading just to tie up the new loose ends that my reading had revealed for me. First, it was English translations of the mythology of the ancient Near East from clay tablet writing. From there, I sought satisfying interpretations of that mythology; failing that, I attempted to understand the nature of mythology more generally. Two academic disciplines, history of religions and anthropology, agree that mythology that treats origins—of man, of his environment, of his society—often called cosmologies, are important as information in gaining an understanding of the particular society itself.

> Myths of origin have always held a certain fascination for the historian of religions, and for many scholars the creation myth has become the chief mode of entry into a foreign culture. The method is a tried and proven one, and any number of rich studies has come as the result of careful investigation of creations accounts. Certainly there is ample reason why this

> should be so, for the cosmogonic myth is the myth which es-
> tablishes the order of the world and thus has important social,
> material, and economic ramifications as well as deep religious
> significance ... and is accorded special prestige and respect by
> those who live the myth. (Lincoln 1972:121)

At this point I had little idea where my studying would take me. And I can't say that it bothered me. I was just unraveling loose ends; I did not really see how the threads might ever fit together. But as I read on, I noticed that the two academic disciplines mentioned above treat mythology quite differently. From the perspective of history of religions, cosmology—or cosmogonic myth in the quotation above—is a formulation of religious and philosophical thought largely independent from the social structure in which it is found. Therefore, its formulation becomes a historic event, especially if it can be found as cosmology for widespread cultures. For anthropology, mythology is merely the "superstructure" of the social order, the charter for and justification of social inequalities already present within that order. For them, this principle was fixed early and the presence of similar cosmologies in widespread societies is not even mentioned. Neither of them allows for what is obviously going on around us. That is, the struggle to maintain or establish ideals is embodied in our two major competing cosmologies. The future of our society will depend on the outcome of this struggle.

Before going on, it is necessary to point out that the meaning of *myth* used in everyday language—that is, that a myth is a false story—will not suffice. *Myth*, as used in the quotations found within this project, whether in story form or not, is myth precisely because it is (or was) true (that is, believed). Myths of origin, that is, cosmology, tell of the beginning of man, the universe, or a certain social order. Within the definition used here, much of Christianity as well as evolution can be called myth. Christianity contains my myth (what I believe); evolution contains most anthropologists' myth (what they believe). It would be better if another, less loaded word could be found. But *myth* is the word used both in and out of academia. If this troubles you, don't be surprised; even anthropologists are squeamish about having their cherished beliefs labeled myth. But those who take a postmodern philosophical stance have certainly done this. In the course of this book, I have usually avoided the use of the word *myth* precisely because of its negative connotation. When speaking of believed origin stories, the more neutral word *cosmology* will generally be used. Of course, within quotations, the word *myth* will not be changed. Often within the quotations, the word *cosmogony* is used. In this book, the word *cosmogony* has the same meaning as *cosmology*.

Over a period of several years, I began to formulate the concept that by using the efforts of these two disciplines, cultural anthropology and the history of religions, I would be able to construct a hypothesis about the development of religion. Perhaps that hypothesis would be unsuitable to members of both of those disciplines, but it might fit within my own presuppositions. Once this hypothesis began to take shape, I found that my study had been given direction. When I started out, I was often disappointed because I was very inexperienced. But gradually things started to fall into recognizable patterns.

Perhaps the two things I learned from the efforts described above were these: one, there is no end to what might be learned or at least read, and two, presuppositions are very important in determining what one will discover in such a study. Not everyone will be motivated to pursue questions in this manner. For the few who might think they would like to, reading of my adventures might either satisfy them or serve as a guide on their quest.

Be warned: I am an evangelical Christian, but I am not claiming to speak for evangelical Christians. Nor am I attempting to somehow make my hypothesis one that will be acceptable to all evangelicals. For one thing, I am allowing that the archaeological evidence covering the material I have pursued is properly dated. This will turn off some of my potential readers. But I do not know how to approach the data in any other way. I fully realize that the genealogy of Shem in Genesis 11 does not appear to allow time for the dates that archaeology proposes. But does this mean that we cannot study what the field of archaeology has to offer in terms of prehistory? Biblical archaeologists are keen to find the points of agreement between the Old Testament writers and their contemporaries as found by archaeology. It seems reasonable to me that, since they have found these points on which to agree, the work of archaeologists considering earlier sites should not be discarded without seeing where it might take us.

Further, I will not be surprised if some of my conclusions have bothersome theological implications. This is especially true when one learns that there are people, with little technological advancement from our perspective, with a concept of God similar to our own as well as the hope to spend eternity with him. But this is what I have found, and I have attempted to report it accurately.

I've tried to distinguish my presuppositions from those of the authors whose works are used. Presuppositions determine more than what one is looking for. They also help one to recognize what he is looking for when it presents itself. I freely admit that my presuppositions have guided me through this journey. At the heart of it, this is why my understanding of the history of the development of the world's religions is radically different from what one finds in the textbooks of academia. This being said, the data that I have used is almost totally the result of their efforts. Not only that, they have also provided statements and observations along with data that encouraged me and helped me over obstacles that would have otherwise stopped me.

While my study touched more than anthropology, I put most of my recent efforts into that discipline. My interest in anthropology was not a general one; and, as a project, it was once more important to anthropologists than it is now. As expressed earlier, my interest has been the origin and history of religion. However, while anthropology has been less interested in that topic, since the 1960s some in the discipline have turned to find an order in the development of social complexity. Since I have focused on the relationship between the social order and cosmology, these anthropologists' recent pursuits have still attracted my interest. I have used cosmologies as reconstructed from ancient writing and from the ethnographies of contemporary cultures that have remained preliterate.

While anthropology is less interested in the origin of religion than it once was, the subject has not been altogether forgotten. In a chapter of his book, American anthropologist Morton Klass (1995) offered his appreciation of the hazards for an anthropologist raised by the subject of the origin of religion. In this chapter, titled "The Noisome Bog," Klass offers this quotation from Anthony C. Wallace: "It is always difficult to set forth in search of the headwaters of human institutions. The unwary scholar is all too apt to find himself soon mired in a noisome bog of speculations, unable to extricate himself with dignity and subject to stoning by his more prudent colleagues on the bank" (Klass 1995:8). The institution that Klass (and Wallace) was about to consider was religion. Then Klass goes on to point out that the anthropologist's problem is "of our own devising." As Klass saw it, anthropologists want to "distance" themselves from any indication that they personally subscribe to the phenomena whose "origin they seek." And Klass adds that this reluctance is based on the assumption that they are *scientists*. But it is in his third chapter that he gets to what he considers the basis of the real problem for anthropology concerning this subject. It is, how is "religion" to be defined? Klass goes on to explain that most definitions offered by anthropologists are very ethnocentric. Anthropology insists on a definition that allows that religion is a panhuman experience yet different in some specific quality from the worldviews that relate the anthropologist to his own world. While most anthropologists still search for truth within their own materialistic perspectives, a few anthropologists have come to a postmodern perspective and have recognized the tenuousness of their own claim to objectivity. A postmodern perspective denies that there is any final truth. But denying reality to all worldviews, including their own, has not really helped the postmodernist to organize and interpret data about the origin and development of religion in mankind's experience.

The approach used by history of religions is called phenomenological. It differs from anthropology in that it is willing to study phenomena without consideration of its "truth." So the historian of religion is not attempting to discover in what way the material he works with is true or useful. He wants to understand it the way it is. For the anthropologist the stories told within a society have meaning primarily as they relate to some aspect of the social and material culture. Usually it is to explain how it is that some are given special prerogatives. Some also allow that certain beliefs might help the actors through crisis experiences.

The approach of secular academia to the study of religion may be sensitively treated. But whether this approach is evolutionary, psychological, or sociological, it will generally find no place for what we as Christians respect as revelation. This is not because the data of anthropology proves that revelation can be dismissed or for that matter proved. Rather it is a prior commitment to the philosophical stance of rationalism. The very definition of that stance is that all truth must come through reason. True, academia has achieved a platform in which many differing persuasions do participate. But even while doing so, much of secular academia is abrasive to those who do not share a humanistic, materialistic, or evolutionary perspective. My motivation in writing is not to criticize their stances, just to present a stance less hostile to my own perspective. My reader will have to decide if it can stand scrutiny.

In spite of an objective reputation, academia has its own presuppositions. Academics pursue those subjects that are of interest to them and ignore those subjects that are not. Thus, hypotheses not easily comprehended within their presuppositions do not even arise to be considered. It is for this reason that

I consider it worthwhile to offer an interpretation of some of the data concerning religious phenomenon with presuppositions that are not materialistic, humanistic, or evolutionary. However, at the end of this study, I do not claim that I have proved that God revealed himself to mankind before people spread around the globe. The data I am considering does not offer information on which to base such a conclusion. I hope that my study does allow my readers to believe, if they so choose, that 1) at one time all of mankind did know God, and 2) mankind has always been ambivalent in attitude toward God.

As I indicated at the outset, I have been pursuing this study for some time. When I have been asked what I was studying, it has been a real struggle to explain it. I have tried on several occasions to distill my insights into something others could understand. On one hand, I had already spent enough time and emotional energy in this study that organizing and writing down my thoughts seemed a reasonable price to pay. But, on the other hand, I struggled to picture an audience for this writing. It is not likely that all of my thoughts will be easy to understand, especially since they were formed after consideration of material that most of my readers would find unfamiliar. Further, they will likely require the reader to make some reassessment of previously held positions. I have tried to present my arguments clearly, but they are my own. They will be new and, therefore, strange. Assessing different ideas always has been both challenging and threatening to me. I assume that my reader will have some of the same discomfort. In other words, because I am aware that the ideas put forward in this book are unusual to the point of being alien, I have hesitated to attempt to make them public. I have kept the book short. But it still covers a lot of unfamiliar territory. I certainly have not put together all of the data that could be used to make my points.

I do have a couple of friends who, over the years, have challenged me to put my thoughts into writing. My response was usually an articulation of my principal concern: to whom would I write them? However, both of them, without consulting each other, challenged me with these words: "Write them to me." One of these men, Timothy Friberg, is overseas. But even from Indonesia he has been a help and great encouragement. The other, however, has interacted with me on a chapter-by-chapter basis. That person is Steve Monson, a long-time friend. He admitted to some difficulty understanding what I was writing about. But with patience he has been able to decipher my hypothesis. To the extent this book is understandable, it has been the result of Steve's efforts to help me make it that way. I am most indebted to him. He has not only helped me birth this book but has assisted me by proofreading it and getting it ready to make it available to others. My son Tom has also helped me make several chapters more easily understood.

This project would not have been possible without my very patient wife, Marilyn. Not only have I put a lot of time into my studies, but also I am a messy student. My books and photocopies often clutter up much more than my share of our living space.

Contents

God and His World

> ... for although they knew God they did not honor him as God or give thanks to him, but they became futile in their thinking and their senseless minds were darkened. Claiming to be wise, they became fools and exchanged the glory of the immortal God for images resembling mortal man or birds or animals or reptiles. Therefore God gave them up in the lusts of their hearts to impurity, to the dishonoring of their bodies among themselves, because they exchanged the truth about God for a lie and worshiped and served the creature rather than the Creator, who is blessed forever! Amen. (Romans 1:21–25 RSV)

And

> Know therefore that the LORD your God is God, the faithful God who keeps covenant and steadfast love with those who love him and keep his commandments, to a thousand generations. (Deuteronomy 7:9 RSV)

Did you know that at one time, all of mankind knew God? Some do not understand this from the header above, and perhaps it is not what the Apostle Paul had in mind when he penned those words. However, the early chapters of Genesis assure us that after the flood, all of mankind did know God and could interact with him.

But did you also know that there was still evidence of a widespread knowledge of God as late as the beginning of the twentieth century? Very few of my acquaintances have ever heard this. The chapter to follow presents the evidence uncovered by anthropologists of that knowledge along with their reaction to it. However, the premise of the book goes further than that basic point. In it, the argument will be made that a single thought system set aside God, a thought system that can be reconstructed from the written literature of the ancient world and oral literature of recent preliterate societies.

According to Genesis 9:1–3, God, through Noah and his sons, gave mankind a mandate to multiply and fill the earth. At that time he also gave them leave to eat the flesh of all animals. Hunter-gatherers did spread over the whole earth, often using ice-age animals (see endnote Introduction, note 1: Ice age or Pleistocene fauna) that are associated with the Pleistocene, the time period that preceded our own, the Holocene. There are many who interpret Genesis 10 and 11 to mean that mankind began to spread out only after the confusion of languages described in Genesis 11 (see Appendix). But is this the proper interpretation?

Archeology does not support the dates that may be derived from Shem's genealogy. However, since the purpose of this book is to consider the data from anthropology, archaeology, and the history of religions without presuppositions that are hostile to biblical traditions, archaeological dating will not be dismissed without an attempt to understand the implications of that data.

Admittedly, the reader may find the general information presented below new and challenging enough without being led through an organization of this data to make a further point. The point, however, reinforces the premise that mankind did spread over the earth with a useful knowledge of God as the Supreme Being (see endnote Introduction, note 2: Concerning the Supreme Being). The book also identifies the way this knowledge was either diminished or lost in many places. This will be done by means of three interlocking observations.

1) The first observation is the ethnographic evidence uncovered at the end of the nineteenth and during the early twentieth century concerning the existence of "the Supreme Being of the Primitives," along with some discussion of controversies relating to this evidence. Since belief in this Supreme Being was found among very widespread hunter-gatherer groups, it is reasonable to infer that they spread over the earth with this belief. This is certainly not a new observation.

However, it remains little known and is controversial because it contradicts both evolutionary and humanistic assumptions of the academic elite.

2) The second observation is the presence of one recurring cosmological theme in the literature of the ancient societies. In particular, it is the theme of the separation of heaven and earth. But this theme is not limited to ancient societies. Ethnographic reports from several continents reveal that this theme was still current in the last century. Anthropology recognizes that cosmology has sociological implications but is not interested in the distribution of cosmological themes. Their materialistic or sociological assumptions cause them to overlook the possibility that the distribution of cosmological themes may have historical significance. At the same time, those who study mythology without the burden of those assumptions—for instance, the discipline history of religions—find this distribution has important historical implications. An eminent scholar in that field has offered that early farmers held this cosmology, while the previous hunter-gatherers believed in a Supreme Being.

3) The third observation is my own. Simply stated, it is that this one particular cosmological theme, the separation of heaven and earth, was the intellectual argument used to set aside the worship of a moral and providential Supreme Being. Of course, this observation will need support. That support is the main thrust of the book.

If you have a background in anthropology, you will recognize that my third proposition stands much of cultural anthropology on its head by holding to the notion that applied ideas have consequences, even ideas advanced long ago. In other words, my hypothesis is idealist rather than materialist. For example, anthropologists committed to materialistic explanations insist social hierarchy will (indeed must) first be in place; only then can its (false) justification be invented and enforced. For these anthropologists, ideas follow practices, not the reverse.

Within our culture, it is quite natural to us that ideas have consequences. But, amazingly, many in the field of anthropology do not allow this simple observation for any group whose history cannot be documented. This includes all ancient literate societies and all groups, including contemporary ones, who have no written record. If cosmology follows practices and is invented to justify them, then cosmology cannot be used to suggest historical links. Further, since with rare exceptions only material culture can be found by archaeology, the implications of cosmology are not within their purview. Anthropology and its child archaeology are both insulated from idealistic interpretations—archaeology by the nature of its data, anthropology by its self-imposed materialistic approaches.

Yet, in spite of my rejection of its approach, anthropology treats a subject that we will examine closely—the organization of societies. This social organization, referred to in this book as social structure, is the focus of many in both anthropology and archaeology. Not only is an understanding of how and why people have organized in fixed hierarchical social structures of interest to anthropologists, but also such an understanding will help us get a handle on what happened to the knowledge of God as the Supreme Being. This knowledge was certainly absent in both ancient literate societies and in many agricultural societies that have remained preliterate.

In contrast to hierarchical social order, an order in which certain members are privileged because of birth, many of the hunter-gatherer groups are said to be egalitarian. This means that they do not recognize any member of their group as more important because of his parentage. Is it a coincidence that the hunters who recognize the Supreme Being as their god are egalitarian? Although anthropologists have concerned themselves with social order, their materialistic approaches prevent most of them from even framing such a question.

Even so, anthropology has related beliefs, as cosmology, to social structure. The circumstances under which the anthropologist Bronislaw Malinowski articulated the proposition that cosmology justifies social inequalities will be described in Chapter One. Malinowski, however, offered that cosmology was part of the "superstructure" of a society created by that society to justify the social inequalities *already* in place.

Here, the contrast between the approaches of materialistic anthropologists and most academics in the history of religions is obvious. For these anthropologists, social structure is of interest; for many historians of religion, the historical order of the cosmologies demands attention. Although some ethnography written by anthropologists include cosmology, few of them acknowledge that their reports resemble cosmological material from other areas. While many historians of religion search this same ethnographic material to support their insights, they do so with little interest in the implication of the cosmology in any particular social structure.

The understanding that cosmology charters and justifies special status along with ritual responsibilities for a selected few of a society affords cosmology with tools that might be used to change the social order. Most anthropologists have chosen to ignore this possibility. On the other side, those in field of the history of religions look only for a historical relationship between cosmologies. The two disciplines do not communicate with each other, nor do there seem to be brave souls who suggest such a welding of these concepts. Further, because of their differing objectives and approaches, neither have a predisposition to interpret cosmology as a vehicle for change in the social order.

Mircea Eliade, a historian of religions who held a chair at the University of Chicago, contrasted the distribution of the two cosmologies of interest to us. These cosmologies are the one Eliade has identified as the "cosmic hierogamy" and the cosmology in which the Supreme Being created everything. The former—that of the cosmic hierogamy, meaning the marriage of heaven and earth—is the same cosmology that I have identified as the separation of heaven and earth. It should be obvious that Eliade and I disagree as to the meaning of the symbolism in this cosmology, and Eliade has not related these cosmologies to social structure. By contenting himself with historical relationships, he has made the generalization that the Supreme Being was the central figure in the cosmology of the hunter-gatherers, while the separation cosmology became the cosmology of the early farmers.

Chapter Five treats these and other differences in interpretation in some detail. Within the discipline the history of religions, a principal concern has been to understand the symbolism. That is also my goal. But we are obviously on different tracks on our way to uncover that meaning. However, for the present we want to explore some of his insights.

In his *Myth, Dreams, and Mysteries*, Eliade identified the cosmological material found in these ancient literate cultures as cosmic hierogamy. However, in his description of this mythic system, he took no particular note of ancient cultures, but rather described the distribution of this cosmology covering all of history.

> The cosmic hierogamy, the marriage between Heaven and Earth, is a cosmogonic myth of widest distribution. It is found above all in Oceania, from Indonesia to Micronesia; but also in Asia, Africa and the two Americas. This myth is more or

> less similar to that which Hesiod tells us in his *Theogony*. Ouranos, Heaven, unites with Gaia, the Earth, and the divine pair engender the gods, the Cyclops and other monstrous beings. "The holy Heaven is intoxicated (with desire) to penetrate the body of the Earth," says Aeschylus in his Danaids (Nauck fragm. 44). All that exists—the Cosmos, the Gods and Life—takes birth from this marriage. (Eliade 1960:172)

As a historian of religions, Eliade was predisposed not to consider cosmology in its relationship to social structure. As emphasized above, consideration of this possibility may have led him to a different meaning and other significance for this cosmology. However, on the next page Eliade followed this observation about the distribution of cosmic hierogamy by noting its absence among those with a Supreme Being cosmology. "Nevertheless, the absence of the hierogamic myth from the earliest strata of the "primitive" religions is of significance from our point of view… At the archaic stage of culture—be it remembered, corresponds with the Paleolithic period—hierogamy was inconceivable, because the Supreme Being, a god of celestial character was believed to have created the world, life and men, all by himself" (Eliade 1960:173). By this observation, Eliade directed my attention to the division between belief in the Supreme Being and Eliade's cosmic hierogamy, which I have called the separation of heaven and earth, or simply separation cosmology. The areas in which these two cosmologies are or were known include much of the earth's surface. Yet one appears to exclude the other. If separation cosmology replaced a Supreme Being cosmology, could it also have served as an argument against it?

As already mentioned, this book develops an interpretation for the symbolism implied by his cosmic hierogamy. This interpretation emphasizes that it is the separation—not the union of heaven and earth, as Eliade suggests—in which its meaning is to be found. The premise of this book is that the Supreme Being was in some places rendered ineffective and in others replaced altogether by the new worldview advanced in the separation cosmology.

Eliade has emphasized the difference in time between these two cosmologies, offering that Paleolithic peoples knew cosmic hierogamy, while Neolithic groups (early farmers) knew separation cosmology. But since it was true that some hunter-gatherers (his Paleolithic peoples) who believed in a supreme being still existed for ethnographic reports in the late nineteenth and early twentieth centuries, there must recently have been places where this contrast of worldviews could also be located geographically. Eliade was content to point out the contrast in history. The possibility of geographic proximity between groups that believed in a supreme being and those that held the separation cosmology led me to consider closely ethnographic literature from places where this contrast might be found. In this context, the polemic nature of the separation cosmology becomes apparent. In fact, in Sudan the separation cosmology was accompanied by parallel arguments (as cosmology) decrying the constraints imposed by the Supreme Being.

Eliade recognized that hunter-gatherers (nonagriculturists) tended to have a cosmology with a supreme being. It must have been an obvious choice to ascribe his cosmic hierogamy to early agriculturalists. Yet, if belief in a supreme being were the basis of an egalitarian social structure for hunters and the separation cosmology a basis for hierarchical social structure for farmers, a certain time period also becomes very important in our quest. This is the time between the beginning of agriculture and the first introduction of hierarchy. What about these people? If the separation cosmology is the product of human reasoning, is there reason to believe that farming itself required a new cosmology, one that supported hierarchy? In the ancient Near East, archaeology has identified a long time period that began after the beginning of agriculture that is without convincing evidence of social hierarchy.

In fact, archaeology has described the circumstances before and after the advent of this first hierarchy in terms that are difficult not to relate to comments about Nimrod in Genesis 10:9–12 and the confusion of languages in Genesis 11:5–9. Needless to say, archaeologists do not interpret the event that way, although some admit that it is a discontinuity difficult to explain. However, details given in Genesis 10:11–12 strongly argue that this was indeed the event. (The Appendix explains that Genesis information is very specific and most unlikely to be general information known by any person who transcribed Genesis.) The confirmation of this event is very important to us who hold a high view of the scriptures. Chapter Two describes the circumstances before and immediately after this event.

It should not be surprising that, if there were one cosmology that held this special place in turning man from God, it would be identified in Genesis. But this event is really only a link in the chain of reasoning described in the body of this book. The premise of the book is this: dependence on God's providence was set aside by the introduction of one new thought system. As stated in the preface, the name we give to older thought systems is *mythology*. Since culturally we have a tendency to dismiss mythology, these thought systems that concern origins have been labeled cosmology in this book, a term that has less negative connotations. Human thought and human thought systems should not be dismissed out of hand. For good or for evil, thought systems are the driving force of history.

How would it be possible to have any knowledge about the thought system that brought a judgment from God so long ago? If this thought system brought great changes to Sumer—that is, biblical Shinar—is it not possible that other societies might also have employed it? Here an observation of importance is the widespread presence of the cosmology, the separation of heaven and earth, and the cosmology that gives its name to this book. If it can be shown to be a polemic against the creator and his heaven, this cosmology itself further demonstrates the once pervasive nature of the belief in a Supreme Being, a being with attributes similar to the God of Judeo-Christian traditions.

This cosmology Eliade called the cosmic hierogamy (see page ix). Others in that field have called it the World Parents' Cosmology. As mentioned earlier, the term *cosmology* usually means "origin story" or "belief." However, when *cosmology* is used in this book, it often has the sociological implications of the origin story as well. This particular origin story, the separation of heaven and earth—as cosmology—justifies positions within the society that have ritual responsibilities. To reiterate my premise, members of the society committed to this cosmology believed that the proper execution of these rituals by the appropriate persons guaranteed their prosperity.

My reasoning follows this line. Instead of recognizing the providence of the Supreme Being, rituals performed by the religious elite were thought to reinvigorate the environment. When a society replaced the providence of the Supreme Being, it also tended to deny individual access and moral responsibility to him. Often, but not always, these ritual responsibilities came to have privileges such as wealth and authority. In short, ritual responsibilities for controlling the destiny of the society usually became the justification for the social inequalities in hierarchical societies.

Although the motivation for writing this book is based on my personal worldview, my hypothesis is based on available published data. I have attempted to carefully use information that is well respected in the field in which it is given.

Even so, since this information can only be considered contemporary, it cannot provide certainty about things that happened long ago. The most one can claim from this kind of information about the past is inference. However, this attempt to offer an idealistic interpretation, even though based on inference, is still worth the effort. Without such an interpretation, the inferential material—organized on evolutionary, materialistic, or humanistic presuppositions of academia—go unchallenged. As far as I know, no group in the Evangelical community is *presently* attempting such an interpretation. Anthropology defines the course material even in our missionary colleges. This is understandable, for certainly anthropology has offered useful insights into the workings of culture. With this in mind, it is not surprising that schools training our missionary candidates have shied away from open controversy with the discipline of anthropology.

Samuel Zwemer did write from an evangelical perspective concerning the Supreme Being in his *The Origin of Religion*, published in 1935. He gathered the evidence then known for belief in a Supreme Being among the "primitives" and argued that residues of this earlier belief could be discerned in rituals and practices in non-Christian religions. This book has lost currency; when it is taken up, it is almost as a curiosity. While I take a different tack from that of Zwemer, I agree with him that the evidence put forward by ethnographic reports supports the hypothesis of an early widespread belief in a creator or Supreme Being. I hope that my arguments are more convincing than those advanced by Zwemer. My project takes note of theory and information not available to him.

Although the order suggested earlier in the introduction seems simple enough, it was certainly not the order of my own path of discovery. My first exposure, as mentioned in the preface, was the mythology and archaeology of the ancient Near East. After a lengthy and careful study of this material, I compared these cosmologies with those of other cultures that were literate in ancient times. I found the similarities in these early cosmologies striking. Yet, for anthropologists these similarities attracted little attention. They are either ignored or lumped together under some form of psychic unity. This treatment did not answer my questions. There was no satisfying interpretation of the intellectual content of these similar cosmologies.

In contrast to this general neglect, I found an author, Rudolf Anthes, an Egyptologist, who offered that the Egyptian pyramid texts suggested that Egyptians used their cosmology in the installation of a new ruler. I also came across the writing of an anthropologist, Stephen Tyler, who interpreted a cosmology with the familiar theme, the separation of the heaven and the earth, as the justification for ritual practices in Vedic India. This first brought this question to my mind: Did this same cosmology serve as justification for ritual practices important to all early hierarchical societies even as it did for Sumer, Egypt, and India? It certainly seemed to do so in much of the recent South Pacific and sub-Saharan Africa.

While a definitive answer to the meaning of the symbolism involved in this cosmology was not forthcoming, the pursuit for that answer encouraged further research for information about the interpretation of mythology, especially cosmology. It was at this point I turned to the writings of Eliade. He not only believed that the first religious orientation was to a celestial creator but also referred to the copious literature on which this conclusion was based.

From this material, I learned that some of the first trained ethnographers who went out as anthropologists near the end of the nineteenth century took as assignment the verification of hypotheses meant to explain the origin and evolution of religion as well as some of our other basic institutions, such as marriage and law. These efforts, in regard to religion, were frustrated by reports of a supreme being among preagricultural groups. Needless to say, anthropology has not given up its presupposition that religion has evolved. As mentioned in the preface, the search for the origins of these institutions no longer occupies anthropologists. From their perspective, a time period too long to probe hides the origins of these basic institutions. Anthropology moved from the pursuit of origins to the more fruitful studies about how a society functions. Anthropology today is not monolithic; there are many subgroups within the discipline. But most of these subgroups present different explanations for the motivations *within* the society, the population, or the environment to account for its ordering, practices, and beliefs. (However, see endnote Introduction, note 3: Linguistics and the movement of ideas.)

It cannot be said that there is a conspiracy against the hypothesis that belief in a supreme being was once widespread. But it suffers such abuse and neglect that most have never heard of "The Supreme Being of the Primitives." The fact that this Supreme Being was often found among egalitarian hunter-gatherers uninfluenced by Western religions is very important. The possibility that all hunter-gatherers may have at one time believed in a cosmology in which the providential Supreme Being had the central role is simply a burden too large for social evolutionists to bear. For this reason, it is not treated in any meaningful way even in cultural anthropology courses, where one would expect to receive this information.

However, those who find Genesis a meaningful account of man's interaction with God should not be surprised to find that mankind spread across the globe with knowledge of God. And, based on Deuteronomy 7:9, perhaps we should not be surprised to find the evidence of God's faithfulness to those who remembered him. But it is surprising that many of the characteristics of the God we worship were still recognizable among widespread groups of hunter-gatherers. Surprising because our Scripture also points out that belief in our God, at least in the Near East, was a very fragile thing. Mankind as represented in the Bible has always tended toward idolatry: belief that nature can be controlled by ritual without moral responsibility to its creator and owner.

How is the project ordered? A rather eclectic first chapter tells of the circumstances under which anthropology was first exposed to the Supreme Being of the Primitives along with a very brief glimpse of the beliefs associated with this being and the adjustments the discipline of anthropology made in response to this information. The second chapter is given to the archaeology identifying the places and conditions under which the earliest obvious hierarchical societies occurred. This part of the project limits its consideration to the Old World. The New World is treated later.

In the third chapter, the earliest cosmologies of the ancient literate societies are compared. In addition, the similarity of later African hierarchy to the hierarchy described in the pyramid texts is underscored. The purpose of this apparent digression is to show that social hierarchy can fit a pattern. This pattern is a good indication that hierarchy as a social structure in Africa has been diffused. It did not come into being merely as a need to regulate behavior or the economy within a particular society. My argument is that some societies adopt a neighboring cosmology with rituals to control the environment; the rituals in turn become the justification for hierarchical social structure.

The fourth chapter is rather philosophical. In it some of my presuppositions are given and contrasted with academia, especially those of anthropology. The chapter underscores the limitations a materialist accepts by denying that ideals imbedded in cosmology are motivation for practices. Thus anthropologists say that the great value hunters place on sharing must be surrendered in the change from gathering to farming. But they ignore the possibility that this value might be based on cosmology. Apparently hunters continued to hold the same cosmology even as they turned to farming. To the idealist, when the cosmology of a society changes, the values of that society change. The fifth chapter treats the myth of the separation itself. It also gives a rather lengthy account of the Maori origin myth with some insight into its social significance.

The sixth and seventh chapters take advantage of the fact that the inhabitants of the Mesopotamian Valley used clay tablets right down to the Christian era. This affords the student of these tablets the opportunity to trace those cosmologies over millennia. The eighth chapter switches back to more recent material and traces the movement of the cosmological concepts and the social order associated with the Austronesian language group.

Chapter Nine compares two Nilotic tribes in Africa, demonstrating conclusively that for them it is the separation of heaven and earth cosmology that distinguishes an egalitarian group of herders from their neighbors who have a "sacred" leader. This chapter, more than any other, demonstrates the point that for these tribes, hierarchy was introduced by separation cosmology. The tenth chapter makes a similar comparison between tribal groups from central and southeast Australia. Again, the results are similar. However, when comparing those with and those without the separation cosmology in southeast Australia, it is obvious that those who believed in a supreme being hoped to be in his care after death. Those with the separation cosmology have no such hope.

Chapter Eleven begins by looking to the earliest evidences for hierarchy in the Americas. Again, as in the Mesopotamian Valley, this hierarchy seems to invade and separate what previously had been one large interacting community. The American anthropologist Franz Boas suggests that the hierarchy found in the Americas is marked by similarities that set it aside from any other in the world. He, therefore, offered a scenario in which this hierarchy overspread the continent and brought many egalitarian hunters and farmers under its influence. In Boas's scenario, the original culture that once occupied the whole of the two continents could still be identified at the extremities. And indeed, ethnographic reports from those areas identified tribes that had still recognized the Supreme Being.

Chapter Twelve draws together some of the points made in the body of the book. It reiterates an idealistic motivation for the prevalence of social hierarchy, the belief that the elites could manipulate the environment through ritual. It is pointed out that ancient hierarchy did not increase the creativity or productivity of the society. It diverted its citizens' efforts into monumental architecture dedicated to the gods, spent its youth on war, and enslaved those it defeated. The chapter also reiterates the polemic quality of the cosmology that initiated the hierarchy and worldview of the ancient world. The cosmology on which that hierarchy was based stated that the conditions before this new cosmos came into being were dark and confining. Our "modern" world looks back before the period of the Enlightenment in much the same way. In each case, it was the creator or Supreme Being and his promises that were diminished. Does this intellectual rejection of the Supreme Being along with his providence and authority bring us closer to reality? And if not, what changes will its imposition bring now?

The appendix compares the event of the first hierarchy as archaeology describes it with the relevant verses from Genesis 10 and 11 concerning the confusion of languages. Genesis offers specific information about the time and circumstances of that event that are difficult to dismiss as accidental.

Chapter One

High-God of the Primitives

> The theory of a soul is a principal part of a system of religious philosophy which unites, in an unbroken line of mental connection, the savage fetish-worshiper and the civilized Christian. The divisions which have separated the great religions of the world into intolerant and hostile sects are for the most part superficial in comparison with the deepest of all religious schisms, that which divides Animism from Materialism. (Edward B. Tylor as found in Lessa & Vogt 1979:19)

In 1873 Edward Tylor published *Primitive Culture*. From the passage above, it is obvious that he had little use for religion, whose origin he sought to discover. He offered that the progress of religion would follow this pattern: animism, then a wider doctrine of spirits, guardian spirits, polytheism, monotheism, and finally materialism. There were others who in fairly rapid succession offered different motivations and starting places for the origin of religion, but each had monotheism near the end of a lengthy progression, just before the pinnacle of their intellectual achievement, materialism. In step with other evolutionists of his time, Tylor expected a systematic, single-line scheme of development, certain inevitable stages through which man would pass. He himself was a theoretical anthropologist, but others went out armed with his theory of origins looking for evidence to support it. Certainly some expected that among the Australian Aborigines vestiges of primitive religion would be found.

Andrew Lang, a student of and an early enthusiast for Tylor's theory, followed these Australian ethnographic reports with interest. Based on those and other reports, in 1898 he wrote a book, *The Making of Religion*, in which he came to differ with Tylor, offering that there was a belief in a supreme being among some of the most primitive peoples on the globe. In this book he pointed out that since this being had always lived, belief in his existence was not likely based on the animism that Tylor had offered. Although Lang's book caused a stir among his readers, he was primarily known as an author and not taken seriously by anthropologists.

A few years later, Father Wilhelm Schmidt took up the chore of collecting and organizing the material that then called into question all origin-of-religion theories. Schmidt argued for a primitive *urmonotheism*—that at one time all on the globe worshiped a single, eternal, omnipotent god whose abode is heaven. This god was not only a provider but also established the moral code and judged men's actions. Often this judgment resulted in reward or punishment after death. There can be little doubt that the god Schmidt described resembled very strongly the God of the monotheistic tradition of Western civilization. Schmidt's early works are not easily found in English. Therefore, the reader is referred to his *Origin and Growth of Religion*, originally published in 1931. But his first major works were published in 1912, and within a decade most anthropologists were forced to consider the possibility that widespread groups knew of a being referred to as "the Supreme Being of the Primitives."

How did anthropology respond to this situation? Almost needless to say, anthropologists were not prepared to surrender the firm belief that evolution accounts for all physical, mental, and social attributes of humans. Nor were they ready to admit that religious traditions similar to those of Western civilization may have been primeval. Further, the notion that such a belief might have been the result of revelation from God himself would undermine materialism and thus, in their minds, signal the end of science itself. Anthropologist Wilhelm Schmidt was also a Catholic priest, and the school he organized trained clerics to go into the field. His motivation was therefore considered suspect. The reports his followers brought back were also disputed. The following is from a collection of anthropological writings edited by William Lessa and Evon Vogt. It introduces a section in which the sixteenth chapter of Schmidt's *The Origin and Growth of Religion* is given:

A large number of Catholic ministers working with native peoples have been trained by Schmidt and devote considerable research toward finding evidence of a high god among their flocks.... Often they have confused monolatry—the worship of one god among many—with monotheism.... They see eternity, omnipotence, omnipresence, creativeness, complete beneficence and righteousness—characteristics of a true supreme being—where they do not actually exist. Radcliffe Brown's material from the Andaman Islands shows, for example, that Biliku does not really deserve to be called a monotheistic deity because the natives threaten and trick him (or her), steal from him, exile him, and even kill him in revenge. The Bushmen of South Africa do not really have a high god, for there both the moon and the stars are worshiped, and they do not only have multiple forms but lack the immortality, unalterable goodness, and other qualities of the monotheistic hypothesis. In short, the facts are not what they are represented to be. They are scanty, unreliable, contradictory, and distorted. Aside from all this, there is always present the objection that "primitive" is not the same concept as "primeval." The culture of the Pygmies is not *Urkultur*.

A unique objection to the high-god hypothesis has been made by Radin (*Primitive Religion*, 1937), who not only argues that true monotheism is extremely rare among primitive peoples but in any case is not really a manifestation of religion at all but the result of philosophic speculation of a small part of the community—the medicine man or shaman among hunting and gathering tribes....

Lang and Schmidt performed a service for the science of religion by stemming the influence of the theory of animism and demonstrating the plausibility of non-animistic hypotheses of religious origins. While their counterproposals are themselves vulnerable, these two writers did help keep the thought on the subject fluid and critical. (Lessa & Vogt 1962:25f)

This reflects the flavor of anthropology's response to Father Schmidt. It is a little amusing that anthropologists, highly motivated to demonstrate that religion evolved, and in this way to undermine it (and defend their materialism), would consider themselves objective enough to suggest that Catholic anthropologists were biased because they found counter-evidence to this theory. The criticisms leveled against Schmidt and his school have some merit. Father Schmidt, in spite of his religious beliefs, was an evolutionist. And following the ideas of his time, he believed that Pygmies represented an early human form. He also believed the concept, now generally considered outdated, that mankind passed through a stage of matriarchy. Perhaps some of his followers were overzealous in their treatment of the beliefs of some groups. Of course, the reports from which Lang found evidence for his high-gods, which were contrary to his earlier beliefs patterned on Tylor's *Primitive Culture*, were written before Father Schmidt and his followers came on the scene.

To be more specific in regard to the critical quotation starting on page 4, is there reason to believe that the intellectual commitments of Radcliffe-Brown investigating the Andaman Islanders in 1909 made him a better ethnographer than E. H. Man in 1882? It was his observations that were used by Father Schmidt. E. H. Man was a prison administrator in the islands for thirty years and pursued a personal interest in the native language, perspectives, and culture over that period. Certainly E. H. Man had a longer and fuller exposure to that culture. In fact, should it be that surprising that Radcliffe-Brown found changes in beliefs among the Andaman Islanders after thirty more years of contact with outsiders? Another example would be the Bushmen, whom Schmidt described as a weak representative of belief in a supreme being among primitive people but a representative nevertheless. However, Katz (1982:39), referencing L. Marshall (1962), who is not a Catholic priest, offered that the !Kung people believe that "Goa Na, the creator, is deeply involved with humanity, constantly aware of what people do. He reacts with pleasure or displeasure to human behavior and favors, punishes, or ill-treats man accordingly." When confronted with such beliefs, does it really matter if these people also have other stories, perhaps from their neighbors? As for Radin, where would you expect to learn the religious sentiments of a people if not from their recognized religious leaders?

When Lang made his arguments, he used the word *degeneration* to describe the religious beliefs of the people who moved from belief in a high-god to gods more related to nature and the ancestors. And in this process they also moved from simple social structures to the more complex. Today, this characterization, "degeneration," does smack of ethnocentrism. Analogously, Schmidt's

"Ethnological Argument" for a supreme being also included other stages of religious evolution suggesting a movement away from and not toward acceptance of a supreme being.

Eric Sharpe has since pointed out that while Schmidt was disqualified because he was a Catholic priest, it remains true that "Pettazzoni, and some years later, E. O. James and Geo Widengren, were to prove the point about 'high gods' with caution and objectivity, that they were *there* in the 'primitive' and ancient religions, but that it is wise not to speculate unduly as to how they came to be there" (Sharpe 1975:185). Not wise perhaps because in academia it is threatening to an evolutionist's perspective to suggest that this may have been a primeval religious belief of mankind, or even worse, that it was the result of divine revelation. And outside academia it may be threatening to non-monotheistic religions; that is, such speculations today may be considered politically incorrect. Mircea Eliade was not able to bring his field, history of religions, along with him. But he, for one, believed that at one time all of mankind worshiped the Supreme Being. A number of his books mention this; indeed, some are offered as arguments for this very point: *Rites and Symbols of Initiation*, 1958; *Shamanism*, 1964; *Australian Religions, An Interpretation*, 1973; *A History of Religious Ideas*, 1976.

As for keeping the thought on the subject of religious origins fluid and critical, the writings of Lang and Schmidt brought noteworthy anthropological speculations about the origins of religion to a rather abrupt end. The last of the presently notable works done on the origin of religion was by Emile Durkheim in 1912. This interpretation of ethnographic material of the Arunta tribes of Central Australia is noteworthy because it is a sociological interpretation, not really so much a treatment of origins as an attempt to offer a role for religion. Perhaps it should be mentioned that Freud also published his *Totem and Taboo* in 1913. In this book he essentially rewrote his Oedipus complex as a primordial event bringing humankind into existence.

How did anthropology respond to the controversy stirred by Lang and Schmidt, and where does that controversy stand today? As mentioned above, further exploration of religious origins essentially ceased. However, the response was even more comprehensive. While the first impetus for professional ethnographers was to investigate the origins of religion and other social institutions, European anthropology underwent a radical change shortly after being confronted by the Supreme Being of the Primitives put forward by Lang and Schmidt. This change gave anthropology a new direction and motivation. Cultural anthropology began to look into the inner workings of a culture. The following excerpt from the British anthropologist Raymond Firth indicates that Malinowski is to be credited with getting past the "aridities" of Wilhelm Schmidt's *Kulturkreislehre*. He did this not by offering a meaningful critique of Schmidt's works but through a course correction for anthropology: "Without him (Malinowski), the aridities of the *Kulturkreislehre* and the fantasies of pan-Egyptianism would doubtless have in due course been corrected and overcome. But for the younger generation of anthropologists in Europe at least, he fought that battle and won it by the end of the 'twenties.' And though now this is dim history, those who were students at that time know what formidable opponents were to be encountered in Elliot Smith, Pater Schmidt, and their adherents" (Firth 1957:2).

This is the Malinowski mentioned in the Introduction. It is true that anthropology had important concepts to discover and contribute, concepts that were not likely to be found in a search for the origins of religion. Malinowski's ethnographic reports and interpretation of the culture of the Trobriand Islanders set a new direction for anthropology. Elliot Smith offered another school of thought, one also opposed to a fixed system of stages through which culture and its concepts evolved. His assertion that Egypt was the source of all civilized thought could not possibly stand. The fantastic assertions and eclectic style of books by Smith's pupil W. J. Perry have indeed been corrected and overcome. But reaction to Smith's hypothesis may have had some long-lasting effects in anthropology. Malinowski found that the Trobriand Islanders, whom he investigated, had an aristocracy with a complex mythology to justify their positions. He insisted that these mythic charters were to be considered as "superstructure" chartering positions of privilege and justifying the social circumstances in the people studied.

This was a good direction for anthropology. It moved its practitioners away from very ethnocentric evolutionary hypotheses into questions of how a society works. Malinowski related myth, including cosmology, to everyday life. Myth was no longer primitive speculations about things the actors did not understand or infantile reasoning. However, at the same time, it nearly forbade consideration of regional similarities in cosmologies and in this way discouraged using a diffusion model as explanation of similar social structures. In other words, perhaps to deny any place to Smith's theory of pan-Egyptian influence on the rest of the world, Malinowski's approach tended to deny history itself to preliterate groups such as the Trobriand Islanders. "The historical consideration of myth is interesting, therefore, in that it shows that myth, taken as a whole, cannot be sober dispassionate history, since it is always made *ad hoc* to fulfill a sociological function. These considerations show us that to the native mind immediate history, semi-historic legend, and unmixed myth flow into one another, form a continuous sequence, and fulfill really the same sociological function" (Malinowski 1954:125f).

For Malinowski the sociological function tended to subsume all other considerations. By contrast, historians of religion generally have attempted to avoid the sociological function in order to keep for themselves a discrete field of study. The following paragraph illustrates in Malinowski's own words his interpretation of mythology. Notice that this interpretation does not label cosmology as speculation, philosophy, or faulty reasoning. Although he puts it into the superstructure of the culture, he identifies its position in the mind of the natives as the intellectual foundation of their culture.

> We may best start with the beginning of things, and examine some of the myths of origin. The world, say the natives, was originally peopled from underground. Humanity had there led an existence similar in all respects to the present life on earth. Underground, men were organized in villages, clans, districts; they had distinctions of rank, they knew privileges and had claims, they owned property, and were versed in magic lore. Endowed with all this, they emerged, establishing by this very act certain rights in land and citizenship, in economic prerogative, and magical pursuit. They brought with them all their culture to continue it upon the earth. (Malinowski 1954:111)

This emergence of man with his social organization and prerogatives in place typically follows the description of the separation of heaven and earth in Polynesian mythology. It has similarities to the Sumerian cosmology in which the kings were granted their prerogatives at the place where heaven and earth were separated and man emerged. It should be underscored that in spite of Malinowski's functionalism and insistence that the Trobriand Islander's cosmology is superstructure invented to justify their own social inequalities, the cosmology as given by Malinowski appears to be merely a shortened form of the separation of heaven and earth cosmology.

Malinowski felt that religion had a social component, agreeing to this extent with Durkheim, but insisted that the social was not all. For Malinowski, religion met individual needs as well as social needs. He suggested that the most important was the rituals concerned with death and treatment of the dead. These ceremonies (at least for the Trobriand Islanders) helped the community to face confidently their own deaths by promising a continuation of life. Malinowski's school of thought was known as functionalism.

So with Malinowski, anthropology moved away from not only the pursuit of origins but also from considerations of the possible history of the people studied. Each social grouping became a stable (unchanging), functioning unit. But although Malinowski denied a place to cosmology as an agent of change, he did recognize its importance in the stability of culture. He observed that this stability was dependent on the daily use of the myth: "It is necessary to go back to primitive mythology in order to learn the secret of its life in the study of a myth which is still alive—before mummified in priestly wisdom, it has been enshrined in the indestructible but lifeless repository of dead religions" (Malinowski 1954:101).

Although Malinowski apparently had little regard for the religious beliefs he had experienced himself, this insight, which in the context concerned the public and repeated use of myth, may well account for *some* of the stability of a few widespread cosmologies among nonliterate people groups. And it is also true that among the literate hierarchical societies there were often significant modifications in the cosmology that justified the hierarchy. How is it that there can be stability within a mythic system without scriptures? His explanation: these beliefs, or myths—myth is not myth unless it is believed—are repeated on certain formal occasions and whenever relevant to the circumstances. In at least Malinowski's primitive society, myth was in daily *public* use; in this way it appears to be both preserved and transmitted with some reliability. Perhaps similar repetition at formal and informal circumstances partially explains a very durable belief in a supreme being among many egalitarian groups as well.

During the 1920s Malinowski's work became a standard for ethnographic reporting, his insights a model for the interpretation of nonliterate cultures. Instead of asserting a fixed pattern of evolution, anthropology moved to a form of historical particularism. While it is easy to see Malinowski through the eyes of his more recent critics, it cannot be denied that his reinterpretation of the place of magic and myth in culture restored to primitives the mental capacity taken away by the earlier evolutionary and racist approaches. Simply stated for Malinowski, ideas communicated as cosmologies are but a mirror of the society's structure and, thus, don't shape but rather reflect it.

Radcliffe-Brown, in his ethnographic report on the Andaman Islanders first published in 1914, offered another interpretation of culture with subtle differences, called structuralism. In this system the social aspects of culture with regard to religious beliefs were given more importance as in Durkheim, but myth retained its position as mere superstructure.

So firmly established was this principle—that is, myth was the creation of the society to justify its practices—that American and British anthropology actually lost interest in myth until Levi-Strauss revived it for a little while in the 1960s. Of course, this lack of concern with the native justification for ritual was in agreement with the materialistic perspectives of anthropology. The anthropologist took as his assignment in ethnographic reporting to tell what the natives actually accomplished (in a material sense) by their activities and rituals, rather than what the natives thought they were doing while paying respect to gods, spirits, or ancestors.

But anthropology has not remained static. Archaeology, a branch of anthropology, spurred a new interest in the evolution of society, called neoevolution. It was without much of the racism and ethnocentric bias of earlier single evolutionary pattern hypotheses except that stages of organizational development were still offered. In 1962 Elman Service authored *Primitive Social Organization,* in which he suggested that people were organized in bands, tribes, chiefdoms, and states. In 1967 Morton Fried published his *The Evolution of Political Society,* offering his order: egalitarian, rank society, chiefdom, and state. Fried did allow that his rank societies were essentially egalitarian, but they had positions whose owners had ritual responsibilities. Proper execution of these responsibilities brought them prestige but not wealth or political power. Fried's ordering certainly had support from ethnographic reports. Yet, there *still* seemed to be little recognition or interest in the worldview of their subjects. This concern with evolving social organization required new research on the starting point of any system of development of organization, the egalitarian hunter-gatherer societies.

This research revealed many interesting and unexpected facts. On the basis of these investigations, the traditional understanding of these groups as brutish savages near starvation turned out to be quite false. Sahlins (1974:1–39), writing about hunters, called them the "original affluent society." He pointed out that they invested only six hours a day to feed themselves, enjoyed socializing, and were quite content with what they could conveniently carry with them. Further, they had strongly developed mores concerning sharing; they enjoyed family relations and were generally bilateral in determining these relations. Another author's assessment of hunters is as follows:

> Ten thousand years ago, hunter-gatherers occupied all the continents except Antarctica; everyone was a hunter-gatherer. Theirs was a very successful adaptation, one that had provided for the enormous expansion of the human species into a wide range of environments all over the world. Hunter-gatherer societies exhibited a diverse range of forms from large, sedentary groups with hierarchical leadership to very small, egalitarian groups moving about the landscape in search of food. In most areas, wild food was readily available to support large numbers of people. Such adaptations have been described as the "original affluent society" by anthropologist Marshall Sahlins (1968, P. 89). Leisure time was plentiful and life must have been reasonably good. Health conditions were significantly better than among early farming populations. (Price & Feinman 1997:172)

But what happened to the concept of the Supreme Being of the Primitives? Anthropology has, so to speak, swept it under the carpet. First, it does not normally come up because the anthropologist tells us how a given social group is structured or how it functions; that for him is how it meets its material needs. The anthropologist sees no need to explore the epistemic considerations of that group. Second, if it is brought up, it is not denied but merely called an anomaly hidden by ages too long to probe. But at least one anthropologist has not shied away from the Supreme Being of the Primitives. Carleton Coon, in *The Hunting Peoples,* offers this analysis of the beliefs of hunters:

> Some hunters believe that there was once a single creator, who after having finished his work retired and withdrew from

close contact with men. He may return now and then to intervene when things were going wrong in order to straighten out
earthly affairs, and perhaps he will some day come again.

Other hunters pay little attention to the creator, if they mention him at all. They attribute the origin of things to their
ancestors, the earth-shaping heroes. If we run through the list
of hunters about whose cultures we have needed information,
we will find that the two poles of belief correspond to two
different kinds of social and political organization, the simple
and the compound....

By and large the believers in a single, lofty, and remote creator live in single territorial groups. Many of them trace their
descent bilaterally and have little concern with the ancient
ancestors....

At the opposite pole stand two kinds of people. Some are organized into unilateral clans and extensions of clans, whose
members may be scattered in mixed bands or mixed villages.
The members of each such clan may have special duties to
perform in common ceremonies. Others are members who lay
great store by wealth and rank, however they may trace their
descent. They care less about an overall creator than about
the fabulous deeds of their particular ancestors, toward whom
their mythology and their rites are directed.

Believers in a single creator include the Bushmen, Pygmies,
Great Andamanese, Semang, Philippine Negritos, some of the
Southeast Australians, probably the Tasmanians, the Yaghans,
Onas, Central and Eastern Eskimo, the northern Algonkians
and most of the northern Athabascans. (Coon 1971:285f)

After distancing himself from Schmidt's monotheism in a note at the foot
of the page, Coon adds, "My purpose was to see if there might be some
relationship between the ways in which different hunting peoples are organized socially and politically and the organization of their spiritual worlds."
In light of the reactions to Lang's and Schmidt's writings, it would seem
that such an observation would attract attention. However, the intervening

development and direction resulted in the discipline's meeting Coon's observations with a yawn; anthropology felt no need to respond to these observations. They were not really inconsistent with Malinowski's explication from his observations about the Trobriand Islanders. However, unlike Malinowski's observations, they did relate the concept of a Supreme Being to an egalitarian social structure.

So we learn that within the world's hunter-gather groups, using Fried's categories, there are not only egalitarian societies but also rank society and chiefdom organization. Several inferences may be drawn from this fact. For our purposes, it is worth noting that while economic conditions are not determinative of religious perspective, social organization and (religious) worldviews are interrelated. However, whether or not such organization was present among hunters before it was known among farming groups is not something that has been settled for some anthropologists. Some have attempted to associate the domestication of animals and plants to hunters with complex social structure, that is, rank and chiefdom organization. For reasons offered in the next chapter, this does not seem likely. However, the theory here presented does not forbid this from happening; it merely requires that within a society, equal access to the creator (or whatever deity) be first set aside by another cosmology that limits this access.

Many have treated these origin theories. For further reading, here are some suggestions: *The Origin and Growth of Religion* by Wilhelm Schmidt; *Theories of Primitive Religions* by E. E. Evans-Pritchard; for a more overall treatment of anthropology on religion, *Ordered Universes* by Morton Klass.

This map shows some of the hunter-gatherer groups found that worshiped a creator-supreme being. Carleton Coon has offered the list in the text. Among other authors who have offered similar lists are Mircea Eliade in *Myths, Dreams, and Mysteries* and Wilhelm Schmidt in *The Origin and Growth of Religion*.

Chapter Two

The Earliest Social Hierarchies

> But the LORD came down to see the city and the tower that the men were building. The LORD said, "If as one people speaking the same language they have begun to do this, then nothing they plan to do will be impossible for them. Come, let us go down and confuse their language so they will not understand each other." So the LORD scattered them from there over all the earth, and they stopped building the city. That is why it was called Babel—because there the LORD confused the language of the whole world. From there the LORD scattered them over the face of the whole earth. (Genesis 11:5–9 NIV)

As the header suggests, we are about to turn our attention to the lower Mesopotamian Valley. In spite of recent political obstacles, some archaeological work continues in this area. However, this area has attracted attention for a time long before these recent conflicts. While over that period today's technologies have not always been available, much useful information has been gleaned from archaeological projects in that area extending back more than a hundred years. Because of the height of "tells," notable sites were easy to locate. Tells are the mounds that result from building on top of partially demolished older buildings. Buildings made from dried clay brick, though buried in preparation for buildings on top of them yield a lot of information. Often the covered buildings show the size and layout of the rooms. Sometimes there are artifacts that suggest the activities carried out in the rooms. Since the dried clay brick walls were painted with a wash to make them more impervious to moisture, the number of coatings suggests the length of time the building was in use. It is obvious, then, that a great deal of information was learned from the excavated tells even without today's technology.

But this is not all the information that was gleaned without recent archaeological techniques. Over time, whole towns and cities have been rebuilt many times. In nearly every level of every tell, pottery shards were found, and on the basis of these shards, date comparisons were made without use of radiometric dating. In a few instances, some clay tablets with cuneiform writing have also been found. Several sites have held collections of tablets that have been described as a library.

The neoevolutionists had this information available. However, they wanted to fit the changes as reflected by the archaeology of the area into their present understanding of how these changes would have taken place. Of course, the starting place for this understanding is always the egalitarian hunter-gatherer. As mentioned in the last chapter, the research on recent hunter-gatherers led to a change in attitude toward those who lived under those conditions. The old arguments for change from a Mesolithic (late Stone Age) to a Neolithic (farming with pottery) economy were certainly challenged. Present-day hunters are neither discontented nor starving. These hunters for the most part are living in places where agriculture is difficult. If hunters thrive under climatic conditions that make agriculture difficult, apparently it would have been easier to feed themselves under more favorable conditions.

Therefore, the question of what circumstances would have led hunters to take the risks necessary to become farmers presented itself. Answering this question has been one of the focuses of recent archaeology. In order to get at the data to answer it, refinements in archaeological technique have made it possible to gain more information from sites. At the same time, improved carbon dating techniques have made age comparisons of widely separated sites possible. Carbon dating is thought reliable (reproducible). Tree ring correction has led those who use the carbon dating method to conclude that the actual date of older materials is older than the technique indicates; that is, the end of the Ubaid Period is not about 4000 B.C. but about 4600 B.C. (This Ubaid time period becomes important in this chapter.) Generally, I will use the uncorrected carbon dates. The reader, however, is advised when researching the subject independently to know what the given carbon date means.

Not only has the methodology changed, but also new explanatory concepts that avoid explanations based on movements of people have been advanced. Perhaps the two most well known are systems theory, an explanation that attempts to incorporate several causative factors, and Marxist theory, with emphasis on dialectic social interaction and change. Both of these approaches are materialistic. They both purport to explain the way men organize themselves as emergent qualities, somehow necessary and positive steps on the way from egalitarian to state organization.

This chapter focuses on the change from egalitarian to hierarchical state organization on the basis of archaeological evidence from the area including modern Iraq, Syria, much of Turkey, and northwestern Iran. Here, several thousand years after the first evidence for a Neolithic economy, there was a sudden move from egalitarian culture to hierarchical state organization. But, in contrast, shortly after this Mesopotamian event, egalitarian hunter-gatherers in several areas on the Atlantic coast moved directly from an egalitarian Mesolithic economy to a hierarchical Neolithic economy using Near Eastern domesticates. In these areas, hunters moved directly into hierarchical social structure even before agriculture had become well established.

It is obvious that mankind generally did move from mobile hunter-gatherer societies without agriculture to farming societies with permanent living structures. With few exceptions, these hunters not only gave up their subsistence strategies but their egalitarian status as well. In short, they often came to be farmers living under a politico-religious hierarchy. But what is the pattern? And what was the impetus for the move away from egalitarianism?

Recent technological advancements have made it possible for archaeologists to learn more about the first attempts at agriculture. In a few areas (mostly in Syria and the Levant), there are sites with evidence for the development of a Neolithic economy without pottery. These levels are called pre-pottery Neolithic. But this is true of only a few sites with early dates. After pottery technology was developed, it quickly spread through all the nearby settlements and was used in most of the settlements established later. The earliest pottery was plain and not well fired. But as skill in the technology increased, an unusual thing happened. Instead of many well-decorated potteries representing the tastes of different areas, pottery became standardized. This is an important observation, and it will be treated later in greater detail. The evidence indicates that clay from certain sites was preferred, yet pottery was primarily a local craft.

As hunter-gatherers, the occupants of this area had traded obsidian over a large area. Obsidian is a hard volcanic rock used for cutting tools that came from the mountains in Anatolia. Now as farmers, people in the same area traded pottery as well. They were willing to be identified with each other rather than trying to distinguish themselves from each other.

The important point here is that both before and after the first domestication of plants and animals, there were widespread systems for trading and all shared in the benefits of this trade. This trade no doubt included food and other perishable materials that have left little evidence. The need for obsidian may have initially motivated this trade, but there must have been social considerations as well for the exchange of pottery. Burial practices changed occasionally from place to place as well as over time, yet there were no graves found with an unusual amount of "wealth." There was little evidence of weaponry that would have been directed at people. From my perspective, then, archaeology has shown that these people who began practices that led to agriculture were egalitarian; they did not have inherited leadership or social classes. And they apparently maintained their egalitarian social structure as they became farmers.

The first standardized pottery that became widespread is called Halaf, named after a site in Syria where it was first identified as a pottery type, and the time this pottery was used is called the Halaf period. Since the subject of this chapter is the first hierarchy, this very brief sketch of the origin and spread of farming with pottery will suffice. The elaborately decorated Halaf pottery became an important tool to gain insight into that period. It has stood the test of time on the sites where it was used; and, because of its distinctive color and designs, its distribution has demonstrated trading areas in a more obvious manner than many of the other cultural materials. Carbon dating of the earliest of this pottery gives a date of the early to middle seventh millennium B.C., or 7000–6500 B.C. It was once thought to be earlier than the Samarran pottery of northern Iraq (site Samarra) but perhaps should be considered contemporaneous with it.

During that millennium Halafian pottery was found widely distributed in Syria, Turkey, and northern Iraq. Archaeologist Peter Akkermans (1994) characterizes Halafian sites as open to trade. Obsidian and basalt were brought in from the Turkish hinterland, along with some crystal rock craft items either as finished products or raw materials, with evidence of pottery from western Syria and local production and exchange of painted wares. Notice that these are all items that have not perished with time. This trade must also have included many perishable items such as food, leather goods, wood, and baskets. Akkermans offers this about the pottery itself: "In general, however, there is hardly any evidence that painted Halaf wares served in elite contexts; the pottery is widely spread and found in vast quantities and therefore seems to have been within the reach of virtually every individual" (Akkermans1994: 287).

With this comment about well-crafted pottery not serving in an elite context, Akkermans joined the discussion within archaeology as to whether or not such fine craftsmanship and the trade necessary to make it available are an indication of the presence of elites (social superiors). In other words, the distribution of fine craft products, in the minds of some, already suggests the need for social management—in a word, hierarchy. But against that position, no Halafian burials have been found that suggest any considerable differential in wealth. Not all dwellings are the same, but none are dramatically larger than others. There are no obvious political boundaries and no special cultural markers to set one group in distinction to others.

The size of this cultural area does not fit well with the evolutionary patterns as offered by either Service—bands, tribes, chiefdoms, and states—or Fried—egalitarian, rank society, chiefdom, and state. Each step in these schemes held that a greater number of participants could be involved than in the previous step. Here, however, it is obvious that the participating area is larger than that of any ancient state. It is not until much later that some of the empires are found to exceed this geographic area. The data does not fit theoretical neoevolutionary assumptions.

Others in archaeology attempting to explain how man would have taken up agriculture in the first place have suggested that a "complex" social order would have been required to draw people into the "disadvantages" that first farmers would have encountered. One such perspective is treated in the paragraph below.

> A change from community to household levels of economic organization may have accompanied the transition to agriculture, including a shift from communal sharing to familial or individual accumulation. Economic intensification and competition were frequent companions of the Neolithic revolution. Wealth accumulation and status differentiation appear

at the individual, household, and lineage levels. The transition to agriculture may well be closely related to the beginnings of hereditary inequality in human society. [There was considerable debate about this social aspect of the transition, and not all participants agreed with this assessment.] (Price & Gebauer 1996:8, brackets in original)

Notice that there was not agreement on the Price assessment above. However, from this assessment, the argument has been advanced that hierarchy was already present, just not showing itself, in early agricultural societies. This matter is treated again in Chapter Four. Archaeologists' concerns about the origins of agriculture indirectly affect the premises of this book. Based on thin evidence, many archaeologists believe that mankind spread out more than forty thousand years ago as hunter-gatherers. At about ten thousand years ago, mankind began domesticating plants in at least six widely scattered areas, in each area using different plants in the process. The anomaly raises the questions: Why then? Why leave their obviously successful strategy at all?

Some archaeologists consider the introduction of hierarchy as helpful in explaining the anomaly. They admit that evidence for the presence of hierarchy is thin. But if hierarchy were the answer to their problem, the questions would change to these: Why hierarchy then? Why leave their successful egalitarian societies at all? My own premise is that the first event of social hierarchy can be well documented by the archaeological data, and this event happened long after the time man began to practice agriculture. Further, this pattern seems to hold in each of the different areas where plants were domesticated. If I need to offer an explanation of why man changed his subsistence pursuits, that is, why he became a farmer, it would follow this line. Mankind spread out provisioned by ice-age animals (see Introduction note 1). Shortly after these animals disappeared, for whatever reason, agriculture became more desirable. Why did hierarchy come at all? My answer is elaborated further in this book.

But without doubt, the cultural values of today's hunter-gatherers would have been modified. For instance, some new sense of ownership would be required if one expected to harvest crops after the labor of planting them. Similar problems would arise with respect to ownership of domesticated animals. Probably the earliest people who planted and harvested crops still supplemented their diets with wild plants and animals, but at some point their movements became more restricted. They lived in either temporary or permanent houses that they must have claimed as their own, and they stored grains for food and seed for the next season's planting. This pattern of behavior would seem to contradict the practice of sharing all their possessions that many hunters today value so highly. However, similar problems would have to be overcome in a hierarchical setting as well. In spite of these necessary adjustments in the cultural values of the hunters, the evidence indicates that the earliest farmers rejected the very concept of inherited social inequalities and remained egalitarian in perspective.

Settlement of the lower Mesopotamian Valley (southern Iraq) began later than in the north, about 5500 B.C. The people apparently moved from earlier agricultural communities, probably from the north, yet settled this area starting from the south to the north. They came to the lower valley with domesticated plants and animals, pottery, and craft skills, as well as the ability to use irrigation for their agriculture. They built permanent houses of dried clay brick and lived in small settlements. Because they used grains both for food and the seed they needed for the next crop, they had large storage facilities. Archaeology has labeled the time periods in this area by changes in pottery patterns. In the lower valley, one of the first is identified as Eridu pottery followed by a group of potteries often identified as Ubaid 1, 2, 3, 4, or early to late. The early Eridu pottery design could probably be traced back to the Samarran ware mentioned earlier in northern Iraq. Eridu is a town located in the lower part of the valley. These pottery types were remarkably stable and take us through about 1,500 years.

The people of the Ubaid period (lower Mesopotamian Valley) of the ancient Near East were apparently religious; they had structures that have been identified as temples, but no obvious evidence exists for social inequalities. Communication apparently had only natural barriers such as deserts, mountains, and distance. There was specialization and exchange of both food and craft products. In the absence of other evidences, a reasonable assumption is that all of these activities, indicating considerable specialization, happened without the management afforded by social hierarchy. This specialization is the only significant argument for hierarchy earlier than the end of the late Ubaid period. Of course, specialization exists even in egalitarian hunter-gatherer societies.

These apparently independently organized group and individual activities were not completely brought under a centralized control after the introduction of hierarchy. When, much later, writing became a source of information for us, traces of this earlier economic organization could still be found (Adams 1984:90–94). For our purposes the argument here is that neither the stages envisioned by Service nor those by Fried fit the situation in the lower Mesopotamian Valley even as they did not fit the Halaf culture area farther north. It may be difficult to recognize Fried's rank society archaeologically, but a chiefdom society of lengthy duration should be obvious. In this type of society, chiefs mobilize some significant portion of the output of the society to use for their agenda, including public building or warfare. When written records became available, remains of an economy independent of chiefdom organization were clearly present. One portrait of the order of this development in the lower valley follows:

> The complex processes that led to the growth of later civilization in Mesopotamia clearly had begun during the Ubaid period. Yet indicators of pronounced social differentiation appeared only at the very end of the period. There are few exotic luxury items at Ubaid sites. And despite many excavated Ubaid burials, no highly elaborate funerary contexts have been unearthed. Not until the subsequent Uruk period (3600–3100 B.C.) did monumental urban centers arise in accordance with clear indicators of social stratification. Eridu remained an important place for more than 1,000 years following the end of the Ubaid period. Yet early in the fourth millennium B.C., other centers, such as Uruk (also known as Warka), rapidly surpassed it in size, monumentality, and political significance. Although for much of its early history the centers and polities of Mesopotamia shared a common cultural tradition, rarely was this region dominated politically by a single rule or core state. (Price & Feinman 1997:390)

A few well-placed *yets* indicate some problems in the minds of the authors who give this material. The archaeologist Robert McCormick Adams also raises questions after his extensive surveys of site size and distribution. For Adams (1981:59) the anomalous feature of his survey was the dispersed pattern of sites. The expectation of irrigation farming would have predicted a linear distribution of sites reflecting watercourses either of natural or even small local canals for water distribution. He did offer that this distribution perhaps indicated that the commitment to irrigation agriculture was not as complete as has been assumed. Some members of that culture must have been "divergently specialized across the full spectrum of subsistence resources." But when considering drastic changes between the earlier Ubaid periods and the following Uruk period, Adams offers,

> What would have led to the considerable emphasis on cen-tralization in a few sites, with social institutions sufficiently formal and complex to favor the development of public archi-tecture, in spite of the prevailingly very low density of popula-tion? These questions raise the question of a major break, a disjunctive step of some kind, between the Ubaid period and what followed. Yet such a break is belied, at least in the best studied aspects of the material culture, by the apparent gradu-alness of the ceramic transition in the deep Eanna sounding in Uruk (von Haller 1932) and elsewhere, and by the manifest continuities in monumental temple architecture at ancient Eridu as well as Uruk. (Adams 1981:59)

Eanna is the name of the largest temple in Uruk. During early historic times it was dedicated to Inanna, the goddess of fertility. Please note that Adams finds a "disjunctive step of some kind" between the Ubaid period and what followed. He calls attention to the fact that this centralization of population in the Uruk period happened when the density of the population was pre-vailingly low. The temple architecture was similar between the two periods, but it became monumental only during the Uruk period. Question: does the continuation of a pottery tradition and architecture pattern argue strongly against the very prominently displayed changes? These changes include war-fare, monumental buildings, and huge walled cities—all strong evidences for hierarchy. It would seem that they only argue that the population itself has not been replaced, that the disjunctive step is the rather sudden introduction of hierarchy. Adams revisits the same disjunction when he offers his summary at the end of his book.

> In the largest sense, Mesopotamian cities can be viewed as an adaptation to this perennial problem of periodic unpredictable shortages. They provided concentration points for storage of surpluses, necessarily soon walled to assure their defensibility. The initial distribution of smaller communities around them suggests primarily localized exploitation of land, with much of the producing population being persuaded or compelled to take up residence within individual walled centers rather than

remaining in villages closer to their fields. Tending to contradict a narrowly determinist view of urban genesis as merely the formation of walled storage depots, the drawing together of significantly larger settlements than had existed previously not only created an essentially new basis for cultural and organization growth but could hardly have been brought about without the development of powerful new means for unifying what originally were socially and culturally heterogeneous groups. (Adams 1981:244)

Adams is uncomfortable with the materialistic perspective that cities with walls came into being merely to protect food surpluses for times of shortages. As will be pointed out below, for nearly all the very long period labeled Ubaid, there is no evidence for the need of such protection. Every Ubaid community, whatever it consisted of, had its own large storage facilities. Adams's survey does make it seem likely that some enclaves were involved in subsistence that did not include irrigation agriculture. But is his assumption valid that this economic diversification indicates the early presence of culturally heterogeneous groups in the lower valley during most of the Ubaid period?

In another article Adams had more to say about this sudden and seemingly unexpected change. This paragraph is interesting because he here presents a motivation that suggests Genesis 11:4. Notice the sentence: "The whole apparatus could equally well be mobilized for expansion and aggrandizement." Here, when speaking of the sudden appearance of Uruk as a large city, he makes the following observations:

> The ostensible purpose of the system as a whole presumably was the protection of urban populations, including their stored agricultural reserves and other forms of wealth, and in a symbolic sense, the city-temple residences of their patron deities. But the whole apparatus could equally well be mobilized for expansion and aggrandizement. In any case, the formation of cities, and not simply their fortification and regimentation of their inhabitants, is clearly part of the same system. Urban nucleation involved the abandonment of less defensible smaller settlements, and the creation of much more potent offensive and defensive concentrations of paramilitary personnel and their provisioners and dependents. (Adams 1984:111)

In 1998 Gil Stein, in an article written for the *Journal of Archaeological Research*, offered these comments about the term *chiefdom* as a stage in the evolution of social systems: "Many of the problems with this term have been addressed by the rejection of a redistribution-based definition of chiefdoms in favor of a less rigid, conflict based model of power relations that recognizes a range of variation in the strategies used by elites to create and manipulate structures of inequality. However, future research must eventually grapple with the extremely difficult problem of fitting this revised chiefdom concept into an explicitly multilinear social evolution framework" (Stein 1998).

Notice his commitment to an evolutionary framework. The implication is that man necessarily moved from social equality to social inequality in the evolution of political systems. Of course, a conflict-based model of power relations does not fit the conditions in this area during most of the Ubaid period. When writing just a few years earlier, Stein offered this neoevolutionary perspective to encompass the data from the ancient Near East. He then advanced a model of chiefdom society that might account for the absence of the usual archaeological markers of chiefdom society while incorporating the data of the Ubaid into an evolutionary perspective. He argued for social hierarchy during the whole of the Ubaid period (Stein 1994), defining the time frame as ca. 5500–3800 B.C. First Stein outlined the typical chiefdom model with its recognizable archaeological features—warfare, long distance exchange, exaggerated symbolization of social ranking, and the resulting cycles of consolidation and collapse. But after doing this, he pointed out the following: "However, it is important to note that these developments all take place at the tail end of the late Ubaid—ca. 4000–3800 B.C., immediately before the transition to state organization in the Uruk period. For the earlier 90% of the Ubaid evidence for warfare, exotic trade goods, and pronounced social stratification is completely lacking" (Stein 1994:40).

The archaeological data from the Near East is not all that one could desire. But it is adequate to locate the traits Stein has identified as typical of chiefdom organization. For Stein, the emergence of social complexity without the social hierarchy associated with chiefdom society was in clear contradiction to his understanding of the path leading to these first city-states. Therefore, he offers this explanation for the archaeological data.

> By focusing on economic control over *local* resources, mobilized through ritual sanctification of authority, Ubaid chiefs

> would have avoided the instability inherent in polities whose political economies depend on wealth distribution of exotic trade goods. What we see archaeologically as a result of this hypothesized strategy is a network of numerous small-scale chiefdoms that exhibit tremendous stability over time….
>
> An egalitarian facade of this sort helps explain the lack of conspicuous display of status differences….
>
> The remarkable stability and uniformity of Ubaid material culture in both time and space suggest that this was an extremely durable and adaptable ideology.
>
> This expansion seems to have taken place through the peaceful adoption by northern communities of an Ubaid chiefly ideology. In other words we are seeing the *replication* of existing small systems, rather than the *absorption* of neighboring areas into a few large expansionistic chiefdoms. (Stein 1994:43)

In order to accommodate his theoretical position Stein offered a hypothetical and otherwise unknown form of chiefdom society. His chiefdoms were not circumscribed by boundaries visible in the archaeological data. The chiefs all pretended to be part of egalitarian systems, displaying no status differences and not competing with other chiefs. No special prestige marked their structural place in the social order, nor were there boundaries of their chiefdoms. No wars were fought to validate these invisible boundaries. Stein's chiefdom societies are utopian; if his assessment is right, these early chiefs had overcome the problems associated with all later chiefdom societies.

Perhaps for Stein the presence of temples implied social hierarchy. Why is it so difficult to speculate that the early temples in Mesopotamia were dedicated to a supernatural being that was equally approachable by the whole of the population, a supreme being whose worship would require the recognition of this equality of access? If this were the situation, all the conditions described above would follow. Such belief systems, usually without permanent temples, have been demonstrated among contemporary hunter-gatherer societies. Based on the data, is it not logical to allow that the economy was based on the activity of independent actors, not a chiefdom-controlled economy, and that the religious ideals were egalitarian up until the intrusion of a different cosmology at or near the end of the Ubaid period? The data of archaeology would be well explained by the introduction of a new worldview allowing, or even requiring, stratified social structure.

While Stein's model may help neoevolutionary archaeologists get a handle on the Ubaid culture, it fails to explain why the Halafian culture pattern (Stein's northern communities in the above quotation), already in place in northern Iraq, Syria, and Anatolia, would need to become chiefdom societies when this area and southern Iraq combined into one very large unified culture area. The fact that this happened will be mentioned again at the end of the chapter. The lower valley practiced irrigation, true. And without doubt, this practice required some additional activities. But evidence for these activities in Ubaid times did not require a change in the structure of society that would then be adopted by the rest of the culture area, especially if that area did not practice irrigation agriculture. At some point there was a discontinuity between the hierarchical social structure of the occupants of the ancient Near East and their egalitarian hunter-gatherer ancestors. The evidence indicates that this discontinuity in social order occurred near the end of the late Ubaid period. Up until that time, there is very little evidence for unequal social order with its attendant characteristics. In fact, there is no archaeological evidence for ethnic differences either.

As mentioned at the start of the chapter, this area has continued to be one of interest and research for archaeologists; the broad outline of the data from this area has been known for more than half a century. This takes us back to a time before archaeologists brought neoevolutionary expectations to the data. How did those who studied the archaeological data then interpret this material?

> How are we to interpret these broad-scale developments? With the greatest difficulty. All we can say is that in that age close ties connected regions of Western Asia, and that these ties were promoted by reciprocal exchange of goods. But is that enough to explain what we see? Everything we know of the historical ancient Near East, where ethnic groups occupy only limited areas, warns us we must think in terms of large-scale migrations. But if there were migrations here, on the edge of history, they would have come from those areas where village culture was as yet unknown: the population density would have been too low, at the level of a hunting and food-

gathering existence or of pastoral nomadism. But the original homeland of the village culture, the rim of the Fertile Crescent with its fast-rising population, would have been forced to expand. We have seen the example of the settling of Babylonia; in Anatolia and Iran, too, farmers opened new areas farther and farther away from their starting point. At this time settlements spring up in territories as climatically ill favored as the northern Negev in Palestine. But whether the village cultures of Western Asia participated decisively in the development of Neolithic villages of Europe, or whether these were original creations of the Middle and Lower Danube, is undecided. The same is true for the rest of the ancient world. (Falkenstein 1967:30f)

New techniques have sorted out some of these problems. It has been determined that most of European agricultural plants and animals were domesticated in the Near East. The "greatest difficulty" that Falkenstein mentions is the obvious presence of ethnic groups after a long period without evidence for them. The mysteries about the origin of the Sumerian language and when it arrived in the Mesopotamian Valley no longer occupy archaeologists; their present theories allow them to ignore this question. But the apparent ethnic unity and its sudden disruption at the end of the Ubaid period were startling before 1960 and still remain startling. It is almost as though some supernatural being brought about this sudden disunity by confusing the languages. Of course, any consideration of such an intervention is outside the scope of "scientific" archaeology, and no one within that body is apt to even allow such a suggestion.

Trade, specialization in both food and crafts, and construction of facilities and buildings for collective uses appear to have happened in the ancient Near East well before evidence for social hierarchy. Whatever the conditions during most of the Ubaid period, firm boundaries have not been identified archaeologically either within this large common culture pattern or on its perimeter. During the dynastic period, no ruler controlled the entire lower valley. Much later, when areas this large were brought under control of one ethnic group, these areas were called empires, but none of these empires were enduring when compared with the time frame allowed for the unified cultural area of the Ubaid/Halaf. In view of this data, it is difficult to argue that the "evolution" of political societies brought more people into a single polity.

But what about the massive temples in Mesopotamia? Before the late Ubaid period it is true that the temple at Eridu, and perhaps several others, had become fairly large. Apparently the sites seemed important to the builders. The temple was rebuilt, as necessary, on top of the demolished earlier temple. In order to include the ruins of the old temple, the temple site naturally became a tell of considerable height and thus size. It is likely that the temple at Eridu was rebuilt only when typical upkeep could not restore it to acceptable beauty or usefulness. The temple at Eridu was rebuilt seventeen times, perhaps ten times before the late Ubaid period. After the Ubaid period massive temples were erected on great platforms whether or not these platforms covered the remains of earlier temples.

What about the large cities such as Uruk and Ur? Some of Adams's observations follow. The settlement pattern before the process of urbanization began was made up of small towns, villages, or hamlets, all less than twenty-five acres. They were scattered at fairly uniform intervals, gradually becoming arranged in clustered enclaves (1973:R16-7). Uruk may have been one of a handful of ceremonial centers "not long after the beginning of the Ubaid period." But even among the later clustered patterns Adams was sure that one could safely conclude that "recognized social units were prevailingly small and highly localized" (1973:R16-8). The urbanization process did not take place equally. The area around Uruk imploded into Uruk more completely and earlier than the area around Ur. The area around Nippur was depopulated even earlier than Uruk, but Adams allows that there may have been other causes (1973:R16-6). He also mentions that his survey did not adequately cover that area.

It is also possible to speak of Uruk pottery (especially a standard bowl) and thus an objective artifact to easily identify Uruk influence. But now, this influence is called intrusive, characterized by archaeologist Guillermo Algaze as enclaves, stations, and outposts (Algaze 1989:577). During this rather long period, the second half of the fourth millennium B.C., there are some sites such as Nineveh and Brak that have long Uruk sequences; others later in the period were more sophisticated when they first exhibited this influence. A more sophisticated site, north of the modern town of Meskene, Habuba-sud and its acropolis were built as a well-planned city with carefully laid-out streets and well-differentiated residential, industrial, and administrative quarters all within a sturdy wall (Algaze 1989:578). Other sites that have been identified as Mesopotamian enclaves of the Uruk period have been located on the Nile delta and a distance up in the Nile Valley, the Persian/Arabian Gulf, and in Transcaucasia (Algaze 1989:593).

The sites of these intrusions were not haphazard: they were apparently chosen for their access to trade routes. The lower valley lacked lumber, minerals of all kinds, bitumen (used frequently in mortar), stone for building, and metals. These were imported by the south primarily in exchange for food products.

> The Uruk intrusion, too, is unintelligible unless we presume the existence of local communities that, initially at least, were willing to participate in the wider network opened by the Uruk outposts. Otherwise, the position of the intrusive settlements in the midst of alien hinterlands would have been untenable in the face of local opposition. Although the Uruk enclaves themselves and their immediate environs are likely to have been dependent on specific Uruk city-states, there is no evidence of Southern Mesopotamian political control of the areas away from the enclaves. Rather, the links between the Syro-Mesopotamian plains and the surrounding highlands and the Uruk world were primarily economic in nature. (Algaze 1989:589)

It seems as though Algaze's presumption of the economic nature of these enclaves is reasonable. However, he is quick to add that the evidence does not support the notion of a single centralized political entity. Instead, there were competing cities in Mesopotamian lowlands. No doubt several city-states were involved in establishing these enclaves while they struggled with one another for superiority back in the homeland. This can be documented by long-term trends of expansion and contraction taking place in the enclaves themselves (Algaze 1989:592).

Algaze (1989:590) lists a number of changes that the Mesopotamian core would have had to go through in order to accommodate the changes in the Uruk period. The last (fourth) of these changes was "new forms of symbolic representations to validate the changes taking place in the realm of social and political relationships." With this assessment I agree, although in my mind the change that marked the end of the Ubaid unity was the greatest of these new "symbolic representations." When considering the literate periods of Sumer, we are privileged to see continual modifications to accommodate new political situations in the land.

At the start of the chapter, mention was made of circumstances of the first hierarchy in Western Europe. Starting even before the lower Mesopotamian Valley was populated, about 6500 B.C., a Neolithic economy with Near Eastern culti-gens, animals, and pottery gradually spread from Anatolia into and across much of Europe. This movement of the Neolithic across Europe exhibited no apparent evidence for social hierarchy. But during the late Ubaid and the Uruk period, hierarchy turned up in a number of places, some already with a Neolithic economy, and some, including Egypt (see next chapter) and the Atlantic coast, with little, if any, evidence for a Neolithic economy (Renfrew 1979:107). This hierarchy was shown in Egypt by unequal grave goods and along the Atlantic coasts of Europe by elaborate burial procedures. In each of these areas, the first evidences for a Neolithic economy appear along with the first evidences for social hierarchy. Later, these coastal hierarchies, marked by their burial practices, encroach on the areas of those already farming but without hierarchy.

How did social hierarchy come to Western Europe? From history we know that people in most of Europe spoke European languages. But from archaeology it is possible to infer that much of Western Europe practiced social hierarchy before this language family came to Europe. One reconstruction of the Proto-Indo-European language would have its expansion begin during the Uruk period, likely from the Pontic-Caspian steppe with their tripartite (hierarchical) social system already in place (Mallory 1994:197). But starting at about the same time, Neolithic Europe was gradually brought under the influence of several hierarchical systems: the megalithic burial chamber complexes from the Atlantic coast, from Varna on the Black Sea, from the Near East itself and the Mediterranean islands, and finally by the Indo-Europeans. By the time history was being recorded, Indo-European language groups had succeeded in leaving their language and evidence of their social organization throughout all but small pockets of Europe.

Neoevolutionary assumptions prevent archaeology from relating the appearance of hierarchy in the Mesopotamian Valley and the sudden introduction of hierarchy on the Atlantic coastal areas. Hierarchy in the Mesopotamian Valley comes about 4,000 years after evidence for the beginning of agriculture. But on these coastal areas agriculture and hierarchy arrived at the same time. An obvious correlation is that this hierarchy appeared in those areas in sync with the events in the Near East. Further, the archaeological evidence from Europe would certainly not rule out a further diffusion of hierarchical influences, their own theories notwithstanding. The archeological record suggests that this Mesopotamian hierarchy, and—if the premise of this book is right—the cosmology supporting it, could be aptly described as scattered.

The word *scattered* is, of course, found just under the header. Is there reason to believe that this introduction of social hierarchy was indeed the event mentioned in Genesis 11:8–9? My argument supporting that conclusion is given in the Appendix: The Confusion of Languages. But if it is, it raises a question: was God's scattering ineffective? You may remember that the whole area of the Euphrates Valley, from its source in Anatolia to the Persian Gulf, during the later part of the Ubaid period came to share a single pottery tradition. This pottery resembled the pottery traditions of the lower valley. Perhaps the lower valley set the trends in other ways. Perhaps when social hierarchy came to the lower valley nothing would have prevented it from spreading quickly through the whole of the Ubaid culture. It did not. This hierarchy was restricted to enclaves that intruded into other places where the population remained egalitarian at least for a while. This action resisted the direction of change but did not deny man his choice of worldviews and social structure.

Since the purpose of this chapter is not to survey all evidences for early hierarchy but to fix the background for the cosmology supporting the earliest one, this very brief and admittedly controversial introduction to the archaeological evidences for early hierarchy in the ancient Near East and Europe will do. As mentioned above, the earliest obvious evidence for social hierarchy was about 4000 B.C. (uncorrected carbon).

Chapter Three

Origins of Social Hierarchy: Europe, Asia, and Africa

The last chapter described the Neolithic culture pattern called Ubaid. This culture covered a considerable landmass without apparent political borders. It continued to develop and expand for nearly 1,500 years. The evidence suggests a society without elites, a culture obviously built on egalitarian principles. All but the very end of this period was without evidence for either political instability (war) or social inequalities. In fact, while the lower Euphrates valley was occupied—only about 1,500 years—taking into account the upper valley and the Levant where agriculture was first practiced, about 4,000 years passed between the time of first farming and evidence of first hierarchy. But immediately after social hierarchy appeared in the lower Mesopotamian Valley, the social structures in many areas, according to archaeological evidence, became hierarchical.

The materialist looks for material causes for these events; an idealist considers the possibility that a new idea, a new cosmology, could have interrupted the unity of this egalitarian culture pattern that had covered the whole earth. (The whole earth was apparently without hierarchy, even though some areas were distant enough not to participate as directly as those living in the area of the valley of the Tigris and the Euphrates.) If such a cosmology came into existence, can it be known? There cannot be certainty about it. But if it left its influence on later restatements of chartering mythologies, it can be inferred. Let us assume along with Eliade that a creator cosmology had been the cosmology of the whole world. This assumption might account for both the presence of widespread hunter-gatherers who knew of a creator cosmology and the apparently egalitarian social structure of the early farmers in all the places where independent domestication of plants and animals took place.

Since justification for the social order will be found within the society's cosmology, it follows that a change from an egalitarian social order to a hierarchical one would require a change in cosmology. The earlier cosmology of the egalitarian order itself would need to be set aside. We can speculate that the new cosmology would have both denied the providence afforded by the creator and introduced a universe that could be manipulated. Perhaps, then, it is not unreasonable to expect a polemic element against the creator in any early cosmology that claimed to control the environment.

How would a population sharing an egalitarian culture pattern be enticed to recognize the presence of elites and come to depend on them? During the Uruk period, with the obvious introduction of social hierarchy, settlements identified as Uruk outposts funneled goods and resources to the lower valley in quantities that they had not known before. In a few places, the Uruk outpost itself appears to have become the nucleus of hierarchical societies. The fame of this rich culture pattern spread. Either the promise of wealth or the threat of unfavorable trading conditions could be motivation to accept hierarchical social organization and its cosmological underpinning.

The Uruk pattern (social hierarchy) quickly brought into play long-distance trading. But political turmoil came with this boon as city-states within the core area of the Uruk civilization struggled for ascendancy. In addition to war, it is likely that slavery and forced labor were soon introduced to build the monumental structures and walls that the Uruk culture displayed.

Yet obviously there were those who saw benefits in incorporating ritual control of nature into the social structure. It is likely that they would use an argument already successful in the lower valley. The same argument (now stated as a cosmology) would have meaning wherever the creator cosmology was in force. And further, the polemic element in these new cosmologies might well continue to mark them even after changes in these cosmologies reflected the needs and tastes, the history if you will, of the particular group. But in spite of these historical differences in the ancient world, the new social structure offered a cosmos in which elites provided for the society in accordance with the rituals they performed.

Is there direct evidence that such a cosmology spread? The evidence as laid out in the last chapter showed that the hierarchical Uruk culture had outposts in places where they expected to profit by trade. Egypt developed hierarchical centers around two outposts of Uruk culture. In the case of the Egyptian outposts, there was little evidence for the existence of a Neolithic economy before burials were found with both Mesopotamian plant and animal domesticates and an obviously unequal distribution of wealth. It is likely that this system of elites in Egypt was justified by a cosmology similar to the home base back in Mesopotamia. Egypt is a singularly good example of the spread of hierarchy and its supporting cosmology. From the pyramid texts in Egypt we have copies of not only their earliest written cosmologies but also the earliest written cosmologies known.

While the earlier Ubaid culture obviously used marks that identified owners of traded goods and the credit for them, their writing was used primarily to meet economic needs. The Uruk culture does not appear to have changed this pattern. The first written formulations that dealt with the structure of their society appeared near the middle of the third millennium. We can speculate that by this time there had been modifications in the original cosmology since, theoretically at least, the king of the whole land was recognized at a single city, Nippur. It is unlikely that the first city-states had such a confederation. Nippur was never the largest city-state, nor did it ever subjugate the rest of the area.

But this is true not only of the lower Mesopotamian Valley; the earliest written expression of the Egyptian cosmology appeared after the unification of the two hierarchical centers in Egypt. This unification is an important topic in early Egyptian cosmology even as the confederation of city-states in Uruk is important cosmological material in forming the state called Sumer. The earliest pyramid texts are from the early second millennium BC.

But do these very likely modified cosmologies have recognizable similarities? And further, do other cosmologies reduced to writing in the ancient literate societies show some of the same similarities? This is the question that will be probed in this chapter.

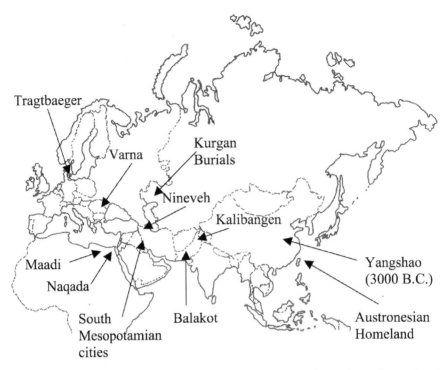

Above are the archaeological sites that are known to have changed to a hierarchical social structure at about the same time. A number of these sites are known outposts of the Uruk culture within Mesopotamia. Within the time constraints imposed by archaeology these all show this social structure shortly after 4000 B.C. uncorrected carbon except for the Yangshao site in China. This site obviously had some contact with the Near East also since archaeologists found in it grains domesticated in the Near East.

As already mentioned, the oldest of the documents that express a cosmology come from the Egyptian pyramids. The texts explained that, by ritual, the dead king became one with the eternal Osiris, Egypt's great god, while the new king became Horus, his legitimate son and ruler of Egypt. The word *Osiris* means "grain." It was the function of the dead king, now one with the eternal Osiris, to provide food for the land. As given by the Egyptologist Anthes, the earliest formulation from 2700 B.C. follows:

> The primeval god, Atum, engendered the pair Shu and Tefnut by himself, in an unnatural though human manner. The children of Shu and Tefnut were Geb and Nut. Father Shu raised up Nut from Geb and so separated the sky from the earth. A quarrel about the kingship in Egypt arose among the sons of Geb and Nut: Seth killed the king Osiris and took the throne until Horus, the son of Osiris and Isis, grew up, fought his uncle Seth, and was acclaimed by the court of Heliopolis as the true king of Egypt and heir to Osiris. (Anthes 1961)

Archaeological efforts in Egypt have suggested that a Neolithic economy appeared in Egypt based on Near Eastern plants and animals. The evidence suggests that this economy was introduced in the middle of the fourth millennium, early in the Uruk period. As mentioned earlier it seems that there were two Uruk outposts in Egypt. It appears that both unequal social structure and domesticated plants and animals were introduced at the same time (Bard 1992:12).

Before the Dynastic Period in Egypt, there appear to have been two hierarchical cultures, one in Lower Egypt, the Maadi culture, and the other in Upper Egypt, the Naqada (Bard 1994:265–269). It is likely that these two competing regions arose around two Uruk outposts in Egypt. An important part of the mythology in the texts recovered from the pyramids recounts the uniting of these two cultures. This was probably accomplished at the start of the dynastic era, 3050 B.C. But unequal social structure was demonstrated by differences in burial practices from the time of the early Neolithic evidence in the Naqada area. Further, these outposts seem to have been the gateway to unequal social structure in the rest of Africa. The last part of this chapter will attempt to strengthen this argument. The material offered in this chapter supports the proposition that after the first explosion of social hierarchy, people in other places were either coerced or found the pattern acceptable. In other words, the premise is that most social hierarchy can be traced back to a worldview first articulated in the late Ubaid period. Perhaps, if this is true, it would not be unusual that this cosmology left its mark on many of the early cosmologies supporting hierarchy.

If hierarchy arrived with the Neolithic economy stimulated by Uruk outposts from the Mesopotamian Valley, the cosmological basis for this hierarchy probably came from there as well. How does it compare with the earliest literature that expresses an understandable cosmology in the Mesopotamian Valley? From the book mentioned above, Kramer offers, "According to the myth of 'Enlil and the Creation of the Pickaxe,' he was the god who separated heaven and earth, brought forth 'the seed of the land' from the earth, brought forth 'whatever was needful'" (Kramer 1961:96).

The material from Sumer will be considered in greater detail in Chapter Six. Here it will merely be added that heaven and earth were separated with the "pickaxe." The place where this happened was the city, Nippur. At this spot it is said that the men emerged and were given the pickaxe, which I interpret to be the symbol of kingship. During dynastic Sumer, the king of the land was recognized at the temple that enshrined this place and event. Is this the same as the Egyptian cosmology? No, even the nature of the king was defined in a different way. The Egyptian pharaoh was the god Horus, his father the great god Osiris. In the Mesopotamian Valley the human king was dependent on the gods; he himself was not (usually) a god. Yet the cosmology of Sumer also incorporated the cosmos into social structure by claiming for its most important city the origin of man and kingship. While the king was dependent on the gods, the people were dependent on the rituals the kings and priests performed to control the environment even as Egypt was dependent on the pharaoh and his father to regulate the environment. Notice that in both situations a stated precondition was separation of heaven and earth.

This observation is worth noting:

> *Social structure that incorporated ritual control of the cosmos originated in the Mesopotamian Valley and was rapidly spread through the outposts of the Uruk Culture. Looking briefly at the cosmological materials of Egypt and Sumer, by far the earliest materials we have, both cosmologies included a separation of heaven and earth theme.*

Certainly in the Egyptian materials, Heaven and Earth were personified and should be capitalized. Whether or not this is true in Sumerian material the reader may determine when looking more closely at the Sumerian myths in Chapter Six.

Although the first Indo-European cosmological material was found in Hittite ruins dating to late first millennium B.C., it is the material from India that will attract our attention. The reason for this is that the Hittite material identifies Sumerian cities (likely Nippur and Eridu) and probably Sumerian gods. Therefore, that material may be an interpretation of the separation of heaven and earth as the Hittites found it among the population in the area. It is also possible to argue that the Greeks merely took their knowledge of the cosmology from the Hittites. Although I believe that the Hittites and Greeks justified their hierarchy by separation cosmology, I have chosen to avoid that question and use the Indo-European version as found in the Rig Veda.

From India the first writing useful for our purpose is not found in the historical context in which it was first used, as in the pyramid texts of Egypt, nor contemporaneously with those who viewed their cosmology as charter for social order, as on the clay tablets of Sumer. The oldest useful literature from India is considered to be their Rig Veda. The history of the people who wrote that literature is sometimes reconstructed in this way. About 1500 B.C. Indo-Europeans came from the north and overran great cities that were already in the process of decay. Archaeology has found script from these cities, but the longest string of symbols is short and their meaning is unknown. These cities are not altogether shrouded in mystery. Two of the most notable are Mohenjo-daro and Harappa. They were planned cities with some evidences for social hierarchy, although the use of their large structures has been identified as grain storage and a public bath rather than the expected temple. These cities are generally dated from the twenty-fifth to the nineteenth centuries B.C.

To the west of these cities in the site of Mehrgarh, archaeologists found evidence for contact both with the Mesopotamian Valley (i.e., grains domesticated in that area) and Afghanistan (i.e., a precious blue stone called lapus luzuli). Price and Feinman believe this site is a precursor village east of the Harappan cities. They argue that because there is record of habitation going back to pre-Neolithic times, the development of hierarchy must have been local. The argument could just as well be made for greater communication between these people and the rest of their world going back to pre-Neolithic times. However, the Harappan cities on the Indus were founded later than less well-known cities—Balakot on the mouth of the Indus and Kalibanga on another branch of the river but farther inland. These walled cities were built earlier, closer to the Uruk period, and may well have been involved in over-water trade with the Uruk civilization. It is certainly more likely that these cities gave rise to the Harappan Civilization.

Although this civilization on the Indus River has left us no written documents, there have been some remnants. "The persistence of many aspects and traditions of the Indus civilization into more recent times is startling. Ceremonial bathing, ritual burning, specific body positions (such as yogic position) on seals, the important symbolic roles of bulls and elephants, decorative arrangements of multiple bangles and necklaces (evident from graves and realistic figures), all are important attributes of ancient Harappan society that remain at the heart of contemporary Hinduism" (Price & Feinman 1997:405).

Linguists have known for a long time that the languages spoken by nearly all Europeans, as well as those spoken in Iran and much of India, form one language family. The implications of this discovery are interesting. The simplest understanding for this situation is that sometime in the past, a single group of people, small enough in number to all use the same language, spoke a language that has been labeled Proto-Indo-European (PIE). Immediately, questions present themselves. Where and how did the PIE speakers live? This language group obviously spread out. So what were the circumstances of their lifestyle at the time they became separate groups? That is, they spread out and their dialects became different languages, so what do the common words in all these languages tell us about their environment, their economy and technology, their family structure, and their social organization? These words are, of course, not the same in all the languages, but linguists are able to trace systematic changes between the language groups and thus predict how these words would have changed. Perhaps there will yet be refinements or even changes in the arguments that have been derived from linguistic studies of the Indo-European (IE) languages. However, according to the New York *Times* article by George Johnson, printed on January 2, 1996, a recent diagram suggesting how these groups spread out offers that the first offshoot of the IE was into Anatolia.

In addition to offering clues as to where the PIE originated, linguists have been able, knowing of the family of languages, to find similar patterns of the social order. Georges Dumezil has been credited with identifying three classes in this social structure and has associated IE gods with these classes. For an English translation of his efforts, see *Mitra-Varuna: An Essay on Two Indo-European Representations of Sovereignty.* Bruce Lincoln has moved in a different direction to offer a reconstruction of the cosmology for the divergent IE groups by analyzing the written traditions of a fairly large number of them (Lincoln 1972–6:121–145).

As to where the PIE lived, Mallory in his *In Search of the Indo-Europeans* has put forward one theory that has been given a good deal of attention. He acknowledged that this theory is dependent on the efforts and reasoning of Marija Gimbutas. That theory relates the PIE people to the Kurgan burials. The first of these burials occurred in the Pontic-Caspian steppe. From there, these burial practices spread to Europe, the area that has generated the most interest, from about 4000 to 2500 B.C. (corrected carbon date) in three waves. The earliest Kurgan burials fall into the late Uruk period; the given carbon date 4000 B.C. is adjusted to a calendar date using tree-ring correction. The area in which these early burials are found is near enough one of the outposts mentioned in the Algaze article, Transcaucasia, to have been directly affected by the events in Uruk.

Within the hymns of the Rig Veda, there is reference to the conquest of fortified cities. In the above scenario, these cities no longer dominated the Gujarat landscape when the IE came. The next large cities in India were built in the Ganges Valley centuries later. It is assumed that the residents of those cities, by then speaking several different IE languages, had passed down by word of mouth hymns (Vedas) over many generations. Several of these hymns are religious in nature, telling of the origin and organization of the Vedic cosmos. The particular cosmology, said to be the oldest, is the "Asura" myth.

> The Asuras originally lived in a house built for them by the god Tvastr (artificer, builder). The house consisted of heaven and earth which at this time were undivided. The sat [orderly rule] and the asat [chaos] were similarly undivided. There are two classes of Asuras: Aditya (antibondage) and Danava (bondage). The Adityas stand for expansion, development, and light, the Danavas for darkness and bondage. Their leader is Vrtra (the encloser). Neither the Danavas nor the Adityas has a parentage; they are personifications of abstractions. Because the Adityas want to release the cosmic waters and the Danavas

want to keep them contained, a war ensues. In this war the three Adityas—Varuna, Mitra and Aryaman (the number varies)—are being worsted by the Danavas and need a champion. They arrange for the birth of Indra, who is kept out of sight when first born, but after drinking soma he enlarges to such an extent that earth and sky fly apart in terror. Indra fills the space in between. He agrees to be champion of the Adityas only if they make him king of the gods. To this they assent. Tvastr forms a weapon (the vaita "thunderbolt") for him, and with it he slays Vrtra, cuts him open and the cosmic waters flow forth—freeing the sat from the asat and making it possible to give it order, light, heat, and moisture. Rta [law] is established and Varuna made the guardian of it. Evil, however, is not completely abolished. The gods still need support in the form of sacrifices for every day the battle with Vrtra is renewed. (Tyler 1973:45)

Tyler proceeds to explain that in the Rig Veda, ethical concepts are derived from the concept of *rta*, the natural order of the universe. For them, the natural order was based on their occupation. This functional division was given as the four *varnas* (Brahmin, Ksatriya, Vaisya, Sudras), priests, warriors, farmers, and laborers. The king was chosen from the warrior class. Each *varna* had some common duties: performance of the sacrifice and combating forces of evil.

This telling of the cosmology does not offer information about the origin of man. From Norman W. Brown this information is available:

When the fight was over it became apparent what the Adityas and the Danavas had been quarreling about for out of the shattered mountain or out of the cave, or variantly out of Vritra's (Vrtra) belly, emerged the cosmic Waters, motherly females who longed to escape confinement. They came out lowing like cattle, flowing over the prostrate body of their former restrainer and lord Vritra, to acknowledge Indra as their new lord. And, astonishingly, the Waters were pregnant and their embryo was the sun (Brown 1961:284).... Later, the first man came into being as a son of Vivasvant "the Wide-shining [Sun]," his function being to perform the sacrifices on earth and so strengthen the gods through the execution of their duties and the frustration of their demonic and human opponents. (Brown 1961:285)

From the Rig Veda (Royal Hymns) we learn that the first man was son of the sun. Notice that in this separation of heaven and earth cosmology the sun did not exist before heaven and earth were separated. When considering the separation myth more globally, this aspect of darkness before the separation seems to be an integral part of the myth. Whether heaven and earth are personified as the mother and father of Indra is not clear in this telling. But it is clear that their separation was necessary for the sun and man (specifically the first king) to come into being. Incidentally following Bruce Lincoln's analysis, when the first king, Yama, was sacrificed, his body became the source of the three varnas: priests, warriors, and farmers/herders. It seems as though the Hindu IE added the fourth, the laborer class called Sudras. Yama himself at this time became lord of the dead. This, along with a sacrificial bovine animal, is essentially the IE creation myth according to Bruce Lincoln (Lincoln 1972:145). In both Vedic India and Sumer, the head of the pantheon separated heaven and earth. In Egypt it was Shu, the father of Heaven and Earth. Again, notice the social structure is incorporated into the cosmos. Further, the society in each case is dependent on the leader for proper interaction with the cosmos.

As noted in a paragraph earlier, Dumezil located a similar structure, three-tiered, with gods corresponding to the three tiers, along with linguistic correspondences for priests and kings between the Romans and the Rig Veda. Further, Lincoln found the chartering cosmology from consideration of several texts, including the Indian Rig Veda, several Iranian texts, and Roman and Norse material. This particular social structure with its chartering mythology was successful in spreading its influence from its origin to the Atlantic as well as into Central and South Asia. Its influence, moderated by Hinduism, swept through much of Southeast Asia. Bali in Indonesia practices a form of the Hindu religion. Buddhism might also be considered an offshoot of Hinduism and is widely practiced in China and Southeast Asia.

In China the cosmology at the time of first hierarchy is even further removed from us than the cosmology of the Indo-Europeans. Archaeological evidence for this first hierarchy is somewhat after the Ubaid period. In China, farming cultures appeared as early as 7000 B.C. The north and south had different farming regimes. In the north, the site Cishan contained evidence of domesticated dogs, pigs, and chickens and domesticated millet. In the south, at Hemudu, rice was cultivated and the southern animal was the water buffalo. In the north, the first obvious hierarchical site is in the time called the Longshan period. "During the subsequent Longshan period (3000–2205 B.C.), significant changes took place in North Chinese social organization, including marked increase in social ranking. Compared to earlier burials, Longshan mortuary assemblages exhibit more variation; some include jade ornaments and ceremonial weapons. For the first time, many of the Longshan period settlements were walled, and the larger communities were much bigger than ever before" (Price & Feinman 1997:420).

The Shang dynasty follows this period and is one of the San Dai—the three dynasties known as the Xia, Shang, and Zhou. Little can be said with certainty about the beliefs of these kingdoms. Derk Bodde, again from the book *Mythologies of the Ancient World*, credits Confucius with a good deal of euhemerization. This means that he restated the mythology he received in such a way as to make it part of early Chinese history. Bodde adds that kernels of mythology traced through Taoism also suffer from reinterpretations conforming to their own biases. After presenting several mythical stories that may have been creation stories, Bodde tells of an incident, supposedly a historic event, that involved the reestablishment of order when a tribal group called the Miao brought about disorder.

> Shang Ti, the Lord on High (name of the most prominent ancient deity), surveyed the people and found them lacking in virtue. Out of pity for the innocent, the August Lord (surely another name for Shang Ti, though the euhemerizing commentators interpret him as either Yao or Shun) had the Miao exterminated. "Then he charged Ch'ung and Li to cut the communication between Heaven and Earth so that there would be no descending and ascending of spirits and men between the two." After this had been done, order was restored and the people returned to virtue. (parentheses in original, Bodde 1961:389–390)

After recounting another text in which similar material is given, Bodde goes on to explain that the mythical element being traced in the two accounts is given in each as "Ch'ung lifted Heaven up and Li pressed Earth down." Bodde at this point brings in Eliade and offers this quotation as Eliade's explanation of this widespread myth. "The myths of many peoples allude to a very distant epoch when men knew neither death nor toil nor suffering and had a bountiful supply of food merely for the taking. *In illo tempore,* the gods descended to earth and mingled with men; for their part, men could easily mount to heaven. As a result of a ritual fault, communications between heaven and earth were interrupted and the gods withdrew to the highest heaven. Since then, men must work for their food and are no longer immortal" (Bodde 1961:392).

Bodde does criticize this interpretation to the extent that he notes that originally, in the Chinese material, only the shaman had access to heaven. Since Eliade has profoundly influenced my thinking, I criticize him with caution. He interprets this cosmology in two different ways: one a "fall" from an earlier paradise in his book *Shamanism,* and the other the marriage of Heaven and Earth as the source of all things in *Myths, Dreams and Mysteries.* Neither of these interpretations allows what the four myths considered here appear to demonstrate: heaven and earth were separated to establish or reestablish (the social) order.

The influence of China's social structure on the rest of Southeast Asia has in the past been considered dominant. Now with neoevolutionary archaeology and the discovery that many innovations were local in development, there is a tendency to claim that social inequalities also developed locally. If it is true that metallurgy, well-crafted pottery, cotton for clothing, and a host of other inventions and discoveries could only be managed under the condition of unequal social structure, perhaps this reasoning is correct. However, if these technologies were developed by local groups without hierarchy, as seems more likely, and were spread through trading channels where the trading partners were first deemed equal, then the argument that hierarchy is required for technological development misses the mark.

There is one system of social hierarchy that is prominent in part of the Old World that has not been considered—that is, the social structure of the Austronesian speakers. This group never became literate. It rivaled the IE in distribution at one time, although it did not likely represent as great a population. It encompasses much of the island world out into the Pacific and had representatives even off the east coast of Africa. It overtook people groups, as did the IE group, and left many of them with an Austronesian language. In some cases, as with the IE, the influence of the Austronesian social structure may be perceived even though their language was not adopted. Further consideration is given to the Austronesians in Chapter Eight.

Now we return to the influence of the Egyptian cosmology and social structure on the rest of Africa. Because the earliest of the Egyptian cosmological materials describes rituals involved in installing the pharaoh in the office of the divine king, there can be no doubt about the relationship between the cosmology and the social structure. The cosmology is not a series of speculative statements; it is the charter for establishment of the institution of the Egyptian god-king. The fact that we do not accept the Egyptian commitment to the meaning of this institution does not make the cosmology false speculation—false perhaps, but a commitment nonetheless. Anthes suggests that the separation of heaven and earth, Nut and Geb, was a cosmological tale. Perhaps in time this became merely a cosmological tale. But when first articulated, this notion that heaven and earth were separated was likely a statement of commitment just as surely as the rest of the text. This text spelled out the rituals from which we gain our understanding of how, at the death of the Egyptian king—the death of Horus, the god-king who ruled Egypt—would now become one with Osiris, the vegetation of the land and Egypt's chief god. Osiris' son was then installed as Horus, establishing the continuity of the god-king of the land.

The question is, what was the intellectual content of the cosmological statement, "heaven and earth were separated"? This formulation is widely used in Africa. To get a further insight into the use of this statement, Edward Parrinder, a mythologist, offers,

> Along the west coast, in the Ivory Coast, Ghana, Togo, Dahomey, and Nigeria there are common myths of God retiring from the earth. In Olden days God lived very near men, in the sky, but just above their heads. He was so close that men grew familiar with him. Children would wipe their greasy hands on the sky when they finished their meals. Women in search of an extra ingredient for dinner would tear a piece off the sky and put it into the cooking pot. Especially women would knock against the sky when pounding their meal.... It is remarkable that right across the other side of Africa similar stories are told. The Nuba of the Sudan say that in the beginning the sky was so close to earth, in fact, that a man could touch it. (Parrinder1967: 34–35)

So it is clear that not only the ancient Egyptians but also modern African groups declare their origins within a separation cosmology. This cosmology is also part of the charter for their hierarchical societies. If it is true that these myths on each side of northern Africa represent the same idea, it follows that *sky* and *God* appear to be used here interchangeably.

The purpose of much of the pyramid texts was to ensure that the dead king became one with Osiris, the source of vegetation for the land. His son was then declared to be Horus, the divine king. This situation is similar to that of many African "rainmaker kings." Henri Frankfort, a specialist in ancient Near Eastern studies, writes, "A rainmaker king is buried in a cattle byre, which continued to be used (as was the royal castle where Osiris was buried).... He is said to take the food of the community into the grave, so when the next season arrives a hole is dug at the side of the byre so that the food may come out again" (Frankfort 1978:33). Frankfort continues with several other examples of African divine kingship. The rainmakers had ritual control of the weather; the Egyptian king had control of the Nile and its inundation of the land.

The example of the rainmaker king given above is from the Dinka, a Nilotic tribe in Sudan. Later we will look more closely at their cosmology and find that it also has the element of the separation of heaven and earth, even as the first texts from ancient Egypt and the first of the translated cuneiform tablets from Sumer. For now it is enough to point out that in ancient Egypt, as well as in Sumer, India, and China, the separation of heaven and earth established conditions that made it possible for the ritual control of the environment, apparently mediated in all cases through the netherworld.

British anthropologists have not been hesitant to suggest that the cultural form taken by these kingdoms is typically African. Since Egypt displayed hierarchy well before any other hierarchy is known in Africa, one can speculate that Egypt was the gateway through which social hierarchy entered the African continent. Marc Abeles, one of these British anthropologists, locates in many African states profound similarities in their systems of legitimation of their rulers. He offers the name Sacred Kingship to the institutions that form this political configuration. In these societies the king has the function of cosmic reproducer on behalf of the entire society. In this institution, widespread in sub-Saharan Africa, the king's position is primarily ritual (Abeles 1981:9). Muller expresses the situation in these terms:

> What is important to note here is that in some cases such prestations of function stem directly from the ideology of "divine

kingship" but the institution is relatively independent from the economic base which is in some ways modeled by it rather than the contrary. Ideology here comes first; it is not a reflection of the economic base or of the relations of production, but the form of the institution (a ruler, a certain centralization, various officers, etc.) seems well suited to smoothing the passage from a chiefdom or kingdom where the king or chief is tightly controlled by the people; to a proper state where such rulers can use the people or their labor for their own benefit since the form can accommodate both provided the ideology changes. (Muller 1981:248)

In the same book, another British anthropologist, Henri J. Claessen, attempts to show that the African institution of the "sacred" or "divine" king is not uniquely African. This is not a surprise. Ethnographic reports showing mythical charters for many (probably all ancient) hierarchical social structures indicate the need for ritual renewal of the cosmos or rituals to guarantee fertility and fecundity. In fact, when this is not true of the ethnographic report, likely the reason is that the ethnographer had little interest in the content of the ritual from the culture's perspective. The person responsible for these rituals may not always be considered sacred, but he must at least be respected as the one able to contact the "supernatural" as the representative of the group. On the other hand, Claessen does admit that there may be specific aspects of the African "divine" kingship that are unique.

> Whether the Ancient Egyptians had "sacred kingship" in the sense that the king had either to be killed or reinvigorated has been debated. There seems to be little evidence for this during dynastic times when written material first becomes available. However, within the Egyptian cosmological materials that are known, specifically: 1) the sacrality of the ruler, 2) the struggle for succession to high office, 3) the position of the royal women, especially the mother of the king, are reminiscent of present ethnographic reports of the institution of the African divine king. [These are three of the list of four fields that Claessen suggests could contain specific aspects that are uniquely African.] (Claessen 1981:63; brackets added)

Apparently the pattern of African social hierarchy spread through the continent. It was neither coerced nor invented locally to fit the needs of the society. As mentioned above, sub-Saharan Africa has relatively recently come to have hierarchical state organization. In Africa it seems as though the pattern that Fried identified as ranked society is not unusual. It is certainly possible that many of the "rainmaker kings" are indeed chiefs in a chiefdom society, but others of these special persons are not accorded special resources or political power; these societies would be labeled "rank societies" in Fried's evolutionary system. In Africa, as noted above by Abeles, this person of rank may be rigidly controlled by his people rather than being in control over them. It is difficult to argue that a position like this came into being to manage and control the people.

The British structural anthropologists who wrote this assessment of African kingship are certainly out of step with much of American anthropology. British anthropologists are still materialists, however; it is just that they are not committed to the neoevolutionary perspective of American anthropologists. Since they are materialists they are not particularly interested in the formulation of the cosmology, just the social structure of those who believe the cosmology.

It is obvious that many important technologies came into being without the impetus of social hierarchy. The products of these technologies were traded without benefit of hierarchy. When hierarchy came into being, apparently war and slavery also became common. Hierarchy does not appear to serve an unambiguously useful function in ordering a population nor need it be considered indigenous to many areas. Indeed, it appears that its spread was either coerced, as typified by the IE language speakers, or spread by diffusion, as in Africa. Neither the neoevolutionary model nor the model of the British structuralists take account of the spread of social hierarchy. A different motivation, an idealistic one, should be considered to account for social hierarchy.

Chapter Four

What Is Social Hierarchy?

> We hold these truths to be self evident: that all men are created equal; that they are endowed by their creator with certain unalienable rights; that among these are life, liberty, and the pursuit of happiness. (Thomas Jefferson: Preamble to the Declaration of Independence)

This is a time of contested definitions. More than words is involved in a definition. Presuppositions get in the way of defining words. They also enter into the discussion of how hierarchy happens and why. After looking at several anthropologists' thoughts about hierarchy, a definition of *social hierarchy* will be offered. Then a few comments will be made about hierarchy of the ancient and/or nonliterate world.

Many consider our nation to be egalitarian. The Preamble to the Declaration of Independence stated the basis of this egalitarianism. There was a time when those in academia also accepted this statement, but it is not true now for many in the secular academy. By their assumptions, secularists must define the social structure of our nation on the basis of its practices. This is not all bad. Certainly our practices often fall short of the expectations based on the statements in the Preamble. These shortcomings should be addressed. But to the secularist, an egalitarian social order becomes one in which all members must be equal. However, if we are speaking of equality, what particular aspect of this equality are we going to protect? Will it be an equality of means? Will it be an equality of influence or opportunity? Will it require gender and age equality?

When the definition of *egalitarianism* is reduced to "equality," it becomes a rather slippery concept.

The Preamble clearly states that our equality is before the Creator; that is, he is the one who has created us equal and given us the "unalienable rights." These are the rights that government is not to take from its citizens. It is in our belief system that liberty and equality are reconciled. The attempt to achieve equality in practice rather than through our belief system will certainly come at the cost of our liberty.

Early in the eighteenth century, Western philosophy in Europe adopted a stance called rationalism. All beliefs were to be subjected to the clear light of reason and rejected if they could not be supported by this reason. This movement was modestly called "the Enlightenment." When Jefferson penned those words, he did so as a rational man. He believed that the notion of a creator was a rational deduction, a belief based on reason. Ironically, five years after the Declaration was written, in 1781, German philosopher Immanuel Kant published his very influential *Critique of Pure Reason*. In this critique he demolished the rationalistic arguments for a creator. Our nation did not follow Kant in rejecting the Creator. After all, while Jefferson may have believed a creator was a rational concept, most colonists accepted the premises of the Preamble because they were ultimately based on Christian beliefs. In the language of this book, they were based on a cosmology, a Judeo-Christian cosmology.

Anthropology has generally chosen to follow the philosophical propositions of the eighteenth century movement called the Enlightenment. This movement has had a number of subtle but meaningful changes. After Kant late in eighteenth century destroyed rationalistic arguments for a creator, authors such as G.W.F. Hegel and Friedrich Nietzsche continued to narrow what was to be construed as "objective reality," the reality that could to be discovered by reason.

Further erosions in this confidence in "reason" have led some in academia to accept a "postmodern" stance. This stance was popularized in this country by the school of thought called Critical Theory, represented in the United States by the New Left during the 1950s. Critical Theory found all reasoning about the cosmos to be metaphysical and thus flawed—that is, without rational basis. Some in anthropology have followed this course; most have not. Where are we going with this digression? Those academics who have taken the Enlightenment seriously must also call into question Jefferson's Preamble to the Declaration of Independence. For them, it cannot be a self-evident truth that the Creator endowed us with unalienable rights. To them, any attempt at a definition either for *egalitarianism* or for its opposite, *social hierarchy*, based on a belief system, is not an objective representation. For them, such a belief system is by definition not rational, not objective, and therefore not scientific. Of course, for those who take a postmodern position, rationalism itself is without rational basis.

What have been the consequences of this enlightened position? With few exceptions, anthropology put all belief systems in the "superstructure." That is, beliefs were unimportant when arriving at the practices prevalent in a given society; they were declared to be only justifications for those practices. From within the "objective perspective" of much of American anthropology, belief systems have no place as motivation for the origin of social practices. The quest for religious freedom within a Judeo-Christian framework must be overlooked as an impetus for the egalitarian social structure that grew in the United States.

But what does this have to do with the definition of *social hierarchy* or, for that matter, *egalitarianism*? If only practices matter, how will materialists ever be able to clearly distinguish between social hierarchy and egalitarianism? The questions are especially relevant to archaeologists with regard to prehistory.

How does this concern our topic? If the definition for *social hierarchy* is limited to "practice," hierarchy is apt to become a general category that can (and does) explain the situation wherever specialization that requires some organization is obvious. Within anthropology and archaeology, there are several schools of thought that treat the transition from egalitarianism to institutionalized social hierarchy. Without consideration of some of these arguments concerning the appearance of hierarchy, the definition that will later be offered would have nothing against which to judge its value. With this in mind, let us look at some of the published material that treats this transition.

Three current approaches will be offered to demonstrate the weaknesses incurred by not recognizing that a change in cosmology, rather than merely changes in practices, motivated the change from egalitarianism to social hierarchy. For the first, some of American anthropologist Timothy Earle's articles have been chosen to represent the ardent materialists' argument for the emergence of chiefdom societies. His extreme materialistic position provokes some controversy even from his colleagues. Nonetheless, his position is a consistent one if practices are the key to understanding the move to hierarchy. A second perspective shared by a number of archaeologists is to link social hierarchy and first farming together. Since both of these changes—from gathering to farming and from egalitarianism to hierarchy—need explaining it would be convenient if some such linking could be established. There are a number of differing ways to do this and two different forms of this approached are treated. The third looks at contemporary perspectives concerning inequalities among egalitarian societies. From this perspective the different roles for men women and children in "egalitarian" societies suggest a form of hierarchy is already present. This approach suggests that the move to hierarchy was not a large one. Hopefully the reader will recognize that none of these approaches actually explain what needs to be explained.

For the first, this survey of Earle's writings (1985, 1987, 1989, 1991a, 1991b, 1997) shows little interaction with Fried's categories: egalitarian, rank society, chiefdom society, state. This is true in spite of the fact that he mentioned Fried (1967) in each article except the 1989 one. Earle (1987:290), citing Fried, offered that "structural differentiation" and "economic differentiation" are best conceived of as a continuum. In this way Earle was able to insist that the "elaboration of clear status markers correlates well with other measures of social complexity" without treating the possibility, clearly underscored by Fried, that ranking not only could precede but also sometimes did precede economic differentiation.

Two of these articles summarize the seminar held at the School of American Research during January 18–22, 1988 (Earle 1989, 1991a). In each, Earle listed the seminar's nine "environmental" preconditions for successful trajectory of political development of chiefdoms. The ninth in this list was "structural preconditions of hierarchy" (Earle 1989:86, 1991a: 10). His summary contained no acknowledgment that this structural precondition may have been embedded in a cosmology. He also recorded interesting differences with other members of the seminar group. "Steponaitis held that in the Mesoamerican and Mississippian chiefdoms no convincing argument could be made for such strict economic control as would be seen in ownership of land or central storage. Rather, populations seem to have been drawn into sociopolitical systems in part by 'smoke and mirror'—an ideology of religiously sanctioned centrality" (Earle 1989:86).

Another participant said, "… the question of any necessary economic coercive power became mute as the cost of refusal need only be minimal and could be ideologically based" (Earle 1989:86). And "Kristansen argued that, prior to true class formation, ideology penetrated social life as cosmology of the natural order and therefore served as a necessary element in the control of labor and production" (Earle 1989:86). It would seem that some of the participants in this seminar might be inclined to recognize social systems akin to Fried's "ranked society." But Earle argues for his own position in this way: "I argued that although alternate sources of power certainly existed, real economic power was basic because only it could be controlled across generations to give stability on which polity must be based. Although I stand by this interpretation, I now feel that it is necessary to determine what constitutes 'real' economic control. As the two cases reviewed here demonstrate, economic and ideological powers come together: the economic base gives the stability for the control as the ideology gives it legitimacy" (Earle 1991b: 98).

But there is little evidence of any later softening of his earlier position as to what constitutes "real" power. Earle, citing Fried (1967) and Webb (1975), writes, "This vision of chiefdoms as coercive and fundamentally warlike contravenes earlier models, broadly accepted by a generation of researchers, of chiefdoms as kin-based societies, voluntarist, peaceful, and religious" (Earle 1997:109).

And again, as earlier, he finds economic control the prime mover toward social hierarchy. "Like kinship and military might, ideology by itself is a weak source of power. Each individual can believe and promulgate whatever he or she sees as fitting and suitable.... To mold beliefs and guide social action, ideologies must be manifested in a material form that can be manipulated centrally and experienced in common by a targeted group. It is this materialization that embeds ideology in the economic process of production and gives it a central role in the competition for political power" (Earle 1997:10).

Earle apparently does not accept the possibility that a cosmology could be the widespread "justification" for rituals to renew or control the environment without prior manipulation of a chief with political and economic means. He writes, "In crude terms, ideas themselves are cheap. Anyone can think whatever he or she wants, as long as that belief does not determine an action that causes swift punishment. People can develop their own ideas about the nature of the universe that position themselves advantageously" (Earle 1997:152).

However it is that Earle comes to this conclusion, it obscures important questions. Do people groups really think just anything is true? Is it possible

55

that similar cosmologies justifying ritual positions are widespread? The second question can be (some would say has been) tested by empirical means. I do agree with Earle that well-established "chiefs" are able to manipulate cosmology to their benefit. But he has dismissed a significant problem. How does one move from the value of sharing that many hunter-gatherers display prominently to the economic control that Earle requires for hierarchy? However, if structural preconditions of hierarchy can be embedded in cosmology, perhaps these conditions may be advanced without prior economic or political control.

The second approach involves a second area of interest to many archaeologists, the introduction of agriculture. When T. Douglas Price offers to locate the emergence of inequality in a chapter by that title, he opens the chapter with these words: "In the history of the human species, there is no more significant transition than the emergence and institutionalization of inequality. Yet, strangely, until recently, this critical issue has received less direct concern in archaeological discussions of social change than the two other important evolutionary questions, the origins of agriculture and the rise of the state" (Price & Feinman 1995:129).

He then offers this useful definition of *hierarchy*: the difference between social hierarchy and egalitarianism is that in egalitarianism, status is achieved and in hierarchy it is ascribed. For those not acquainted with the terminology, anthropology has long recognized that even among egalitarian communities there are leaders. This leadership is recognized in terms of the leader's wisdom or skill and will often be moved from member to member depending on the activity to be performed. This is called "achieved status." Price points out that in a hierarchical situation there exists an institutionalized status that is given to a person on the basis of heredity. This is called "ascribed status." Price then goes on to claim that this circumstance, hierarchy, is "closely related to the intensification of subsistence and more specifically with agriculture." (Price & Feinman 1995:130)

In order to support his thesis, Price uses the southern Scandinavian Mesolithic culture called Ertebolle and its conversion to a hierarchical Neolithic culture identified as the Tragtbaeger (TRB) culture as an example. Within the TRB culture, sometimes called the Funnel-beaker culture, archaeology has found a burial practice that in Price's article is called long barrows. In the previous chapter, similar burial practices were identified as passage graves. These long barrows required a considerable expenditure of effort in the burial of just a few members of the culture. This considerable labor invested in the burial of a few has always been considered a convincing sign of the presence of social hierarchy. Price locates this change in burial practice to 3900 B.C. (calibrated carbon date), which falls near the middle of the Uruk period of 3600–3100 B.C. (uncalibrated carbon).

The problem with his illustration is that the approaching wave of farmers to the south, the Linearbanderkeramik (LBK) culture, has not yielded conclusive evidence to identify it as hierarchical in social structure. Archaeology has shown them to be organized, trading with each other—although perhaps little with the Mesolithic cultures they had infiltrated—and with similar culture patterns, down to small details, over a large area extending from Hungary to France, north of the Alps. But do these features make the LBK culture hierarchical? From the chapter of another book, co-authored by the same T. Douglas Price, along with Anne Birgitte, and Lawrence H. Keeley, we learn that, "No wonder most recent students of the LBK would rather discuss, at some length, invisible LBK-Mesolithic interactions or restrict themselves to inferences of LBK economics, settlement patterns or, more rarely, social organization, and demography. In such a theoretical vacuum, one is forced to speculate" (Price & Gebauer 1995:103f).

This vacuum is not a lack of archaeological evidence. It is a lack of evidence that supports clear markers for social hierarchy. There is little evidence for conflict between the LBK settlements and a great deal of evidence for communication and trade. The LBK farmers used only loess soils, wind-blown soil that is easy to plow, along river valleys, so we need not assume that all the contact with the earlier Mesolithic cultures in the area that they moved into was hostile. Further, although there is good evidence for trade between the LBK and the Ertebolle culture before it became Neolithic, there is no evidence that the LBK had burial practices similar to those adopted by the Scandinavian Mesolithic culture as it became both Neolithic and hierarchical. There is as little evidence for social hierarchy during the spread of the LBK culture across Europe as there was for most of the Ubaid period in the Mesopotamian Valley itself.

Price recognizes that the changes in social and religious spheres that came along with agriculture to this Scandinavian area were more profound than the changes in subsistence, starting with the first evidence for farming. He cites that the earliest evidence for farming was found in the earthen long barrows with wooden funeral structures. Generally there was only one grave, or a very few, in each of these large, elaborate, and labor-costly structures. "The appearance of the barrows at the onset of the Neolithic suggests substantial changes in social organization. Nothing like these elite, mound-covered burials are known from the Mesolithic period; Mesolithic cemeteries reveal a distinction based on criteria of age and sex, but there is no indication of status differentiation beyond these criteria ... subsequent megalithic burial constructions (Megalithic burials) were a continuing elaboration of this earlier tradition" (Price & Feinman 1995:138f).

Price concludes from his consideration of the Danish data that demography, climate, or environment cannot account for the introduction of agriculture. In turn we could ask whether the demography, climate, or environment account for the introduction of hierarchy. Apparently he concludes that agriculture and hierarchy (without archaeological markers) moved together across the European continent (Price & Feinman 1995:146). Then he asked a question about "how and why the rules enforcing egalitarian behaviors were relaxed among prehistoric hunter-gatherers and why elite individuals emerged among these groups toward the end of the Pleistocene, particularly in contexts involving the domestication of plants." He has offered one illustration of hierarchy and change in subsistence arriving together. But how does that prove they were always linked? Musing on this successful egalitarian pattern that rapidly spread agriculture across both the Old and the New World, he leaves unanswered his question of where the "more hierarchically organized groups originated" (Price & Feinman 1995:147).

Apparently, hierarchy first originated in the Mesopotamian Valley, but in time sequence, it did so only after egalitarian farmers had moved across most of Europe. The LBK culture did show evidences for hierarchy later as Megalithic burial practices began to appear in their area. Incidentally, this is rather neutral with regard to Price's question, but it was not only in Denmark that early long barrow burial practices started at this time; they also became apparent on the Normandy coast of France, the Iberian peninsula, and the British Isles across the channel from Normandy. These burial practices came into being in such a short period of time that it is difficult to know where the practice originated. But they all appeared shortly after the first obvious social hierarchy in the Mesopotamian Valley.

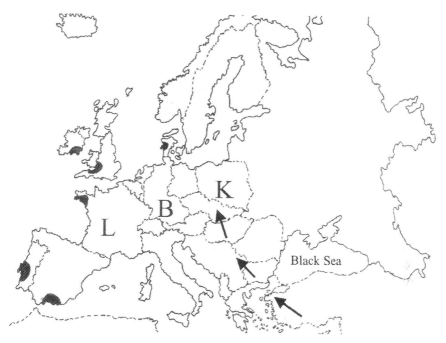

The movement of Neolithic technology without apparent social hierarchy followed the Danube River and its tributaries into the plains of Northern Europe. This group had a uniform culture pattern including pottery types called Linearbanderkeramik or LBK. At about 4000 B.C. the coastal areas shown in black first adopted this Neolithic technology but with obvious indications for hierarchical social order. These are the areas that first built elaborate burial chambers known as long barrows or passage graves. Later innovations in these areas included megalithic burial chambers. Did the charters for social hierarchy arrive by ship from the Mesopotamian Valley?

Price argues that hierarchy comes with agriculture, but in the same book edited by Price and Gebauer, another theorist considering the origin of agriculture, Brian Hayden, links first farming to hierarchical hunter-gatherer societies. Perhaps it would simplify the anthropologist's quest for origins if it could be demonstrated that first farming and institutionalized social hierarchy were linked, although I am not sure how. There is a general observation to be made about linking agriculture to socially complex hunter societies. In all the areas of independent domestication of plants or animals located by archaeologists, clear evidence for social hierarchy appears only well after that domestication. Price correctly points out that farming and social hierarchy appeared simultaneously in the Danish context. But the Danes used already domesticated plants and animals; they did not domesticate them. Further, all agree that the evidence for hierarchy there is decisive. But then, if evidence is necessary to demonstrate social hierarchy, where is the evidence that the LBK culture was hierarchical? The LBK culture furnished the Danes with the domesticated plants and animals.

The pattern as envisioned by Hayden suggests that the "accumulator principle" of the "big man" of either New Guinea/Papua or the Pacific Northwest in the United States could encourage the introduction of agriculture. In this type of society a person, identified as a "big man," lends valuables to members of his group to help them meet social needs. By doing this he accumulates a number of debtors on whom he can call when he desires to show an impressive amount of wealth. In New Guinea this wealth would be in pigs. This wealth makes possible a large gathering for a feast at which some community effort can be advanced.

There are two areas in which the classic accumulator principle was recognized. In North America the Native Americans of the Pacific Northwest showed hierarchical social structure. But this pattern appears about 2,000 years after the first evidence for hierarchy in Mesoamerica and a much longer period after agriculture was widely practiced on the continent. There, in fact, the accumulator principle did not result in the practice of agriculture. When the people did finally raise potatoes, they may have hoped to improve their trading position with the whites that used them. As for New Guinea, apparently Hayden would have the big man complex, a system of leadership, develop from within an egalitarian setting. Of course, in New Guinea there was extensive use of cultivated root crops and domesticated pigs, hardly pre-Neolithic circumstances. In their book *Big Men and Great Men: Personifications of Power in Melanesia,* published in 1991, Maurice Godelier and Marilyn Strathern make the argument that great men—men with inherited positions of prestige—likely preceded the accumulators, the "big men." These accumulators served by facilitating the collection of goods needed by the society: bride price, satisfaction of the ancestors, war. Some articles in the book even argue that "the big men configuration" only followed the breakdown of more elaborate chiefdom societies.

Lawrence Keeling in the same book by Price and Gebauer also took issue with Hayden. He attributed first farming to subtle changes in the environment in the few areas on the globe where useful wild plants capable of domestication were present. But the most telling of Keeley's arguments against linking first farmers to complex hunter-gatherer societies is as follows: "Despite the near simultaneity of agricultural beginnings in both areas [Mesoamerica and the Near East], sedentary villages (and other evidences of social complexity) did not develop until several thousand years after plant domestication in Mesoamerica (i.e., during the early Formative, ca. 4000 bp) whereas in the Near East, there is evidence that sedentary villages existed before plant domestication or even cultivation (e.g., the Natufian, ca. 13,000–10,000 bp). Any general theory must account for these ... features of agriculture" (Keeley 1995:267; brackets added).

The third approach offered by Gary Feinman involves redefining the egalitarian concept (Feinman 1995:261). He offered that "current views highlight differences in gender, age, authority, skills, and prestige in egalitarian social forms.... These contemporary perspectives question the existence of truly egalitarian social formation." Earlier models (prior to 1970) for emergence of inequality that depend on "exogenous conditions" are not necessary if one locates social inequality in these nonstratified societies. According to Feinman, this insight releases one from the restraints that ignoring external factors once imposed. But after this, he says,

> Yet, alternatively, if the seeds of inequality are recognized to be present in egalitarian human groupings, then the focus of this central research question must be shifted. Rather than endeavoring simply to account for inequality, the emphasis should be expanded. Attention must be placed on those mechanisms in non-stratified societies that have served to level extant inequalities before they become institutionalized, as well as on the internal and/or external conditions that work to negate those leveling strategies and sanctions so that existent inequalities are permitted to become more institutionalized.

> The institutionalization process cannot occur unless social and ideological conceptions are transformed. (Feinman 1995:262, with credits to Cashdan, Flannery, and Marcus)

So Feinman allows what we see in our own culture, inequality in many areas even though, ideally, we are an egalitarian society. And he comes close to allowing that social and ideological conceptions might be based on the cosmology or religious perspective of the egalitarian society. However, materialistic presuppositions do not allow, at least not openly, that the motivations for the recognized "leveling mechanisms" are indeed ideologies based on worldview. Inequality and egalitarianism are not necessarily opposed to each other. They may be reconciled as in our own nation by recognizing our equality before God. Certainly this recognition can be considered either a religious worldview or a cosmology. This equality does not rule out leadership in different arenas of social contacts. But if the cosmological basis for equality is discarded, then perhaps institutional hierarchy has been given a pathway. Needless to say, Feinman does not go on in his article to say anything like this. However, many of those treating this notion of inequality within egalitarianism look for leveling mechanisms within the culture to maintain egalitarianism. It is merely that cosmology, which they say is not "objective reality," is not usually considered in this search for leveling mechanisms.

So with this long introduction to the questions that anthropology has been asking, these observations follow. Hierarchy, like egalitarianism, is a social phenomenon. The hierarchy we have encountered in the ancient world was based on the principle that society recognized certain elites who had ritual control of their environment. This pattern extended well into historic times. It was not only true of the ancient literate societies, but it was also true in ethnographies yet to be considered from Africa and the Pacific Islands. In fact, Japan of the early twentieth century held to this pattern. Its emperor was recognized as the direct descendant of Amaterasu, the sun. Because of this relationship, the emperor had ritual responsibilities on which his nation depended. From these considerations, I offer this:

> *Earliest social hierarchy is chartered by a cosmology that designates some member or members of the society to perform certain rituals that sustain, guarantee, or renew the environment; in some cases the rituals are meant to renew the cosmos itself.*

In order for this cosmology to be effective in justifying hierarchy, it must limit those who are able to perform these rituals. It is not necessary to deny a single creator, but he must either be made distant or disabled in such a way as he is thought no longer interested in or in control of his creation. The belief in a transcendent and providential creator who created an essentially inanimate physical creation in which he placed his creatures and cared for them must be, and was, supplanted by a cosmos that could be influenced by ritual. An animated cosmos that could be manipulated by ritual is generally recognized to be the worldview of the ancient world. Therefore, the articulation and introduction of such a cosmology brought into being the hierarchical "Ancient World."

This definition of *hierarchy* answers several of the questions that have puzzled anthropologists. How or why would people fall into a trap that robs them of their dignity and independence? They exchanged these for the hope that they would be taken care of with little attention on their part. Worship of the Creator usually required a rigorous concern for the welfare of others, an ideology that fulfills the anthropologists' quest for a leveling mechanism. Anthropologists have long wondered at the value shown among recent hunters for sharing whatever they have. Apparently, difficulties in changing from gathering to farming were overcome without giving up the basis of their egalitarian social order. This is illustrated not only in the Ubaid period of Mesopotamia but also in all the places around the globe where domestication was an independent invention. The pattern in these places always has archaeological evidence for hierarchy located well after the first domestication of plants occurred.

If there was just one source for the first interruption in egalitarian social structures in all the places reached directly or indirectly by the Uruk outposts (see Chapter Three), how is it that the hierarchical social structures resulting from this interruption were dissimilar? Any answer to that question is speculative. Perhaps the mission of the Uruk outposts was purely economic in nature. Then those areas probed by the economic tentacles of this wealthy society might only be imitated, instituting a pattern of social hierarchy they assumed to be similar to this first pattern for social hierarchy in the Mesopotamian Valley. In short, the earliest justification for social hierarchy was probably diffused rather than borrowed directly or imposed.

This brings up another point. There is a difference in the spread of these various hierarchical structures. The IE languages were accepted by nearly all of Europe. Perhaps these people were coerced into their social order. The IE king was of the warrior class, and within his person he was thought to represent the whole of the society. Before the Christian era, Indo-Europeans left their language in India, Iran, and most of Europe. They also occupied some areas without changing the language of the population, for instance, the ancient Near East. They quickly spread across regions that did not have social hierarchy and overran hierarchical societies as well. Included in these societies would be the Mediterranean hierarchies as found in the area of modern Greece and those groups along the Atlantic coast that buried their elites in passage graves and megalithic chambers. It appears that they lent their social order to many of those with, and all those without, hierarchical social order. It must have occasionally been done with the application of force. But other hierarchical groups with different structural formation, such as those in Africa, probably did not for the most part overrun their neighbors. Their style of rainmaker kings served more as a model for other groups to emulate.

Yet, looking at these various systems of hierarchy that have survived for us to consider either in literature or in practice, there are some remarkable similarities. The Dumuzi cult (Tammuz in Ezekiel 8:14) from the Mesopotamian Valley was actually based on the worship of the dead king who was identified with the grain of the land. That is very similar to the dead king of the Egyptians, whose name (and responsibility after death) was the grain of the land. Again, Egypt and the Indo-Europeans have rulers with a special relationship to the sun. This is also true of the Japanese emperor and many of the heroes of the Polynesians. I take these similarities to be related to the cosmology of the separation of heaven and earth since in its usual form light, symbolized in the myth as the sun, does not appear until after heaven and earth are separated.

Why did man give up his position in an egalitarian society? Some were forced, but many did so willingly. Mircea Eliade and Charles Long use neutral language by saying that they gave up the transcendent Creator for animistic "strong gods"—gods who controlled the environment and could be influenced by ritual. As a believer in the God of our traditions, I am inclined to use ethnocentric language and say that they gave themselves to idolatry (see Romans 1:20–25). They accepted a new cosmology that today would be described either as animism, polytheism, or pantheism. All of these systems of thought lent themselves to hierarchy through a form of institutionalized idolatry.

Both archaeology and history suggest that once a society gives up its belief system supporting egalitarianism for one in which they are supported by social superiors, it is difficult to reclaim the freedom and equality they lost. It almost requires a new start with full agreement by the population on a cosmology that declares all to be equal. Within such a belief system, and likely only within such a system, liberty and equality could be once again reconciled.

Chapter Five

The Cosmology Identified

In this chapter, first myth in general and then the cosmological myth, the "separation of heaven and earth," will be considered further.

With all that has been written about mythology, what is the criterion used in this book to sort out meaningful interpretations of the subject matter? Although it has been some time since Christians have been at the forefront in defining and interpreting mythology, their influence on this subject is still in evidence. A story concerning the activity of the gods could safely be dismissed since for Christians there was only one God. For these stories the Greek word for our word *myth* sufficed. When someone wanted to distinguish between myth and heroic tale, the standard still has mythology as the story of the gods and their activities. The heroic tales become legends. In this way the stories of the gods of the Greeks and Romans compared unfavorably with our Scripture.

Under the influence of the eighteenth century Enlightenment, our Scripture as well has been relegated to the position of myth or heroic legend. Now it must be understood that in this context, myth is mere falsehood and heroic legend is exaggeration at best. There were a few who claimed to find some kernel of history or wisdom from the myths. But for the most part, mythology came to represent a problem in the sense that it was irrational, childish, silly, and apt to extensive discourse about nonexistent beings. In short, the question became, how do we account for the men who first articulated these stories, and how were others ever moved to believe them? But, by taking this stance—that is, mythology itself is meaningless, the result of immature or flawed mental activity—one must assume that little information is to be gained by a careful consideration of mythology. In fact, this has been pretty much where anthropology has remained, except for recognizing the notion that cosmology rationalizes the special privileges of the elite.

Clearly distinguished from these attitudes about cosmology, the assumptions used in this book about cosmology include the following: 1) cosmology is the creative product of mankind from men with normal mental abilities; 2) since certain categories of cosmologies are very widespread, their distribution is important for historic implications as well as their use in particular societies; 3) cosmologies can be expected to justify social facts; 4) the attempt to discover what is meant by the symbolism in a widespread cosmology is a worthwhile pursuit.

Does this mean that reflections about mythology by those who do not share these assumptions are to be ignored? If so, there are probably no other authors whose material is worth reading. Some collections and interpretations of mythology were undertaken specifically to undermine Christianity, such as Frazer's *Golden Bough,* first published in 1890. Even this book, however, was extremely influential in both religious and academic circles and could hardly be dismissed as not worth considering. It was gradually discredited as more information about ancient near eastern cultures became available. Archetypes springing from a Jungian "collective unconscious" are sometimes used to explain widespread similarities. The decision in this book to ignore a Jungian approach is a deliberate one. Allowing such explanation takes away man's choice and responsibility in his belief system.

Freud, the psychoanalyst, explained myths as the product of a neurotic or infantile mind. Even his contributions contain something of interest. The myth, which I've called the separation of heaven and earth, is sometimes considered an illustration of his Oedipus complex. Freudians were quick to point out the adversarial role between heaven and those freed when heaven and earth were separated. This was a relationship that Eliade did not seem to explore, choosing merely to allow the conjoined heaven and earth to be a symbolic representation of plenty for early agriculturalists. To answer the question then about what may be dismissed as without merit, the study of mythology as a whole has grown in many directions. There have been many contributions to my thinking about mythology from authors who would certainly find my particular assumptions without merit.

But even with the identification of assumptions about cosmology, unraveling the meaning of its symbolism is difficult. The meaning sought in this book may not correspond with the meaning asserted by the very people who believe the cosmology and live under its influence since the original articulation or implementation of the cosmology may have addressed "problems" long ago forgotten. If there was a place of first articulation and diffusion from there, it is the meaning the cosmology had when it was first articulated or first accepted by another group that interests me. The cosmology we are pursuing is of wide distribution. If it is true that myth in general and cosmology in particular are the creation of normal human minds, the mere existence of a single cosmology with global distribution is a nearly insoluble problem for those who insist that groups with the cosmology did not respond to similar problems. However, this problem of similar cosmological themes is more often expressed in words such as these:

> Considerably earlier than Jung, as we have said, Adolf Bastian propounded the theory of "elemental ideas." The unanimity of myths is the result of an inherently uniform disposition of the human mind….
>
> Very recently, Kilton Stewart—an anthropologist—has stated his conviction that all men develop according to a single mental pattern….
>
> Other aspects of this are discussed by Alexander Lindsay, who comments: "Identical archetypes can be found in sample tales from the South Seas and in the sophisticated pages of Ovid's *Metamorphoses*. (Freund 1965:291f)

It is partly because contemporary cosmologies have such widespread similarities that developmental mental theories or prerational archetypes are used to account for these similarities. In the conclusion of his book, Freund does allow that this type of accounting for cosmology will necessarily involve questioning the soundness and creativity of our own thinking as well (Freund 1965:290). As a Christian, I have no doubt that my thinking is limited and flawed by the fall. Yet, to use explanations that deny human creative thought lessens man's responsibility for his own beliefs. For this reason, the irrational or infantile mind as suggested by Freud, the collective unconscious as offered by Jung, or some mental developmental pattern as offered by Kilton Stewart must be rejected as explanation for the similarity of widespread cosmologies. Remember from Chapter One that belief in the Supreme Being, a god very similar to that of our own traditions, was found among widespread hunter-gatherer groups. Is it also to be accounted for in one of these ways? Charles Long calls attention to this phenomenon in the following quotation. "For example, the symbol of completeness in high agricultural communities is often expressed by the union of earth mother and sky father. Such symbolism has a specific meaning for man in agricultural societies, but among non-agricultural peoples, the pastoral nomads, this meaning is expressed in terms of a powerful sky deity or by a Lord of the Animals" (Long 1969: 22).

This is roughly the same information that was given in the quotation from Eliade in the Introduction. Long added the Lord of the Animals title although it is doubtful that this title fits any of the groups mentioned by Carleton Coon, discussed in Chapter One. Perhaps Long has added some groups to the list such as the Ainu of Japan to justify this characterization. In the same book, Long makes this perceptive observation about cosmologies.

> The cosmogonic myth is an attempt to resolve these antagonisms and to bring about a definitive structure of meaning for the entire culture. The cosmogonic myth is the myth *par excellence* precisely because the beginnings of all things within the culture are modeled on the pattern of the myth.... While this centeredness which is described within the cosmogonic myth orients, synthesizes, and integrates the world, a complete harmony is seldom achieved....
>
> Furthermore, there remains the threat of the older structure which the new creation ostensibly destroyed.... This critique and qualification of the old cosmos by a new myth enables us to understand the history of mythological forms and symbols. Eliade believes that the oldest religious structures are symbols of sky phenomena. These symbols are usually seen in the myth as supreme beings, creators and all-powerful gods. These symbols in the more advanced stages of cultures are relegated to the background, their places taken by deities of fertility, ancestor worship, and spirits and gods of nature. The appearance of these deities represents the thirst for concreteness and specificity over against the passivity of the celestial gods. (Long 1969:32)

This observation, if applied to the myth of the union of Father Heaven and Mother Earth, would almost require that it be a critique of the cosmos as the creation of an all-powerful celestial supreme being. Further than that, one would expect that it is this myth that establishes a cosmos in which less powerful beings come to have control of fertility and the more "concrete interests" of the "more advanced" cultures. However, Long does not offer the observation that this cosmogony probably supplanted the celestial creator. But by identifying the function of cosmology as both a critique and a setting aside of an earlier cosmology, Long does move us away from the notion that it is simply the practice of agriculture that requires the rejection of a celestial supreme being. Nor does farming require the worship of ancestors, fertility deities, or gods that are moved by rituals performed by elites within the social structure.

In the second chapter of the same book, Long treats the cosmology that he calls the World Parents myth. This is the same cosmology that has been called in this book the separation of heaven and earth cosmology. After referring to the cosmology of the Maori and comparing it with that of the cosmology of Egypt, Long goes on to say, "The symbol of sky-earth in union is expressive of completeness, totality. For this reason, the myths which present us with this motif never stop at this point, for creation means a qualification of totality whether totality is conceived of as chaos or primordial unity. The myths which portray the World-Parents motif always relate how and why the parents have been separated" (Long 1969:68).

The quotation in the paragraph above is a combination of an objective statement that can be observed by examining the World Parents motif in the cosmological myths of the Egyptians and the Maori along with the introduction of the author's interpretation of the symbols used in the cosmologies. This is that tendency for mythologists and historians of religion to explain symbols as though the symbols themselves stand alone outside of history as implanted in the human psyche. This quotation does, however, clearly delineate how it is that Long and Eliade can call this particular cosmology expressive of completeness. It does not matter that everywhere the motif is found in a cosmology, the conditions within the conjoined heaven and earth are identified by the mythtellers as intolerable. As an illustration of this, consider the following quotation from Long, still from his chapter on the World Parents myth. "In the Egyptian, Zuni, Polynesian, and Northeast Indian myths the World Parents is a synonym for chaos and confusion. But the two symbols of the union are related. Light and order occur when the parents are separated. Light is the symbol of knowledge and order. It is for this reason that solar deities—bringers of light—dominate after the separation of the World Parents" (Long 1969:79).

Once again Long objectively relates details from the cosmology as given in four areas of the globe, but then he follows this observation with a mythologist's interpretation of the symbols involved. Here, however, it is possible to agree with the assessment that light and order symbolize knowledge. The earlier interpretation leads us to believe that chaos and confusion are synonymous with completeness.

Notice how widespread these areas are: Egypt in the ancient Near East, and among more recent cultures the Zuni in the southwestern United States, several tribal groups from the Northeast Frontier section of the Indian subcontinent, and New Zealand in the South Pacific. In a quotation earlier in the chapter, Long had given us these words: "This critique and qualification of the old cosmos by a new myth enables us to understand the history of mythological forms and symbols." Identifying the conjoined heaven and earth with chaos and confusion could easily be interpreted as a polemic directed toward the earlier conditions. Both Eliade and Long have suggested, at least indirectly, that the old order included a supreme being and a created world order. But neither has asked the question: specifically what of this old order was being rejected? To me this question is worth considering.

Some things have already been suggested by one of the quotations from Long earlier in the chapter, in which he said, "These symbols are usually seen in the myth as supreme beings, creators and all-powerful gods. These symbols in the more advanced stages of cultures are relegated to the background, their places taken by deities of fertility, ancestor worship, and spirits and gods of nature." Apparently, access to the Supreme Being somehow limited the formation of a social order that could be organized around rituals used to manipulate an animated world. Although neither Long nor Eliade consider social order in their purview, it is obvious that the "more advanced stages of culture" are those with an established hierarchy. The relationship between elite status and ritual performance has already been established in early hierarchical societies. But is this all that can be learned from a consideration of the cosmology of the separation of heaven and earth?

Before further consideration of that question, the reader should gain a better understanding of the myth itself. First, it should be obvious that not all the separation cosmologies are identical; there is considerable room for creativity from area to area. However, there are recurring motifs that are not easily dismissed as coincidental. What are these recurring motifs? How many of them can be found linked together in widespread places?

The literal picture drawn by the cosmology often takes this form: heaven, whether personified or not, is capable of covering earth in such a way that the sun (and light) are prevented from reaching those beings trapped between earth and heaven. When heaven is made distant, the beings held in between are freed from constraint and darkness. Often within the telling, social relationships will be given if men are said to emerge as well as the other beings. If men are not involved, their "creation" will itself figure into the fixing of social relationships. Frequently, the place where this is accomplished or where men emerge will be identified and have social importance.

Although Eliade and Long proceed as though heaven and earth are always personified and have parented the beings contained within them when they are conjoined, this is not always the case. The source of the beings is not always explained, or they may have been the product of a creator who also created heaven and earth.

So if we were to select several of the features and use them as the standard collection of motifs linked together, what would they be? 1) The nearness of heaven had placed constraints on the gods and/or men, keeping them in darkness. 2) When the desired separation had occurred, light, usually from the sun, either first comes into being or for the first time is seen by the previously constrained beings. 3) The constrained beings have usually organized hierarchically before the time of their emergence from the union of heaven and earth. 4) Earth is now considered their home and *final destiny*. Whatever heaven symbolized in the original condition has become distant from them.

The cosmology of interest to us can be found or inferred in ancient texts from Egypt, Sumer, India, Anatolia (Hittites), Greece, and China. Of course, few were acquainted with any of these except the Greek cosmology as given in Hesiod's *Theogony*. But when ethnographies, reports written about little-known people groups, became available for the present-day Polynesians, these ethnographies revealed cosmologies strikingly similar to Greek material. Spurred by this discovery, greater attention was given to cosmology in other areas. Now mythologists also point out that this cosmology was present in recent times in the Northeast Frontier of India, the southwestern United States, and in a slightly modified form in much of Africa. And in spite of Long and Eliade's inference that it is a cosmology of agriculturalists only, some of the hunter-gatherers of Australia also held a separation cosmology.

The present distribution appears to approximate those areas where a single, all-powerful supreme being is also known. If one allows that those who believed in a supreme being tended to live in egalitarian societies, then the presence of the cosmology of the separation of heaven and earth was likely the first step in moving away from egalitarianism into social hierarchy.

Since it is possible that my reader has not looked at mythologies in detail, perhaps the reading of one will be instructive. Extensive ethnographic reports have been made about several of the Polynesian Islands, including their religious traditions. Certainly, these traditions are to us mythology, and in particular their origin teachings can be considered cosmology. The Polynesians were a curiosity for they were "discovered" by some of the early Western explorers who traversed the Pacific in the middle of the nineteenth century. They were a fascination to anthropologists because well-organized and hierarchical groups occupied some of these islands. Often their rulers had severe taboos separating them from the common people. They practiced human sacrifice, some perhaps cannibalism as well. Their word for taboo, *tapu,* and the Melanesian word *mana,* interpreted as power intrinsic in an object, actually had a run in anthropological literature when the concern was to find the origin of religion.

The reader should note that the symbolism in their cosmology requires some thought to follow. The traditions of the Polynesians across the Pacific have remarkable similarities, in spite of the fact ethnographers found that the traditions within each group had several variations, apparently some reserved for experts in their lore and some for the common man. In any event, not just any of the group were allowed to recite the traditions, and the ones who were did so only under certain circumstances.

The Maori of New Zealand can serve as an illustration of the points made in the above paragraphs. Note the presence of the motifs common in the cosmology of the separation of heaven and earth. For the convenience of the reader, Long's rendition of Maori cosmology with further additions from Elsdon Best will serve our purposes. For this first version, Long credits Sir George Grey, 1885.

Men had but one pair of primitive ancestors; they sprang from vast heaven that exists above us and from earth which lies beneath us. According the traditions of our race, Rangi and Papa, or Heaven and Earth, were the source from which, in the beginning all things originated. Darkness then rested upon the heaven and upon the earth, and they both clave together, for they had not yet been rent apart; and the children they had begotten were ever thinking amongst themselves what might be the difference between darkness and light; they knew that beings had multiplied and increased, and yet light had never broken upon them, but it ever continued dark. Hence these sayings are found in our ancient religious services: There was darkness from the first division of time, unto the tenth, the hundred, to the thousandth," that is, for a vast space of time; and these divisions of times were considered as beings, and were each termed a Po; and on their account there was yet no world with its bright light, but darkness only for the beings which existed.

At last the beings who had been begotten by Heaven and Earth, worn out by the continued darkness, consulted amongst themselves, saying, "Let us now determine what we should do with Rangi and Papa, whether it would be better to slay them or to rend them apart." Then spoke Tu-matauenga, the fiercest of the children of Heaven and Earth, "It is well, let us slay them."

Then spake Tane-mahuta, the father of forests and of all things that inhabit them, or are constructed of trees, "Nay, not so. It is better to rend them apart, and to let the earth lie beneath our feet. Let the sky become as a stranger to us, but the earth remain close to us as a nursing mother."

The brothers all consented to this proposal with the exception of Tawhiri-ma-tea, the father of winds and storms, and he, fearing that his kingdom was about to be overthrown, grieved greatly at the thought of his parents being torn apart. Five of the brothers willingly consented to the separation of their parents, but one of them would not consent to it.

Hence, also, these sayings of old time, "The multitude, the length," signified the multitude of the thought of the children of Heaven and Earth, and the length of time they considered whether they should slay their parents, that human beings might be called into existence; for it was in this manner that they talked and consulted amongst themselves.

But at length their plans having been agreed on, lo, Rongo-ma-tane, the god and father of the cultivated food of man, rises up, that he might rend apart the heavens and the earth; he struggles, but he rends them not apart. Lo, next, Tangaroa, the god and father of fish and reptiles, rises up, that he may rend apart the heavens and the earth; he also struggles but he rends them not apart. Lo, next, Haumia-tikitiki, the god and father of food of man which springs without cultivation, rises up and struggles, but ineffectively. Lo, then Tu-matauenga, the god and father of fiery human beings, rises up and struggles but he too fails. Then, at last, slowly uprises Tane-mahuta, the god and father of forests, of birds, and of insects, and he struggles with his parents; in vain he strives to rend them apart with his hands and arms. Lo, he pauses; his head is now firmly planted on his mother, the earth, his feet raises up and rests against his father the skies, he strains his back and limbs with mighty effort. Now are rent apart Rangi and Papa, and with cries and groans of woe they shriek aloud, "Wherefore slay you thus your parents? Why commit you so dreadful a crime as to slay us, as to rend your parents apart?" But Tane-mahuta pauses not, he regards not their shrieks and cries; far, far beneath him he presses down the earth; far, far above him he thrusts up the sky.

Hence these sayings of olden time, "It was the fierce thrusting of Tane which tore apart the heaven from the earth, so that they rent apart, and darkness was made manifest, and so was the light."

No sooner was heaven rent from earth than the multitude of human beings were discovered whom they had begotten, and who had hitherto lain concealed between the bodies of Rangi and Papa. (Long 1969:95f)

The story continues with Tawhiri-ma-tea, the father of winds and storms, taking revenge on his brothers. Only Tu-matauenga, the fiercest of the children of Heaven and Earth, is able to stand before the fierce storms. He was angry with his brothers for their failure and was said to eat all of them except Tawhiri-ma-tea, the father of winds and storms. Now this eating at first seems to be cannibalism, but it is to be remembered what each represented—cultivated food, uncultivated food, food from sea, food and products from the forest. By his eating them he made each of them common—no longer sacred or *tapu*—now accessible to mankind as food. "He assigned for each of them fitting incantations, that they might be abundant and that he might easily obtain them" (Long 1969:103). In this telling of the cosmology, Maui-tikitiki, by attempting to deceive Hine-nui-te-po, brought death to all mankind. Maui-tikitiki is the first man, Hine-nui-te-po is guardian of the dead. Both are mentioned later in quotations from Best.

How well does this story fit the pattern of motifs mentioned above? 1) The nearness of heaven to earth had placed constraints on mankind, even hidden them, and kept the brothers in darkness. 2) Light, desired by those so constrained by the presence of heaven, finally came, but only after heaven was sent away. Best gives a lengthy story about how the sun was finally positioned so as to be useful and not destructive to mankind. While light, generally the sun, was a consideration in the separation, the Maori said they did not worship the sun. 3) The god Tu-matauenga, the fiercest of the children of Heaven and Earth, in Grey's telling is the stand-in for mankind and is represented as the tutelary god connected with the art of war. In this telling his actions in eating his brothers became the basis for the rituals to provide food for the common man. 4) Although it would seem that "let earth only be our home" might already have been enough to fix man's final destiny, the Maori story of how death came to be was told in other areas of the South Pacific. Maori rituals appealed to the ancestors. Man, living through these ancestors, was in a condition we call animism. He was related through his ancestors to his food supply; it was not supplied him by a creator. Through the cosmology and social structure, mankind had gained ritual control over his food.

But was there any evidence for the presence of a supreme being? For the Maori, this being was Io. As ethnographer Elsdon Best explains,

> The cosmogonic myths of the Maori folk of New Zealand
> contain elements of much interest to anthropologists, and

the same may be said with regard to the origin of man as explained in the mythology by the race. One of the most remarkable features connected with these subjects is the fact that there are two versions of both, and this peculiarity is, at first, somewhat disconcerting to the student. A close study of the matter, however, shows clearly that these differing versions are quite in accord with Maori procedure, and the result of the intense spirit of conservatism displayed by high-class experts in ancient lore, combined with a high degree of *tapu* pertaining to such teachings. (Best 1924:85)

While the story told by Grey may be the version for the common man, there was also a version reserved for experts in the mythology. In this version, heaven and earth and all in them were the creations of Io, not the result of a gradual process, as in Grey's version above. Early on, some doubted that Io was part of a conservative mythological tradition of the Maori; however, a creator has been found in the traditions of many Polynesian societies. How in the South Pacific these two cosmologies remained intertwined is difficult to imagine, but it is consistent with the earlier statement that in the preliterate world the separation of heaven and earth cosmologies roughly approximate the distribution of belief in a supreme being.

In the other tradition, Tane the separator, rather than Tu, remains the chief of the secondary gods. It is he that finally ascends into the twelfth heaven to receive from Io the three "baskets of knowledge" and the "supernatural stones" after he builds the appropriate structures in which to store these stones and sacred information. This information included the ritual and arts used in agriculture as well as those used in war. Tane is also identified as the one responsible for ordering the lights in the sky. A special messenger of Io, perhaps Io himself, caused Earth to turn over so that she would not see and grieve for Heaven, her lover. This grieving had made it necessary for mankind to be in constant mist and clouds (Best 1924:108–109). Further, in this tradition it was said that Tane, after fruitless search for a mate from which to give birth to mankind, made a woman from the earth and with the help of Io brought her to life. This Earth-Formed Maid and Tane, with proper rituals, gave birth to a number of human beings. These rituals were used in a marriage service and were symbolized in a charm to bring fertility to the married couple. After a very complicated story, Best offers this explanation about the firstborn of the Earth-Formed Maid and her relationship to mankind.

The name of this first-born daughter of Tane the parent and the Earth Formed Maid had been Hine-titama in the upper world. When she took up her abode in Rarohenga, the subterranean world, she discarded that name and adopted the name Hine-nui-te-Po. She was now the great dame of the Po, or spirit world, the important being of that realm. She had constituted herself guardian of the spirits of men, protector and champion of the spirits of the dead as against dread Whiro [declared source of evil] and his henchmen. Tane cares for his descendants in the upper world, but when decay and dissolution come to them, they pass to the spirit world of Rarohenga, there to be guarded ever by the great Hine. (Best 1924:119; brackets added)

In this tradition as given by Best, Tane pursued this Earth-Formed Maid across the sky each day. She assumed different names depending on whether it was morning, noon, or evening. In this story Tane becomes identified with the sun, and the same Hine-nui-te-Po when she retired in the west was also known as Hine-titama, the beautiful dawn maiden in the morning. Best also mentions the "secondary" cosmology attributing the origin of man to Tu-matauenga, as suggested by the cosmology given by Grey. Apparently this myth was not given by the experts in Maori lore but was known among the commoners. Best speculates that Tu was given this honor in that, as god of war, he might have been associated with the setting sun. That Tiki was the first man fits with the cosmology given by Grey in which Maui-Tikitiki brought death to mankind by trying to deceive Hine-nui-te-Po.

Perhaps the separation cosmology can stand alone without the nearby presence of a supreme being, but it is interesting to note that in each of the four cosmologies that Long mentioned above—the Egyptian, Zuni, Polynesian, and Minyong (from the Northeast Frontier of India)—a single creator is acknowledged. A heavenly creator is one of five types of cosmologies found in the Northeast Frontier of India (Elwin 1958:3). From the pyramid texts in Egypt, Atum is given this place even though he is often interpreted as the primeval hill. Ptah, in the Memphite theology, is claimed to be the source of all. For the Zuni, although Long mentions them in his emergence from earth cosmologies (Long 1963:53), he also mentions Awonawilone, the Zuni creator, in a later chapter titled "Creation from Nothing" (Long 1969:159). This particular case is interesting because the American Southwest is considered to have an emergence from earth cosmology. Clearly, from Cushing's report, the Zuni's emergence is only a partial telling of the separation of heaven and earth cosmology (Sproul 1979:284). The question comes to be whether all emergence from earth myths are actually merely shortened forms of the separation of heaven and earth cosmology. This possibility has already been mentioned for Malinowski's Trobriand Islanders, where the people came up from various places with their social distinctions in place. It will be mentioned again in the chapter considering the other South Pacific cosmologies.

To summarize the chapter, the cosmology of the separation of heaven and earth has combined several motifs in an orderly fashion. Heaven and earth, personified or not, are conjoined in such a way as to keep those beings between them confined and in darkness. When these constraints became unbearable, one of the beings successfully separated heaven and earth. If this being was a god, this being usually became the head of the pantheon of the gods. After the separation, the beings freed for the first time came into light. Along with this freedom and light, there was also a social order and rituals that, properly performed, maintained this newfound order. The distribution of this cosmology found in the last two centuries seems to be related to areas in which a single heavenly creator was acknowledged.

Chapter Six

The Cosmologies of the Mesopotamian Valley

The previous chapter treated cosmological material of recent groups, specifically the Maori of New Zealand. In this chapter, some of the earlier written cosmological material of the Sumerians will be addressed. The objective is to show the similarities between one of the earlier of these from the Sumerian cosmological literature and the recent telling of the separation of heaven and earth cosmology as found in the ethnographies of the Maori as representative of the Polynesians. These similarities are striking even though more than 4,000 years intervene. Some of the other Sumerian material will also be given. The argument advanced in this book is that the separation of heaven and earth cosmology served a particular purpose—to introduce a cosmos that could be influenced through a social structure, one suitable for the growth of social hierarchy. When this had been accomplished, other written cosmologies more suited to the needs or aims of the mythmakers could be created.

In Chapter Two, the argument was advanced that during the late Ubaid period, positive archaeological evidence for social hierarchy appeared rather suddenly in the area that later came to be known as Sumer. Archaeologists have discovered a number of sites away from this area that served as outposts, likely to trade first with Uruk and then with other cities in the Mesopotamian Valley that had similar economic interests. The evidence for this was that these outposts reflected the rising and waning of several warring city-states in Sumer. Many of these outpost sites in turn formed their own social hierarchy, some during the Uruk period, others slightly later. It is true that, if the cosmology supporting early hierarchy was spread by diffusion, this diffusion happened well before literature useful to us was produced in Sumer. The assumption that social hierarchy in literate Sumer was based on a cosmology similar to that of the Uruk culture is speculative. But if all the other ancient literate societies knew of a similar cosmology, the argument favoring that assumption is certainly strengthened.

In fact, while there are earlier cylinders with cuneiform writing on them that may be considered texts, the first extended literature that scholars confidently translated did not appear until the Neo-Sumerian period. Archaeology dates this material to about 2100 B.C., and much of the known Sumerian literature has been found in settings well after that. The Sumerian language continued to be the vehicle for conveying religious writing even after Semitic languages replaced it as the spoken language. The earlier cylinders, from perhaps 2600 B.C., already named Enlil as head of the pantheon and Nippur as central in the organization of Sumer. When literature finally reached a point that it was able to help us reconstruct history, Sumer, at least in theory, was a state with one king. His right to reign had been granted at Enlil's temple. Remember, temples were not a new innovation. The temple at the southern city of Eridu had been in use for a thousand years before the first evidences of social hierarchy. It is not that religion came into existence then, rather a new religious perspective did. The argument is that this new perspective allowed, perhaps required, social hierarchy; the old perspective, judging from archaeological evidence up until the late Ubaid period, valued egalitarianism.

From the Sumerian literature available, it is possible to reconstruct several cosmologies. For the student of these cosmologies, there is an obvious interdependence, a certain conservatism. Yet each cosmology apparently confronted a felt (sociological) need. Since Enlil was recognized as head of the pantheon and his city, Nippur, the place where the king of the land was recognized, the cosmology chartering that temple and city should be considered first; it appears to reflect some of the earliest themes known in written cosmologies. One of these myths used to construct that cosmology has been named *The Myth of the Pickaxe*. The following lines are from S. N. Kramer's translation with some corrections as given by T. Jacobsen in his review article of Kramer's book.

> The lord did verily produce the normal order,
> The lord whose decisions cannot be altered,

Enlil, did verily speed to remove heaven from earth
So that the seed (from which grew) the nation could sprout
(up) from the field;
Did verily speed to bring the earth out from (under) heaven
(as a) separate (entity)
(And) bound up for her (i.e. the earth) the gash in the "bond
of heaven"
So that the "flesh producer" (*uzumua*) could grow the
vanguard of mankind. (Jacobsen 1970:117)

He brought the pickaxe into existence,
The "day" came forth,
He introduced labor, decreed the fate,
Upon the pickaxe and basket he directs the "power,"
Enlil made the pickaxe exalted,
The pickaxe of gold, whose head is of lapis lazuli,
The pickaxe of his house, of ... silver and gold,
His pickaxe whose ... is of lapis lazuli,
Whose tooth is a one-horned ox ascending a wall.

The lord called up the pickaxe, decrees its fate,
He set the kindu, the holy crown, upon his head,
The head of man he placed in the mould,
Before Enlil he (man?) covers his head,
Upon the black-headed people he looked steadfastly,
The Annuaki who stood about him,
He placed it (the pickaxe?) as a gift in their hands,
They soothe Enlil with prayer,
They give the pickaxe to the black-headed people to hold.

And the last lines read:

The pickaxe and the basket build cities,
The steadfast house the pickaxe builds, .
The steadfast house the pickaxe establishes,
The steadfast house the pickaxe causes to prosper.

The house which rebels against the king,
The house which is not submissive to the king,

> The pickaxe makes it submissive to the king.
> Of the bad ... plants it crushes the head,
> Plucks out the roots, tears at the crown,
> The pickaxe spares the ... plants,
> The pickaxe, its fate decreed by father Enlil,
> The pickaxe is exalted (Kramer 1952:52f)

And another telling of apparently this same cosmological event is given in the prologue to *Gilgamesh, Enkidu, and the Nether World*. This also is from Kramer with slight corrections by Jacobsen.

> After heaven had been moved away from earth,
> After the name of man had been fixed,
> After An had carried off heaven,
> After Enlil had carried off earth,
> (And) after it (earth) had been presented as dowry
>   to Ereshkigal in the netherworld
> (var.: to Ereshkigal and the netherworld.)
>   (Jacobsen 1970:122f)

> After he had set sail for,
> After he had set sail,
> After the father for kur had set sail,
> After Enki for kur had set sail;

> Against the king the small ones it (kur) hurled,
> Against Enki, the large ones it hurled;
> Its small ones, stones of the hand,
> The large ones, stones of ... reeds,
> The keel of the boat of Enki,
> In battle, like the attacking storm, overwhelm;

> Against the king, the water of the head of the boat,
> Like a wolf devours,
> Against Enki, the water at the rear of the boat,
> Like a lion strikes down. (Kramer 1952:37–38)

Kramer and Jacobsen are both comfortable with fixing Enlil's attributes on the basis of this cosmology. Kramer identifies Enlil as Lord Air, with *En* = "lord" and *lil* = "air." Jacobson rejects that proposition, insisting that the concept that air should support heaven was not known (in spite of Egyptian material with the air-god Shu supporting heaven) and suggests that Enlil was a storm-god, Lord Wind or Storm, that blew heaven and earth apart. Kramer and Jacobsen are the authors that have provided most translations of Sumerian material in books accessible to the American public. Because they occupy this place with respect to the material, their interpretations of the material have been influential. However, their assumptions differ sharply from the ones used in this book. Before considering these translations from this perspective, it would be best to spell out the interpretative perspectives of these translators. Perhaps the translations, and certainly the interpretation of what is meant by them, are influenced by their assumptions and their interpretative vision. Kramer finds in the myths of origin, especially those dealing with the cosmos (heaven, earth, and the origin of man), the philosophical speculation of gifted minds. "The more mature and reflective Sumerian thinker had the mental capacity of thinking logically and coherently on any problems, including those concerned with the origin and operation of the universe" (Kramer 1959:81).

Jacobsen explains his interpretive vision in at least two of his writings, "Notes on Nintur" in *Orientalia NS 42* and *Treasures of Darkness*. In these he recommends the ideas put forth by Rudolph Otto in his book *Idea of the Holy*, especially in the sense that man originally apprehended his universe in terms of the "numinous," the mysterious and the powerful. Jacobsen says, "The Ancient Mesopotamians tended immediately and unreflectedly to see a numinous experience as revelation of power to, and in, a dominant phenomenon of the situation of experience. The power was, so to speak, the numinous élan vital of the phenomenon, a will in it to be and thrive in its particular form and manner. Only with the advent of the ruler metaphor did a new 'transitivity' of certain gods appear: Will to social justice and morality, will and power to victory over enemy armies etc." (Jacobsen 1973:276).

Clearly, their interpretive approaches led both Jacobsen and Kramer to believe that originally the gods of Sumer were particular aspects of natural phenomena. Both of them concluded that the Sumerians believed in a personal Heaven and Earth who had been separated. Therefore, both conclude that, sometime before literary records were made, Enki (*En* = "lord," *ki* = "earth"), another important Sumerian deity, replaced a goddess, Earth, or "Ki." Both admit that there is no textual evidence for this assumption. Especially Kramer allowed his psychological analysis of this god Enki (or his priests) to influence his interpretation of

Sumerian literature. This is clearly seen in his article "Enki and His Inferiority Complex" in *Orientalia NS* 39and in the book he coauthored with John Maier, *Enki, the Crafty God*, in 1989.

Both recognized the separation of heaven and earth theme as major cosmological material for the Sumerians. This cosmology established Enlil as head of the Sumerian pantheon while identifying his temple, the Ekur, at Nippur as the place where men emerged from the earth. The Sumerian separation cosmology not only freed man (third line p. 105, through the *uzumua*) from the burdens of heaven, confinement, and darkness; but it also established a link to the authority of heaven, the Dur-an-ki "bond of heaven and earth" in Enlil's temple. The king of the land was recognized at Nippur. Therefore, the Sumerian version of the story contains important information about the relationship of the gods to the social structure. Neither Kramer nor Jacobsen have drawn attention to this sociological link. (See endnote Chapter 6, note 1: Enlil and his attributes.)

Neither Kramer nor Jacobsen view the pickaxe, in spite of its composition as more than an agricultural implement. (lines from above)—

> He brought the pickaxe into existence,
> The "day" came forth,
> He introduced labor, decreed the fate,
> Upon the pickaxe and basket he directs the "power,"
> Enlil made the pickaxe exalted,
> The pickaxe of gold, whose head is of lapis lazuli

And not only is the pickaxe exalted and somehow related to bringing into being the "day," it also represented authority.

> The house which rebels against the king,
> The house which is not submissive to the king,
> The pickaxe makes it submissive to the king.

Nor do they note that the introduction of (forced?) labor may have had political and social implications. The only hint of the coming of light in the material above is "He brought the pickaxe into existence, the 'day' came forth." However, from other Sumerian material, Bendt Alster offers this information: "A small Ur III literary text ... describes the world before the separation of heaven and earth. An, the god of heaven was 'lord' (en), information which could have been obtained from another early text.... The 'Anunna gods did not walk around.'... No light existed" (Alster 1976:122).

Alster goes on to explain that when Enlil separated heaven and earth, he moved the Anunna gods to the netherworld to be judges there. He compares this with the reign of Ouranos in Hesiod's *Theogony*.

Now as to Kramer's interpretation, with information from one other cuneiform tablet, he concludes the following:

1. First was the *Primeval Sea*. Nothing is said of its origin or birth, and it is certainly not unlikely that the Sumerians conceived it as having existed eternally.
2. The *Primeval Sea* begot the cosmic mountain consisting of heaven and earth united.
3. Conceived as gods in human form, An (heaven) was the male and Ki (earth) was the female. From their union was begotten the air-god Enlil.
4. Enlil, the air-god, separated heaven from earth, and while his father carried off heaven, Enlil himself carried off his mother Ki, the earth. The union of Enlil and his mother Ki—in historic times she is perhaps conceived to be identified with the goddess called variously, Ninmah "great queen"; Ninhursag, "queen of the cosmic mountain"; Nintu, "queen who gives birth"—set the stage for the organization of the universe, the creation of man, and the establishment of civilization. (Kramer 1952:40–41)

Jacobsen also responded to this interpretation in his review article. He criticized Kramer's interpretation by stating that the text Kramer used for his information about "Nammu," TRS 10, which is a catalog of divine names, suggests three other possibilities that Kramer did not explore (Jacobsen 1970:116). From this same text Jacobsen points out that a genealogy of both Enlil and An can be found. Neither of these genealogies suggests Kramer's cosmological concepts. Jacobsen's point was to nullify Kramer's assertion that the Sumerians had such an organized perspective. From my perspective TRS 10, a later document, does not offer either that Nammu gave birth to the cosmic mountain, heaven and earth, or that Enlil was son of either An (heaven) or Ki (earth).

After briefly giving these objections to Kramer's interpretation of Sumerian cosmological speculations, Jacobsen turns specifically to the name Nammu, which Kramer interpreted as Primeval Sea. Jacobsen pointed out that her name indicated not the sea, but fresh water. He follows this observation with this:

> The point made is not unimportant, for it places the ideas with which we are concerned in a particular group of Mesopotamian cosmogonic speculations. That group envisages the origin of the world along lines suggested by the manner of formation of alluvial Mesopotamia itself: through continual deposits of silt in the riverine marshes, Nammu, the deep which deposits the silt, is to this day "giving birth" to earth in Mesopotamia. By identifying Nammu with the sea, Dr. Kramer must necessarily lose site of the basic meaning of the speculations which he treats. The answer is not difficult. In the text to which Dr. Kramer has reference man was made—as one would make a clay figurine—from "the clay above the *apsu*." This clay typifies the silt which the watery deep of the marshes (Nammu) deposit on the shore (Ninmah), and correspondingly Ninmah (Kramer correctly identifies her with Ki, "the firm ground") is in the myth to "stand above" to receive the child—the clay—when Nammu gives birth to it. The deposited clay owes its plasticity, its ability to receive form, to its content of water. This explains the presence of Enki, who represents the sweet waters and who himself issued from Nammu. Just as the deep which deposits the clay, the firm ground which receives it, and the water which gives it plasticity are all involved in the making of man, a process which the myth sees as entirely analogous. (Jacobsen 1970:117–118)

It is not necessary to criticize this fanciful interpretation in detail. However, both authors point out that their theory of an earth-goddess, *Ki*, is not based on evidence from Sumerian literature. I believe it is only in the mind of these translators. Enki, in the literature, is the god of the temple, called the *apzu*, at Eridu. His temple is recognized as the oldest in the land both in the literature and by archaeology. If his worship extended before the time of hierarchy, was he a creator—a supreme being? In considering Enki's attributes, Kramer points to the myth *Enki and the World Order*. From this myth we learn that Enki ordered all things in the world according to the decisions of

Enlil. Interestingly, Enki, in this myth, is said to have created everything, and his creative powers were not limited to Sumer. Kramer concludes this section on Enki by saying, "(A)ll are ascribed to Enki's creative efforts usually by merely stating what amounts to 'Enki did it.' Where the creative technique is mentioned at all, it consists of the god's word and command, nothing more" (Kramer 1963:122).

Notice that Enki is said in the prologue to Gilgamesh, *Enkidu, and the Nether World* (above) to be under attack when Enlil separated heaven and earth. There is no doubt that Enki's position among the pantheon of Sumerian gods was awkward. He was the god of wisdom, the only god who was said to know everything; in the myths where man was said to be made from clay, he was often required to accomplish this creation even though he was assisted by a birth-goddess. He was said to be the friend of man. It was he that confused the languages in *Enmarkar, Lord of Aratta*, saved the flood hero from Enlil's flood in *Atra-hasis*, and provided the cultural *mes*. The *mes* were said to be the knowledge required for the civilization to flourish. Although it is useless to speculate further on the attributes of the god of Eridu before social hierarchy invaded the area, it does not seem unreasonable to consider that he was once the creator of all and accessible to all. At least it can be observed that during historic times, Enki may have occupied a position in Sumer similar to that of Io for the Maori. (See previous chapter.)

Since the *Myth of the Pickax* and the *Gilgamesh, Enkidu, and the Nether World* were present in the Ur III libraries, it seems reasonable to use them together to gain an insight into their meaning. In such an interpretation, heaven and earth were separated so that man's "name could be fixed." This was interpreted to mean that man came into being when heaven and earth were separated. With this in mind, the earlier lines from *Gilgamesh, Enkidu, and the Nether World* are startling in that they state both man's origin and destiny in such a terse manner. It would seem that a synopsis of these lines of the myth would be this: heaven and earth were separated so that man could come into being; and man's place, earth, or *ki*, was (necessarily in the process?) given to the netherworld. One would think that the religious implications of these lines would completely overshadow the merely cosmological ones. Jacobsen has Enlil present the earth, *ki*, to Ereshkigal, queen of the netherworld, as a gift or perhaps even as a dowry, although he does not associate any particular religious significance to his own interpretation.

Some observations about the Sumerian separation are as follows:

1) Although there was no lengthy tale concerning the difficulties involved while heaven and earth were conjoined, early Sumerian material does state that movement was constrained and darkness prevailed (Alster 1976:122).

2) Enlil was the father of *Nanna*, the moon, who in turn was the father of *Utu*, the sun, even as Tane, the Maori separator of heaven and earth, was instrumental in putting the sun and moon into place. In short, the separator of heaven and earth was also responsible for the coming of light.

3) Enlil, the separator, was recognized as the pre-eminent god even as Tane, the separator, was in the Maori belief system.

4) In Sumer men emerged into a world in which at least the concept of cities already existed. The offices of ruler and priest were either already present or immediately established. Man's destiny was the netherworld, not as a place of judgment in the sense that Christians have about the dead who are lost, but a dreary place of no return nonetheless. While the Sumerians enjoyed a much more advanced civilization than the Maori, the similarities in those particulars listed above are undeniable. (See listing of associated motifs in the previous chapter.)

Another very important and apparently early myth in historic Sumer was the myth of Inanna, the goddess of fertility, and Dumuzi, an early king, her consort. For obscure reasons, Inanna chose to visit Ereshkigal in the netherworld. She left this instruction with her vizier, Ninshubur: if she did not return within three days, go first to Enlil, then to Nanna, and if they did not help, to Enki. Of course when the fertility goddess was taken and hung as a corpse in the netherworld, the earth was smitten by her absence. After neither Enlil nor Nanna helped, Enki fashioned two creatures, gave them the water and food of life, and Inanna was revived. However, she could not leave the netherworld without a substitute. She left promising to furnish this substitute. When she returned to Dumuzi, he was celebrating, not mourning, her plight. In anger she chose him to be the substitute required by Ereshkigal. Immediately in this telling the demons took him to the netherworld (Kramer 1963:153f). The story was very popular and had many variants. This story tells us that the dead king, who had each year during his reign ritually played the part as lover to Inanna, the goddess of fertility, in death became her substitute. In this way the dead king, as well as the living king, were instrumental in the fertility of the land.

The story was later given in roughly the same way in Babylonian times; but then, Ishtar and Tammuz were the chief actors. Weeping for Tammuz is the idolatrous practice mentioned in Ezekiel 8:14.

It is worth pointing out that this story and others resembling it are limited in distribution to the Mesopotamian Valley and the eastern Mediterranean area. While the elite of the social structure are held to be responsible for the fertility of the land in many widespread areas, this belief is not usually based on the leader's ritual sexual relationship to a goddess of fertility. This myth, then, does not hold a place similar to the separation cosmology. An inference based on this observation is that this myth came into being in Sumer after hierarchy had already become well established.

Another creation of man cosmology was found in the Sumerian language, although later than a neo-Sumerian context. This is the story that Kramer offered in *Sumerian Mythology* and for which Jacobsen offered his very creative interpretation. Both Kramer and Jacobsen identify Ninmah, whose name they consider to be one of the earth goddess's names during literate times, as a birth-goddess. I agree to this extent; she was a birth-goddess. She identified the newborns' place in the society. In Kramer's words,

> The story begins with description of the difficulties of the gods in procuring their bread, especially, as might have been expected, after the female deities had come into being. The gods complain, but Enki, the water god, who, as the Sumerian god of wisdom, might have been able to come to their aid, is lying asleep in the deep and fails to hear them. Thereupon his mother, the Primeval Sea, 'the mother who gave birth to all the gods,' brings the tears of the gods before Enki saying: "O my wise son, rise from your bed, from … work what is wise. Fashion servants of the gods, may they produce their …" (Kramer 1952:70)

> Enki gives the matter thought, leads forth the host of 'good and princely' fashioners, and says to his mother, Nammu, the Primeval Sea:

> "O my mother, the creature whose name you uttered, it exists, Bind on it the image(?) of the gods;

> Mix the heart of the clay that is over the abyss,
> The good and princely *fashioners* will thicken the clay,
> You, do you bring the *limbs* into existence;
> Ninmah will work above you
> The goddesses (of birth) ... will stand by you at your fashioning;
> O my mother, decree its (the new-born's) fate,
> Ninmah will bind upon it the (mould)(?) of the gods,"
> (Kramer 1963:149–150)

Apparently, Kramer did not accept Jacobsen's earlier correction that Nammu represented the fresh water. Kramer's 1963 offering did not change his translation except to substitute you for thou. Perhaps, as Jacobsen suggested, Enuma Elish, the Babylonian Genesis, which we will consider in the next chapter, influenced Kramer. However, if he had been influenced by it, it seems reasonable that he should also have recognized that what was bound on man was the toil of the gods. Notice in the translated portion above that Kramer is not certain of the word following either "bind on it" or Ninmah "will bind on it." The word may be borrowed from the Akkadian meaning "basket." This notion was expressed and translated in *Atra-hasis* as the toil of the gods. And this is consistent within the context of this story. But neither Kramer nor Jacobsen seem willing to ascribe to the Sumerians' stories such forceful sociological implications. Neither allow that the task of Ninmah was to attach to man the toil of the gods, while Enki was to furnish man. It was the duty of one of the many birth-goddesses to "fix the destiny" in the case of each newborn. In the context, Kramer does note that man's creation in Sumerian material has very different implications from the almost similar description of man's creation in our own scripture. In ours, man is made to rule over God's creation; in the Mesopotamian, man is created to relieve the gods of their labor (Kramer 1963:149). The reader should note that—in the animistic, pantheistic, or polytheistic systems the myth of the separation proclaims—man becomes (merely) a servant through a social structure designed to assist the gods in their duties.

Chapter Seven

Three Later Cosmologies from Mesopotamia

In this chapter we will consider some of the other cosmological material from the Mesopotamian Valley. While the earliest of this material was committed to writing shortly after the Sumerian material available to us, it obviously differs significantly from it. This is in spite of the fact that the first of these cosmologies did not offer a significant change in political alignment. That is, the Akkadian cosmology, *Atra-hasis*, still recognized Enlil as head of the pantheon, and his city remained the place where the ruler of the land was recognized. The reason for the change appears to be cultural; that is, the people living there then spoke a Semitic language and are believed to have come from an Amorite (West Semitic as opposed to Akkadian, East Semitic) background. Whether or not this material gives us an insight into Amorite traditions, it does demonstrate that the separation of heaven and earth cosmology is not somehow fixed as the only way that men of the time could think.

The author who first wrote *Atra-hasis* expressed it as a history rather than a religious affirmation to be used in the cult, yet he certainly included cosmological material. Perhaps the first few lines of this piece will help the reader get a flavor of it. If the separation of heaven and earth is mentioned at all, it is expressed in lines 11 through 18.

> 1 When the gods like men
> 2. Bore the work and suffered the toil-

3. The toil was great,
4. The work was heavy, the distress was much -
5. The Seven great Anunnaki
6. Were making the Igigi suffer the work.
7. Anu, their father was the king:
8. Their counselor was the warrior Enlil;
9. Their chamberlain was Ninurta;
10. And their sheriff Ennugi.
11. The gods had clasped their hand together,
12. Had cast lots and had divided.
13. Anu had gone up to heaven,
14. [. .] … the earth to his subjects.
15. [The bolt], the bar of the sea,
16. [They had given] to Enki, the prince.
17. [After Anu] had gone up to heaven
18. [And Enki] had gone down to the Apsu
    (Lambert & Millard 1969:43)

The story line is as follows: After a mutual decision to divide the spheres of influence, Enlil was still the one effectively in control of the earth. This is the setting for the drama that follows. The minor gods, the Igigi, had to support Enlil and the Anunnaki, the major gods. Those supported may not have included Anu or Enki, although they were listed as king and prince. The labor mentioned was the digging of canals for irrigation. The Igigi rebelled, and Enlil (chief god) became angry and wanted the leader of the rebellion put to death. He approached Anu and Enki; both were reluctant to do this. Finally it was decided to put one of the gods to death in order to make man—specifically, to make man who was to bear the toil of Enlil. The process of making man to be a servant of Enlil required clay from the Apsu along with the "personality" of the slain god. Seven males and seven females were made from this clay mixed with the flesh and blood of the slain god. Mankind filled their role and multiplied for 1,200 years until Enlil became annoyed by their noise. First Enlil sent a plague to control the population; Enki thwarted it. Then he ordered a famine; and again, Enki thwarted it. Finally he ordered a flood to eradicate man altogether. All the gods took an oath to participate in this flood, but Enki prepared his protégé, Atra-hasis, by telling him to build a boat for his family and some animals. The gods, who were dismayed at man's destruction, were elated to discover that one family had survived. However, Enlil was furious, and Enki stepped forward to claim the deed.

Enlil stipulated that childbirth must be limited to control the population in the future.

Lambert and Millard offer an approach to this story that is worth considering. They set up this paragraph by comparing the differences in the Sumerian and the Babylonian perspectives. The following is from their description of the background of the author who composed it:

> The author used what was the generally accepted of this matter among those who wrote in Akkadian, that man was formed from clay mixed with the blood of a slain god. To understand what the author of *Atra-hasis* was achieving in his account one must know not only this fact, but also the implication, though no ancient text formally offers a commentary on the meaning of creation. "Clay" in this context is the material substance of the human body. This can be learnt from a number of passages that speak of death as a "returning to clay." Exactly the same context is shown in the Hebrew account of man's creation where the penalty for disobedience was laid down: "You are earth, and to earth you shall return" (Genesis 3:19). The present writers have not found any similar Mesopotamian clue explaining the blood, but this does not mean that speculation is out of place. (Lambert and Millard 1969:21)

The part of the epic that we are particularly interested in is the creation of man since by definition this is cosmological in nature. Lambert and Millard's suggestion that clay and the blood of a slain god were a west Semitic notion is without known basis, as they acknowledge. It cannot be from Hebrew sources. Nor is it from the Sumerian story of the creation of man with clay from the Apsu considered in the last chapter. The use of the blood of a god does, however, become a standard explanation for the creation of man in the next two cosmologies to be considered. Incidentally, one of the variant names of the Sumerian god Enki, or his Semitic counterpart, Ea, is Nudimmud. This name has been translated as "the creator of man." If we assume the tradition that Enki (or Ea) created man, it becomes clear that the real accomplishment of the story is the new population's subjection to Enlil, head of the pantheon. Perhaps then, to overcome Amorite sensibilities, the death of a god subject to Enlil was incorporated into the cosmology, in the creation of man, in order to justify their obligations to the head of the Sumerian pantheon.

Lambert and Millard tell us the epic was first known from Assyrian sources, as many of the Sumerian and Babylonian stories also were. The date of its first composition is uncertain, but it is probably Old Babylonian (after 1800 B.C.). They mention that the great-great-grandson of Hammurabi (Amorite) was a contemporary of Ku-Aya (Lambert and Millard 1969:5), the scribe who was responsible for the most complete copy of the epic found. The story starts with the words "When the gods like men," and that is the title they apparently used. The title, *Atra-hasis,* which is given it today, is the name of the flood survivor in the story.

The opening lines tell us that Anu (Sumerian An, the heaven god) had been given heaven as his domain; Enki was given the deep (subterranean water?) as his domain. Enlil controlled the space between. Enlil and the Anunnaki were making the Igigi suffer hard labor. At length the gods rebelled, burning their tools and storming Enlil at the Ekur. The complaint of the gods angered Enlil.

> 168. Enlil … his words
> 169. And addressed the warrior Anu,
> 170. "Noble one, with you to heaven
> 171. Carry your authority, take your power,
> 172. While the Anunnaki are present before you
> 173. Summon one god and have him done to death."

Anu objected, saying, "Their labor was hard, their distress much." Then Enlil turned to Enki with the same complaint. Enki also defended the oppressed gods. Finally the solution was offered that man could be created to bear the toil of the gods.

> 194. "You are the birth-goddess, creatress of mankind,
> 195. Create *Lullu* [common word for man] that he may bear the yoke,
> 196. Let him bear the yoke assigned by Enlil,
> 197. Let man carry the toil of the gods."
> 198. Nintu opened her mouth
> 199. And addressed the great gods,
> 200. "It is not possible for me to make things,
> 201. Skill lies with Enki.
> 202. Since he can cleanse everything

203. Let him give me the clay so that I can make it."
204. Enki opened his mouth
205. And addressed the great gods,
206. "On the first, seventh, and fifteenth day of the month
207. I will make a purifying bath.
208. Let one god be slaughtered
209. So that all the gods may be cleansed in a dipping.
210. From his flesh and blood
211. Let Nintu mix clay,
212. That god and man
213. May be thoroughly mixed in the clay,
214. So that we may hear the drum for the rest of time
215. Let there be a spirit from the god's flesh."

223. We-ila, who had personality,
224. They slaughtered in their assembly,
225. From his flesh and blood
226. Nintu mixed clay
237. "You have commanded me a task, I have completed it;
239. You have slaughtered a god together with his personality.
240. I have removed your heavy work,
241. I have imposed your toil on man."
    (Lambert and Millard 1969:57f)

There are several things to notice about this creation of man story. It starts with the gods already in a hierarchical system, supporting themselves in a human manner during a time in which man is said not to exist. Enlil along with the Anunnaki was in charge. The labor was described as digging canals or rivers on which their agriculture depended. The origin of the gods and the landscape on which they labored is not mentioned. While the creation of man is cosmological in nature, it did not offer a major political change from the Sumerian system; the head of the pantheon remained in charge, and his temple was the seat of power. Taking our prompt from Lambert and Millard, it was designed to bring a new population into the political system and labor force as well as to answer questions about how this situation came into being. Although written in Akkadian, an east Semitic language, the Babylonians as a group were probably a west Semitic group with traditions significantly different from the people for whom the earlier cosmologies were written. If so, this might account for the flood tradition as well. It is not certain that any similar flood details appeared in Sumerian literature before this time. Nor is it certain that the creation of man from clay was given before this time in Sumer; the story given by Kramer and criticized by Jacobsen in our last chapter is known from a Babylonian, not a neo-Sumerian, context. The birth goddesses were certainly Sumerian goddesses. What had been their function? They assisted the mother and emphasized the newborn's station in the society. That would not require an original creation from clay.

Lambert and Millard did not ask why Enki, not Anu, was chosen as the god in this pantheon to help create man from clay. If the west Semitic people shared an understanding with the Hebrew population, they would have looked to one similar to El, likely their creator, who apparently was also head of their pantheon. The Sumerian god, An, was represented in cuneiform by a star shown as four intersecting lines. This same symbol, the "dinger" symbol, if used in conjunction with another name, indicated that the being was a god. *El* was the common word for a god among the Semites as well as the particular name of the head of their pantheon. As an aside, the symbol for the deep according to Mallowan was a rectangle, and it was distinguished from the oval sign for the earth. The symbol for heaven and the deep was this rectangle with the star of four intersecting lines, the dinger, within (Mallowan 1965:60). Mallowan continues with a listing of several symbols, including the dinger in the rectangle, pointing out that it had been represented on pottery well before the literate period. I believe this symbol was also the early symbol for the Apsu (temple) at Eridu. This leads me to speculate that when Enlil divided heaven from earth, heaven was taken from the Apsu. In short, at that time Enki, the god whose temple was called the Apsu, was declared to no longer be the god of heaven. The Semitic El also has been identified as the god of the two deeps, one being heaven. This is another argument suggesting that Enki held the same position in Sumer as El did for the west Semites.

Is it also possible that a sacrificial substitute would fit into their understanding? The notion that man was created by mixing clay with the remains of a god, or his blood, became a standard narrative in the Mesopotamian Valley. Lambert and Mallard suggest that it was west Semitic in origin; if so, what is the source for their speculation?

Notwithstanding, there are several things to notice about this story. As with all Sumerian and, indeed, all known Mesopotamian myths, culture precedes man. In a number of Sumerian myths, before man came into being the gods moved from city to city, traveled by boat, and had temples. While this is not spelled out in *Atra-hasis*, it was probably traditional enough that it did not need to be. Perhaps the complaint of the overworked gods was already present in Sumerian material. Here, however, the execution of a rebellious god whose substance was used to make man appears as a new thought. Effectively, the lesser gods are redeemed from their toil by the death of one of their own, the one guilty of leading the rebellion. His blood, however, does not "cleanse" the gods of their wicked deed. Enki probably accomplished that with his purifying bath, which was almost certainly water, not blood—at least not We-ila's blood.

Why was Nintu, the birth-goddess, unable to accomplish the task by herself? It was Enki that furnished man as the (living) clay. The "personality" of the god, We-ila, was to remind mankind specifically of his role, the toil of Enlil. Although the story follows by offering interesting instruction about childbirth and their rituals concerning it, it does not tell us much about the social order—how Enlil expressed his orders to mankind. It does not justify social privileges as the anthropologist Malinowski taught. It merely explains how it is that man must endure forced labor. Social hierarchy was already well established.

The second cosmological myth to be considered is *The Babylonian Genesis*, or *Enuma Elish*, the first line of the "hymn" meaning "When above." This piece of literature was used in the cult, and that is why it is sometimes called a hymn. ("Used in the cult" means that it was repeated at an annual celebration installing or invigorating the king.) It is the most well known of these cosmologies since it was the first translated into English. Before *Atra-hasis* became available, it was the cosmology most often compared with the Old Testament. For the account of the story from the cuneiform, Alexander Heidel's *The Babylonian Genesis* has been used. As with the other material, the first order of business is to put it into historical perspective. Heidel offers that it was probably written during the time of Hammurabi, the Babylonian king who in the eighteenth century B.C. established a dynasty that lasted four hundred years. He was a west Semite, usually identified as Amorite; he unified Sumer under his rule and extended the state to include more area to the north. Heidel offers that the *Agum* inscription seems to indicate this.

> When the exalted Anu, the king of the Anunnaki, (and) Enlil, the lord of heaven and earth, who determine the destinies of the land, committed the sovereignty over all the people to Marduk, the first-born son of Ea; (when) they made him great

> among the Igigi; (when) they proclaimed to Babylon his ex-
> alted name; (when) they made it unsurpassable in the regions
> of the world (and) in its midst established for him an ever-
> lasting kingdom whose foundations are firm as heaven and
> earth: at that time Anu and Enlil called me, Hammurabi, the
> reverent prince, the worshipper of the gods, by my name, to
> cause justice to prevail in the land, to destroy the wicked and
> the evil, to prevent the strong from oppressing the weak, to
> go forth like the sun over the human race, to enlighten the
> land and to further the welfare of the people. (Heidel 1942:14,
> credits Bruno Meissner 1904)

This dating would allow that its creation was before *Atra-hasis*. Since Heidel wrote, this dating has been reconsidered. Lambert has argued that during Hammurabi's reign, there is no evidence that Marduk, city god of Babylon, was elevated within the Anu-Enlil pantheon. In fact, while it is accepted that *Atra-hasis* was written during the Babylonian period, neither Marduk's name nor Babylon are even mentioned in that text. Lambert offers that in the *Agum* inscription itself (above), Marduk was elevated among the people, not among the gods. He was great among the Igigi, not the Anunnaki or great gods. He continues by suggesting that it was during the reign of Nebuchadnezzar I, ca. 1100 B.C., after Marduk's statue had been recovered from Elam, that the hymn elevating Marduk to the head of the pantheon was composed. There has been little challenge to this reasoning. Further, only an Assyrian version has been found in an older context than the library collection of Ashurbanipal (668–630 B.C.) in Nineveh, and that is well after the event he alluded to (Lambert 1964:11).

As for the hymn, this is a summary of Heidel's account of the story line. The original condition was Tiamat, Apsu, and their offspring Mummu, which are most often said to represent the salt water, subterranean freshwater, and the clouds. They gave birth to Lahmu and Lahamu. Shortly after, another pair came into being, Anshar and Kishar. They gave birth to Anu (Sumerian An, the sky-god) who in turn gave birth to Ea (Sumerian and Akkadian Enki). Ea, god of exceptional wisdom, had no rival among the younger gods. The younger gods, who by this time were many, were by nature boisterous. Apsu and Mummu planned to do away with them so they could sleep and presented this plan to Tiamat. Although she would not agree to their plan, they proceeded to set it into action. The young gods were terrified, but Ea, master even of Apsu, put a spell on Apsu, took his tiara and supernatural power from him, killed him, and imprisoned Mummu. Since Tiamat did not agree to the plan of Apsu and Mummu, she was not molested. From Apsu's remains, Ea built his abode and named it the Apsu. There Ea and his spouse Damkina gave birth to Marduk. Ea conferred on him a double equality with the gods, so that "he was exalted among the gods." Eventually, restless Tiamat was led by Kingu with some of the gods to avenge her husband's death. This divided the gods, some siding with Anshar, some with Tiamat. Tiamat brought many monsters into being and planned an assault against the gods who were responsible for the death of Apsu. When Anshar heard of the plot, he was benumbed with dismay. Anshar went to Ea, asking him to save them by peaceful measures. Ea failed. Then Anu went with his authority, but he also failed.

After all the gods had been notified of their dire position, Anshar remembered the mighty Marduk. The gods got together to confer on Marduk the supreme position in the pantheon. In single combat Marduk, armed with great weapons, overcame Tiamat and killed her. He sliced her body in half, making heaven and earth, and then established Anu, Enlil, and Ea in their respective domains. He took Kingu prisoner and made the rebel gods servants to provide sustenance for the victors. In time the gods who had sided with Tiamat asked for relief from their labor. In solemn court Kingu was indicted as the one who caused the strife. Ea, following the ingenious plans of Marduk, created man using the blood of Kingu and imposed the service of the gods on him. Next Marduk divided the Anunnaki into two groups of three hundred each and assigned one group duties in heaven, the other on earth. Out of gratitude they built Marduk the Esagila, his temple at Babylon. Here they held a banquet and recited the fifty names of Marduk. The instructions to the listeners were to study these names and rejoice in Marduk so that things would be well with them. (Heidel 1951:3–10)

The dependence on *Atra-hasis* seems obvious. But here a new political and religious order was established. Enlil was given a place, but he was no longer head of the pantheon. His city, Nippur, was no longer the city where kings were recognized. Marduk became the chief son of Ea; yet Ea, the father, assumed the second place. This is not unlike the Ugaritic texts of the West Semites, where the preeminent gods Baal, Anath, and Dagon are called children of El. West Semitic material on which to build a typical cosmology has not been found. Perhaps some translation of the Ebla material will yet yield such material.

Apparently, Marduk's position as given in this hymn was accepted for some time in the lower Mesopotamian Valley. There are a number of other texts likely from these times that acknowledge the preeminence of Marduk and his temple, the Esagila, at Babylon. As to the treatment of Ea, the Sumerian Enki, one of his Sumerian titles, Nudimmud, meaning "the creator of man," is used even at the start of the hymn. When he overcame Apsu, he merely reclaimed his domain, the deep, which he had in the earlier Sumerian and Akkadian cosmologies. Although Heidel has offered a symbolic meaning for Mummu, the vizier of Apsu, as "mist or cloud" to account for the fifth line in the hymn, "they mingled their waters together." He also authored a journal article in which he argues that the word is derived from the Sumerian word *mud-mud*, meaning "creator." Heidel said, "This seems to indicate *mummu* is a divine name or appellative. If our deduction is correct, there can hardly be any doubt that the word *mummu* is identical with the one we have just considered, and that in the case we have just considered it has reference to Ea, who was not only present in the *bit mummu*, but who was himself *mummu*, the creator of all things, *mummu*, the creator of ordinances and ceremonies, the lord wisdom, the creator of creation, the fashioner of all things" (1947:104).

True, Heidel goes on to point out that there may be several homonyms—roar, thunder—all derived from the Sumerian *mud-mud* signifying "creator" or "fashioner." However, seeing that Ea captures his own temple (Sumerian Abzu) and domain, that is, underground freshwater, why would he not also recover his traditional titles and attributes in the hymn? The use of symbolic speech often makes for two or more meanings at the same time.

The order of the hymn is interesting. It reverses the order in *Atra-hasis* in at least two ways. The great gods do not start out with their attributes. In the case of Ea, he acts to capture them. Later Anu, Enlil, and Ea are given their respective places in the heaven and earth that Marduk makes from Tiamat's body. This reversal serves to establish Marduk's authority. There is also a reversal in the literary sense. In *Atra-hasis* the gods rebelled against Enlil in the first few lines, and only near the end did Enlil bring the flood to destroy noisy mankind so they would not disturb his sleep. In the *Babylonian Genesis*, Apsu and Mummu set out early to destroy the noisy gods who were interfering with their sleep. Another motivation was given to Tiamat and the gods who accompanied her—that is, vengeance, not rebellion. But when she came to avenge Apsu, she surely was filling the role of the Igigi gods who had rebelled against Enlil in *Atra-hasis*. Kingu obviously filled the role given We-ila in that story. He does this rather completely. He was said to be the one guilty of causing the conflict even though it was only his blood that was used to make man; it was Ea who accomplished it. The man so created was directed not to the service of one god, as in *Atra-hasis*, but to the service of all the gods.

Those who are looking for a way to discover the Babylonians' cosmological speculations about the physical universe will find the meaning for Tiamat nicely filled as the "sea" or "oceans." However, those who are looking for a sociological meaning for Tiamat will find in her the disorder that existed before Babylon became both the political and religious center of the land. During earlier times, Nippur was consistently the religious center, but it had never been important militarily. It was respected as the place that reconciliation could be accomplished after one or another city had established supremacy by military means. I believe the similarities between this story line and *Atra-hasis* make the choice of the latter interpretation, the sociological one, closer to what the mythmaker had in mind. Again, as with Mummu, symbols can have more than one meaning.

How does this compare with the earlier cosmology of Sumer, the separation of heaven and earth? Some do find it to be another separation of heaven and earth story. While there are lines that indicate Tiamat's insides were disturbed, it does not appear that the gods were contained within her. Where and how they lived before Marduk made heaven and earth from her body is not explained, only hinted at by the opening words of the hymn, "when above." But they were not in distress because they were constrained or kept in darkness. In line 25 we are told, "Apsu could not diminish their clamor" (Heidel 1951:19). In fact, as Heidel interpreted his translation, Anu and Ea were to make peace with her, not to split her open (Heidel 1951:6). And finally Tiamat was killed, not merely separated. Her position is better compared to other myths in which a god or goddess is killed, resulting in benefit for all. Yet, all in all, while it became a traditional cosmology for the Neo-Babylonian Empire and with minor changes for the Assyrian Empire as well, it remains unique as a cosmology accounting for the creation of heaven and earth.

The third cosmology is short enough that the whole translation of it may be given. The Sumerian cuneiform signs used in this one suggest a late date. It was found in the ruins of the city of Ashur, dating to about 800 B.C. There were three columns, one whose signs have not been deciphered, one Sumerian, and one Babylonian. It is of interest because it is believed that, some time after early Assyrian and Babylonian dominance in the area, the area returned to a pantheon with An and Enlil at its head. This would indicate that during Babylonian supremacy there were still those who remembered the Sumerian pantheon. The translation as given in Heidel follows:

1. When heaven had been separated from earth, the trusty twin,
2. (And) the mother goddesses had been brought into being;
3. When the earth had been brought forth (and) the earth had been fashioned;
4. When the destinies of heaven and earth had been fixed;
5. (When) trench and canal had been given (their) right courses,
6. (And) the banks of the Tigris and the Euphrates had been established,
7. (Then) Anu, Enlil, Shamash, (and) Ea,
8. The great gods,
9. (And) the Anunnaki, the great gods,
10. Seated themselves in the exalted sanctuary
11. And recounted among themselves what had been created.
12. "Now that the destinies of heaven and earth have been fixed,
13. Trench and canal have been given their right courses,
14. The banks of the Tigris and Euphrates
15. Have been established,
16. What (else) shall we do?
17. What else shall we create?
18. O Anunnaki, ye great gods,
19. What (else) shall we do?
20. What (else) shall we create?"
21. The great gods who were present,
22. The Anunnaki, who fix the destinies,
23. Both (groups) of them, made answer to Enlil:
24. "In Uzumua, the bond of heaven and earth,
25. Let us slay (two) Lamga gods,
26. With their blood let us create mankind.
27. The Service of the gods be their portion,
28. For all times
29. To maintain the boundary ditch,
30. To place the hoe and basket
31. Into their hands
32. For the Dwelling of the great gods,

33. Which is fit to be an exalted sanctuary
34. To mark off the field from field,
35. For all times
36. To maintain the boundary ditch,
37. To give the trench (its) right course,
38. To maintain the boundary stone (?)
39. To water the four regions of the earth (?)
40. To raise plants in abundance,
41. Rains(?) [...]"

And on the reverse side the story continues.

1. "To maintain the boundary (?),
2. To fill (?) the granary,
3–5 (*destroyed*)
6. To make the field of the Anunnaki produce plentifully
7. To increase the abundance of the land,
8. To celebrate the festivals of the gods,
9. To pour out cold water
10. In the great house of the gods, which is fit to be an exalted sanctuary.
11. Ulligarra (and) Zalgarra
12. Thou shalt call their names.
13. That they should increase ox, sheep, cattle, fish, and fowl,
14. The abundance of the land,
15. Enul (and) Ninul
16. Decreed with their holy mouths.
17. Aruru, the lady of the gods, who is fit for rulership,
18. Ordained for them great destinies:
19. Skilled worker to produce skilled worker (and) unskilled worker for unskilled worker,
20. (Spring up) by themselves like grain from the ground,
21. A thing which, (like) the stars of heaven, shall not be changed forever.
22. Day and night
23. To celebrate the festivals of the gods
24. By themselves,
25. These great destinies
26. Did Anu, Enlil,

27. Ea, and Ninmah,
28. The great gods, decreed (for them)
29. In the place where mankind was created,
30. There Nisaba was firmly established.
31. Let wise teach the mystery to the wise." (Heidel 1951:68–71)

There are a number of interesting things about this cosmology. It is perhaps the only Mesopotamian one in which the first humans were given names. In a footnote Heidel offers that the names probably meant "establisher of abundance" and "establisher of plenty." These names are suggestive of their purpose from the perspective of the gods. They were made from the blood of Lamga gods; Heidel offers that they were craftsmen gods (Heidel 1951:69). Something of the original separation story is preserved in the opening lines. Uzumua again was the place in Enlil's temple where mankind came into being, perhaps still the place where heaven and earth had been separated. The Anunnaki address Enlil as the head of the pantheon. The purpose for mankind remains as defined as in *Enuma Elish,* the service of the gods. Ea is not directly involved in the creation of man; only Aruru, a Sumerian birth-goddess is given this position. The chief gods of the pantheon are, once again, Anu, Enlil, Ea, and Ninmah (another name for Aruru).

In this particular cosmology, skilled and unskilled laborers are distinguished as different classes in the social order. Here the notion that these laborers spring up like grain from the ground was likely poetic. There is no indication that anything other than the usual reproduction of humans was intended. It is easy to wonder if this has also become an interpretation of the earlier material stating that the first of mankind did spring from the earth when heaven was moved away. Notice that the cosmology identifies permanent class distinctions among laborers.

17 Aruru, the lady of the gods, who is fit for rulership,
18. Ordained for them great destinies:
19. Skilled worker to produce skilled worker (and) unskilled worker for unskilled worker,

20. (Spring up) by themselves like grain from the ground,
21. A thing which, (like) the stars of heaven, shall not be changed forever.
22. Day and night

23. To celebrate the festivals of the gods
[...]
30. There Nisaba was firmly established.
31. Let wise teach the mystery to the wise.
  (Heidel 1951:70f)

The closing line of this cosmology references Nisaba, no doubt as the goddess of writing and wisdom. Effectively, it is saying to let the wise hear and take note of how things are. Two observations may be made about all three of the cosmologies treated in this chapter. They do not directly justify positions of authority, as Malinowski would have them. However, this authority and hierarchy were certainly present. The cosmologies were concerned about explaining how it was that man had to meet the needs of the gods. These needs appear to include the labor done both to raise food for sacrifices and to maintain the temples. There was little in these cosmologies to explain what the gods contributed beyond the original order, which was already in place when man was created. It was man's responsibility to follow the order established by the gods. The other observation is that all three of these cosmologies required the death of a god for the creation of man. This notion is not of widespread distribution, but the notion that man was created from clay or dust is, of course. In spite of Jacobsen's fanciful interpretation of man's origin in the previous chapter, this creation usually required an actor, most often the creator himself, to bring man into existence from the clay. These later cosmologies, in contrast to the separation of heaven and earth cosmology, are of very limited distribution.

Chapter Eight

The Austronesians and the Cosmology of the Separation of Heaven and Earth

At roughly the time of the sites of earliest social hierarchy listed in Chapter Three, linguists estimate that a group of people in Taiwan spoke a language that today is called proto-Austronesian. This language group spread over a great area even as the Indo-European speakers spread across Asia and Europe. Austronesian speakers spread into the Philippines, Vietnam, Malaysia, Indonesia, sections of the Island of New Guinea, the islands known as Melanesia north of New Guinea, the Polynesian Islands in the far expanses of the Pacific, and as far west as Madagascar off the coast of Africa. Anthropologists, in studying the social ordering of these people groups, have found certain similarities that seem to belong specifically to the area of the South Pacific Islands.

Let me review how this fits into the general pattern underscored in the book. The Indo-Europeans had a system of social ordering that lent itself to the label pantheism since its leader was said to embody the whole of the society. The Mesopotamians and those in their sphere of influence are identified as polytheists because of their beliefs concerning the activity of the gods. The Africans have been called ancestor worshipers because of their particular institution of sacred leaders and the ideology surrounding it. Further, my position is that all of these groups, different as they obviously are from each other, each started from a similar cosmology. As far as the data allows us to know, a separation cosmology in each instance chartered a position or positions that were invested with responsibilities to ritually control the environment. The cosmology as a charter for these positions must have been articulated in terms the target groups understood. That is, the symbolism represented by the terms *heaven* and *earth* must have been culturally relevant for the charter itself to have meaning. Likely there was at one time a similar understanding of the symbols involved in this cosmology. If this is true, what did *heaven* represent?

This chapter offers the proposition that the island world of the South Pacific has a social order influenced by certain basic principles unique to that area. And those principles might reasonably be associated with the spread of the Austronesian languages. Remember that the cosmology of the separation of heaven and earth is very well represented in the Polynesian Islands. Archaeology has verified that as the Austronesians migrated, they first occupied the coastal areas without moving inland. Here they were able to exploit the coastal resources while establishing the plants and animals they brought with them. They were also in position to maintain trade with other like groups. Often the whole population of the islands came to be included in their culture pattern, and in many places the aboriginal population adopted their language as well. When they moved into the open Pacific, they were not colonizing but merely settling unoccupied space. Their cosmological myths are best represented among these inhabitants, the Polynesians.

This chapter assumes, with considerable support, that the distribution of this myth in the Pacific area, with a distinctive Austronesian social ordering, can be associated with this one language group. The area includes nearly the entire island world of the South Pacific. Even Australia, whose people do not speak an Austronesian language, was influenced by this cosmology with the result that the social structure of a large part of the continent is consistent with that of the rest of the South Pacific. While changes happened that differentiated them from one another, there remained an underlying similarity within the cultures in the area. This similarity can be distinguished from the other social orders that have been described.

With anthropology's acceptance of Malinowski's work with the Trobriand Islanders, *Argonauts of the Western Pacific,* published in 1922, schemes of widespread influence fell into disrepute. But linguistics, the study of languages, revived the possibility of a widespread diffusion of social order by demonstrating the widespread distribution of several language groups. For some time there have been anthropologists who have participated in arguments about the Indo-European language and the importance of social structure in the spread of

Much as the Indo-Europeans spread their language throughout Europe and central and south Asia, the Austronesians spread out from Taiwan throughout the Pacific. Their language is well represented in Malaysia, Indonesia, New Guinea, the Island north and east of New Guinea called Melanesia and the small islands north of them called Micronesia. Fiji and New Zealand along with islands farther to the east are called Polynesia. Included in these, but not shown on the map, are the Society Islands, Hawaii, and Easter Island. The inhabitants of Madagascar off the coast of Africa also speak an Austronesian language. Australia, however, does not.

that language. It has been a much shorter time that this argument has been advanced with regard to spread of the Austronesian languages. But it has now surfaced. In fact, in a book written as part of a comparative Austronesian Project sponsored by the Australian National University, one of the authors proposed my claim as a possibility.

Bellwood poses this question: "Is it possible to correlate the earliest colonizing of Austronesian speaking peoples into Taiwan, the Philippines, Vietnam, Malaysia, Indonesia and the myriad islands of Oceania with the existence of a hereditary elite stratum of society?" (Bellwood 1996:18). Before considering the answer Bellwood gives to this question, this is his description of the starting conditions for the Austronesians. "The Early Austronesians began their ethnolinguistic career as subtropical coastal and riverine peoples with a Neolithic economy based on cereal and tuber cultivation and a set of domesticated animals. Their ethnographic descendants in island Southeast Asia managed to create for themselves a much wider range of subsistence economies, including rainforest foraging and collection-for-trade" (Bellwood 1995:103).

Bellwood ties linguistic, ethnological, and archaeological evidence together as he attempts to support an answer to his question. He does not feel that he can give this answer with confidence for the Austronesians as they left Taiwan. However, he suggests that the extension of their influence later "cannot be accounted for without an essential component in the sphere of ideology" (Bellwood 1996:28). He names this ideology "founder rank enhancement." This rank enhancement would then be a motivation for a group with an appropriate leader to break off and start a new colony where the founder would be afforded greater prestige and his people promised greater prosperity. And indeed, when considering some of the Polynesian origin stories, this would be a possible interpretation of their motivation derived from some of their cosmology that they interpret as their history.

How well does this founder rank enhancement specify the social order we see among the Austronesians? Certainly this generalization is too broad to identify a specific cultural complex. What makes the "founder" special in the eyes of the founding group or the place where he is said to have founded a colony? Several traits have been suggested. Each clan of an Austronesian group is said to have had a separate origin. At the time of these separate origins, the clan ancestor came with what is sometimes called a "competence," a ritual way of assuring success in agriculture, canoe making, war or peace, etc. This particular competence was recognized as the specialty of that clan and was passed by inheritance, usually to the firstborn son of the clan leader. How is this described in the literature?

Fox, another contributor to the Austronesian Project sponsored by the Australian National University, describes this Austronesian social ordering this way.

> In most Austronesian societies, however, a multiplicity of origins is assumed and groups as well as individuals are allowed to trace their origins as deemed appropriate for social differentiation. The sharing of origins is socially defined and thus always circumscribed. Thus in a now classic ethnography, Michael Young reports that the eight clans of Kaluna of Goodenough Island emerged from the earth in a specific order "bringing with them the customs and competences by which [they] ... are still identified."
>
> The same description would hold for the hundreds of name-clans of the Atoni Meto of Timor, most of whom trace their separate origins to emergence site marked by a rock and tree.... The notion of multiple origins is a prime means of social differentiation. Such a notion may operate at many levels within a society.... I use the phrase "origin structure" as a general designation for the diversity of social formation by which the Austronesians explain and order their derivation. (Fox 1995:216)

Often the social order is based simply on the assumed order of "emergence" from the earth within a separation of heaven and earth cosmology. Sometimes merely an emergence story or some more bizarre story explains the origin of the first ancestor of the clan, and sometimes within the myth/history a reason is given to account for a clan's pre-eminence beyond the order of emergence. The pre-eminent clan has claim to the proper telling of all the origin stories (they are socially circumscribed). If there are scatterings or journeys, it is this clan that keeps track of them. But the origin is not the only concern; there is also the matter of the competences that they possess along with their separate origin. Such a competence, again, is a special knowledge or power concerning some plant, animal or skill (e.g., canoe building, war, etc.). These competences usually include the secret ritual and/or the paraphernalia required to promote success in whatever venture is being attempted. The clan will often be identified by its competence. Within the clan itself, birth order is very important; it is the firstborn who becomes the caretaker of the competence. Use of these various competences is coordinated by the pre-eminent clan and specifically by the firstborn of that clan.

With regard to technological capabilities, the Austronesians were able to move across open water when entering Taiwan. When launching from there to the Philippines, they probably had large canoes with sails. As they progressed to the south, they perfected huge outrigger canoes with which they were eventually able to cross vast expanses of the Pacific. They encountered people who already shared some of their seafaring skills and had already been trading with other island dwellers for obsidian and other useful stone materials. Obsidian is a volcanic rock that flakes into very sharp chips and is useful for cutting instruments. The Austronesians were able by 1000 B.C. to transport Talasea obsidian from New Briton across a distance of 6,500 kilometers from northern Borneo to Fiji (Bellwood 1995:106). This long-distance trade certainly exceeded any trading done earlier by the natives of the Melanesian Islands. Archaeologists have identified the culture that accomplished this long-distance trading as the Lapita culture. Although the Austronesians at first occupied only the coastal areas, at some point some of them mixed with the original natives, and the whole population of these islands often adopted an Austronesian language and social structure.

The Lapita culture is the culture from which the Polynesian Island groups sprung. The Polynesians themselves are thought to be descendants of the original colonizing Austronesians and not part of the group that mixed with the natives of the islands they colonized. Distinctive pottery forms serve to identify the Lapita culture. This culture pattern broke into two groups, and it was the eastern group of islands that that became the first of the Polynesian Islands. Linguists call the language spoken there proto-Polynesian. This eastern part of the Lapita culture, in the islands that make up Tonga, Samoa, and Fiji, became an elaborate Polynesian chiefdom with all the archaeological markers for social stratification. But as Kirch pointed out in *The Evolution of the Polynesian Chiefdoms,* first published in 1984, from the first, the ancestral Polynesians had inherited titles that indicated the "sacerdotal character" of the firstborn of the chief as well as words for *mana* and *tapu* (Kirch 1996:64). One is said to have mana if he is known to have success in his "competence." The great leader will have about him a number of tapus, which isolate him from things that might lessen his mana. Kirch pointed out that mana and tapu were with little doubt respected as prerogatives of the chief (Kirch 1996:62–65). For a further discussion about the meanings of *mana* and *tapu*, see Shore 1989:137–173.

Since the Lapita culture included the many islands that are now called Melanesia and Polynesia, the question that Bellwood framed, given at the start of the chapter, becomes a somewhat more modest one. It is obvious that the Tonga, Samoa, and Fiji islands were for a long period of time, perhaps 500 years, part of the same Lapita culture as those islands now called Melanesia. It is generally thought that the distance over which the pattern was observed was simply too large to be efficient and broke apart when new sources of stone-tool materials were discovered. Likely, communication over so great a distance proved too difficult, but both the Austronesians living in the Melanesian Islands and those living in the Polynesian Islands have similar terms to express their ideology. Further, many of those terms are shared by the wider world of the Austronesians.

The Austronesian language group, including its migration to Madagascar, circumvents more than half the globe. But it is not merely that this group extended its influence over a great distance that is significant; it did so without the development of a writing system. Hinduism, Islam, and more recently Christianity have influenced many areas occupied by peoples who speak Austronesian languages. However, some of these areas still show the remnants of an Austronesian worldview. During the Second World War, the Western world learned of many preliterate people living in isolation in the center of what was then called New Guinea. Not all the natives of that island, now divided into Indonesian Papua and Papua New Guinea, speak Austronesian languages, but it seems fair to characterize much of their social structure as Austronesian. Since there were very few remaining groups of people who were preliterate, they attracted both anthropologists and missionaries. Many ethnographic reports are available from both of these sources.

The distribution of Austronesian languages is strong evidence to the expansion of this group. In this sense this expansion was similar to the prehistoric Indo-European expansion. Unlike that expansion, the Austronesian expansion also included areas that had not been previously occupied, the Polynesian Islands. The reader is reminded that in Chapter Five, the cosmology of the separation of heaven and earth was very prominent in the Polynesian Islands. In those islands it is reasonable to believe that the people would have most perfectly preserved their origin mythology, the basis for their social structure.

The further observation here is that the influence of an Austronesian culture, or one very similar, is obvious in the South Pacific even among people who did not adopt their language. Some of the places they colonized, such as Vietnam and parts of New Guinea, already had a Neolithic economy and apparently were more resistant to their influences. It will be argued in a later chapter that the Australian aborigines, who do not speak an Austronesian language, have been influenced by the Austronesian social order. Specifically, this social ordering is found among those whose religion and social order has been identified as Australian totemism.

But before moving in that direction, some other observations seem in order. The argument developed by Bellwood and Fox, among others, identify a unique array of characteristics that could specify the social structure associated with Austronesians. They may be summarized in this manner: 1) the clans each claim an ancestor who emerged from the earth or had some other singular origin; 2) these clans are often ordered in importance by the order of their emergence or some special competences (ritual knowledge) they possess; and 3) the success of the society depends on the proper performance of the ritual used in expressing these competences. If the society becomes hierarchical in the classical sense of the word, the firstborn of the leading clan is accorded his high position and authority because of his ownership and proper, that is, successful, use of these rituals.

As illustration of these principles, let us consider the pertinent parts of the myth system of the Trobriand Islanders as given by Malinowski. Malinowski was the anthropologist, mentioned several times earlier in this book, who successfully guided anthropology away from its preoccupation with the evolution of religion. He paid close attention to these details for he recognized that the stories were important in the social ordering of these island dwellers. The Trobriand Islands are in the general region of islands known as Melanesia.

> The problem of rank which plays a great part in their sociology was settled by the emergence from one special hole, called Obukula, near the village of Laba'i. This event was notable in that, contrary to the usual course (which is: one original "hole," one lineage), from the hole at Laba'i there emerged

representatives of the four main clans one after the other. Their arrival, moreover, was followed by an apparently trivial, but in mythical reality, a most important event. First there came the *Kaylavasi* (iguana), the animal of the Lukalabuta clan, which scratched its way through the earth as iguanas do, then climbed a tree, and remained there as a mere onlooker, following subsequent events. Soon there came out the Dog, totem of the Lukuba clan, who originally had the highest rank. As a third came the Pig, representative of the Malasi clan, which now holds the highest rank. Last came the Lukwasisga totem, represented in some versions by the Crocodile, in others by the Snake, in others by the Opossum, and sometimes completely ignored. The Dog and Pig ran around, and the Dog, seeing the fruit of the *noku* plant, nosed it, and then ate it. Said the Pig: "Thou eatest dirt; thou art a low-bred, a commoner; the chief, the guya'u, shall be I." And ever since, the highest sub-clan of the Malasi clan, the Tabula, have been the real chiefs. (Malinowski 1954:112)

On the next page in his book, Malinowski spelled out what we have referred to as competences owned by each clan, but he called them magical proficiencies. He explained that each village not only had a chartering myth but also its own magical proficiencies and place rank in the totemic charter. They would resist encroachment in their occupational assignment and the competences that guaranteed their success. This clearly identifies the social structure of the Trobriand Islanders, Melanesian islands, as Austronesian in pattern even as we would expect them to be.

According to Kirch (1996:43), linguists have placed some of the Austronesian languages found in Papua in the proto-Oceanic subgroup of the Austronesian language. Surprisingly, it is estimated that that group broke off from the rest about 3,500 B.C. This means that New Guinea has potentially more than 5,000 years of Austronesian interaction since there are still seafaring people occupying the Melanesian Islands who look for trading partners on the large island.

In New Guinea, anthropology has described a secular position that is filled by a leader called a "big man." He is respected as a leader because he is able through "economic" manipulation to meet the needs of others as they fulfill the ritual requirements of their culture. These requirements include wealth, often in the form of pigs, used up in the ritual situations associated with naming, initiation, marriage, war, or rituals directed to the ancestors. Yet in New Guinea there are also the specialists who inherit and practice the rituals necessary to control the environment, initiate the youth, and appease the ancestors. These appear to be the competences associated with the Austronesian pattern. They are called "great men" in some of the anthropological literature. For a further discussion of this subject, see Godelier and Strathern, 1991.

For an understanding of the groups in the central highlands of New Guinea, let us consider the reports of early missionaries from that part of the island that is now Indonesian territory. The missionaries' intimate knowledge of these people gives us insight into the way these people understood their world. This of course is true of all careful ethnographers. Needless to say, neither missionaries nor anthropologists were interested in the questions treated here. But the missionaries' interest did mention some beliefs of the people that anthropologists find unimportant. Some of those beliefs and aspirations are of special interest in our quest. The first of several authors is Russell T. Hitt. His book is about the pioneer missionaries to the central highlands. They were Christian and Missionary Alliance people who gladly gave him the information he sought.

> When the missionaries came and talked about Christ, the Son of God, as the Creator and Redeemer who was able to restore true life to man, the Danis linked the message to their myth and the messengers to Bok, their god-man ancestor. In their strange legends Bok came up out of a hole at a spot in the Baliem Valley between Seinma and Hetigima. As Bok came forth he walked westward, standing the mountains in their places as he traveled. His footprint still may be seen, say the Danis, in a stone of the North Baliem near Tiom and Maaki. Bok finally disappeared when he reached the coast and now lives on the other side of the ocean.

> In the Dani concept, the ocean is an extended river that surrounds the entire island. The world, as they know it, is confined to their island, which is encircled by a wall with the sky overhead as a roof. They have vague ideas of north and south coasts of New Guinea, but have no conception of the distance from east to west. In their little world, the sun climbs a tree in

the morning, crosses the sky during the day, then crawls down a tree at night and goes underground. The sun is regarded as a sort of female deity and the moon a male that watches over her during the night.

When Bok arrived in those far-off days, he brought along with him "real" people, the Danis, who accompanied him out of the ground loaded down with the original sweet potatoes, the taro, the tobacco, sugar cane, pigs, and dogs. The Danis then moved westward and settled in various areas.

Originally a man and his younger sister were born into one moiety [small part of tribe], and another man and his sister belonged to the opposite moiety. Thus they became the original ancestors of the two moieties of the clans that continue to exist. (Hitt 1962:177)

Notice the similarities with the general Austronesian pattern that are obvious from this missionary report. First, each clan had its own ancestors who emerged from the earth. If one could not derive this from the long quotation, above it was more obvious in another telling of their origin myth. "The first people came clan by clan, each clan carrying something. The Aso (mythical being) brought sweet potatoes" and so on through clan ancestors and their contributions, accounting for the important cultural assets—taro, pig, dog, etc. (Hitt 1962:118). This ownership of ritual secrets brought with them from the time of the emergence also follows the Austronesian pattern. The difference here may have been that the clan as a whole may have shared the secrets and charms to control these assets. This community ownership became obvious when some of the converted Dani felt the need to consult with other clan members before burning their charms and fetishes. Some apparently shared ownership with men who had not been converted.

Just how the chief leader of the Dani came to power is not spelled out in Hitt's book. His leadership seemed to be unquestioned and with substantial impact. In spite of this, he did not openly display his authority and was soft-spoken to the missionaries. Nonetheless, he recognized that his power was derived from the people's belief in the ancestors' ability to control their food supply and give them success in war. He remained an adversary to the missionaries throughout the time frame covered by Hitt's book.

Gordon and Peggy Larson were missionaries who moved among the Dani in the Baliem Valley. In due time, they saw results from their labor. After conversion, the people were encouraged to worship God only. This brought about a crisis, as they would have to abandon their old practices. Remember, since the community was interdependent on the competences of each clan, the whole community would be affected when a significant number of any one clan converted. Therefore, conversion itself often became a community event. The witness to this event was the destruction of their charms and fetishes.

> When a community announced a charm burning, the believers from other areas would gather with them. Marching in a company, the visiting Danis would sing and dance to express their joy at the latest evidence of God's power in their midst.

> Larson realized that there were mixed motives behind the charm burnings. Like the Uhundunis, the Dani had myths with religious significance. In ridding themselves of their magical past, some undoubtedly thought that they were opening the door for *natelan katelan*, their expression for eternal life, that literally translated means "my outer skin, your outer skin." By this idiom they referred to the shedding of the outer skin, and they linked this to the story of the race between the snake and the bird. To the Dani the snake, which sheds its skin year after year, is a symbol of eternal, or at least non-ending, life. Thus *natelan katelan* meant, "We've shed the outer coating of death and will keep on living forever."

> According to the legend, the snake and the bird had engaged in a race across the valley at the beginning of time. Since the bird, who died, won the race and the immortal snake lost, the people were deprived of their original eternal life. "Oh, why did the snake not win?" the Danis still ask.

> With these myths in the background of their thinking, the Danis regarded white men, and the missionaries in particular, as the descendants of Bok, who had come to restore their *natelan katelan*. (Hitt 1962:176–177)

The first of mass conversions among the Dani happened after they heard about another nearby tribe, the Uhunduni, who had already burned their charms and fetishes. With the aid of these charms and fetishes, the Dani believed they were able to control the production of their foodstuffs, communicate with their powerful ancestors, and in general control those elements on which their community depended. Although the Uhunduni also believed in their charms and fetishes, they had a much more direct longing for "heaven" expressed as a chant, and what they longed for was called *hai*. It was thought to be a wonderful place; it was both eternal and a better place to live. Because of this longing, they were the first group able to overcome their fears and burn their charms and fetishes. Once they had done it without the feared outcome of disaster, others were emboldened to follow. Following is a chant of the Uhunduni recorded by one of the missionaries.

> O Friend, up in the sky is a large boat on a great lake,
> A-wai-wae,
> And to this wonderful place we want to go,
> A-wai-wae, A-wai-wae (Hitt 1962:164)

Although this is the only group that Hitt mentions with such a tradition, other groups in a nearby valley knew it as well. Don Richardson's book, *Lords of the Earth*, concerns the missionary efforts in a valley close to the Grand Valley. Among his well-known books are *Eternity in Their Hearts* and *Peace Child,* which have been featured in *Reader's Digest*. Richardson reported that Ekari sages in the Yali Valley announced that the gospel was a fulfillment of *ayi* (Richardson 1983:155). *Ayi* was another pronunciation for the *hai* of the Uhunduni. It appears that this myth concerning *ayi* was known to at least two tribes in the Yali Valley. Richardson mentioned that the Damal tribe, who were represented in this valley, knew it as well. The name Damal is another name for the Uhunduni.

While this expectation worked well for the missionaries, conversion presented other problems to the natives. The leaders of reputation recognized that their position of authority was based on the system of competences, the ritual knowledge by which the social structure itself was defined. Other problems that the local population faced were more immediately cultural. Success in their culture had been measured in terms of pigs and wives, probably in that order. And women were excluded from even the knowledge of the men's religious practices on pain of death. The missionaries made it obvious that the women would also be included in this new religion. Although it was not practicable immediately, men were to be limited to one wife. In the minds of the natives, this was a sure way to be committed to poverty. The wives raised the sweet potatoes that the pigs ate, the pigs could be "sold" for cowrie shells, the shells were used to buy more wives to raise more sweet potatoes, and so on. This was the way to wealth for them.

Among the Dani in the Grand Valley, the founder emerged from the earth, but there are other stories of how the original (founder) ancestors came into being among some of the groups. The argument here advanced, although certainly not demonstrated, is that the basic institutions of the entire island formerly known as New Guinea have been altered by Austronesian influence. Is it possible that the inhabitants of these areas had been egalitarian before Austronesian influence? Did some of their animals, for instance pigs, come from early Austronesian migrants?

Is there any evidence that the Polynesian cosmology, that of the separation of heaven and earth, had been present? Richardson opened his book with several chapters about recent conditions in the Yali Valley as told later by a convert. This introduction included an account of events that led one Yali youth to rebel against the spirit world of his tribe and, therefore, be killed. Leading up to this event a young girl innocently stumbled into the most sacred *osuwa*, was found there, and was put to death because she had violated the law of the *kembu* spirits. However, this same girl, in an earlier conversation with her uninitiated brother, gave this information about their thoughts of what went on in the sky. This conversation was introduced by the boy's curiosity about the pointed center pole of a house. The boy's father told him it was there "so that the sky could not fall directly unto them." With this in mind, the children were looking at the "gardens in the sky," wondering what it would be like to be a *domil-mil*. This does not appear to be their word for the spirit of a dead person; rather, it seems to describe the little white people who lived at peace in the sky. The children mused that they did not want the place of the *domil-mil* to fall on them. This story emphasizes that this tribe may have had traditions that involved people living at peace in the sky. (Remember the Uhunduni chant about the wonderful place to live in the sky.)

The next part of this story used by Richardson gives information about the brother's (brother of the little girl killed) initiation ritual. Our interest is in what was described as the *kulamong*, which was the condition that the people in the valley suffered before they were saved by the *kembu* spirits. When the boy asked what the *kulamong* was, he was told it was a plague of darkness. People who were caught in their gardens could not find their way home. As they groped in fear, a terrible flood came and swept them away. Later their bones were found lodged under rocks and trees uphill from their villages and gardens. Yekwara (the boy to be initiated) showed surprise, and Kebel (the initiator) continued.

> "Even many who were sheltered in their homes died suddenly, without symptoms of illness. They just died from the darkness!" Yekwara winced at the vision of horror his father conjured.

> "But then the *kembu* spirits gave mankind the *wene melalek*— the ancient words—and taught us that if we obeyed them, the *kulamong* would not return. But still sometimes wicked men among us forsake the ancient words, causing us to suffer under an *o-sanim*."

> "*O-sanim?*" [asked Yekwara.]

> "Yes, when heavy rain continues for a long time, that is an *o-sanim*. If the cause is not discovered and removed, it may turn into *kulamong* and mankind will have to start all over again from a handful of survivors." (Richardson 1983:59f)

This is little to build an argument on. However, it could be an interpretation of the conditions before the emergence. In the Polynesian world, the darkness before the separation continues to be the place of the gods and perhaps the dead. Here, this does not seem to be the case. But this might be carryover about the darkness before the separation in the Polynesian separation of heaven and earth cosmology. This sort of story should not be unexpected if the myth of the separation was the inspiration for the form of origin myth (emergence from earth) that was recognized here.

The last part of this story includes something of traditional thought of the Yali expressed by another youth, Bukni. He rebelled at the conditions of life imposed by the *wene melalek* given by the *kembu* for violating the sacred taboos. Bukni knew firsthand about the little girl's transgression into the *osuwa* and the death imposed on her; he was her uncle and told her mother her plight when she was brought to her. He also knew about the senseless death of a young warrior sent on a raid to satisfy the ancestors. He watched as his leader determined that it was a respected man of the community who had caused the *o-sanim*. He was accused, probably falsely, of incest with his daughter. That whole family—father, mother, and daughter—were put to death to satisfy *kembu* spirits. To rebel against the *kembu*, he performed a number of outrages. One finally caused his fellows to kill him. He had climbed unto a sacred *osuwa* and shouted information so that both women and children heard the secrets learned by boys at their initiation, saying, "Women and uninitiated children! Listen while I teach you these names. *Unga woooo! Kolongat woooo! Besal-ma woooo!* These are the names of the places where mankind first came forth from the earth" (Richardson 1983:87f).

And while he received the blows that killed him, he continued: "May the sky - fall upon" - and died Yekwara, later a convert and character mentioned frequently in the rest of the book, was a witness of these events. Perhaps we can piece some of this information into a pattern to see how the sky (heaven?) fits into their traditions. Some creatures were living in it at peace, perhaps eternally. Yet the possibility of the sky falling was thought to be a threat to their lives. Breaking the code of the *kembu* spirits, the *wene melalek,* apparently could be the cause of the coming of the plague of darkness—or the sky falling. Were darkness and the sky falling thought to be one and the same? Darkness was the condition before heaven and earth were separated in the Polynesian origin myth (as well as many other separation origin myths—see Chapter Five). It is my position that the separation of the sky and earth was an integral part of the cosmology necessary to establish the new social structure where this cosmology was used.

Alice Gibbons recorded this story. She and her husband Don were also Christian and Missionary Alliance missionaries in the pioneering work with the Damal tribe. This is the same tribe, also called Uhunduni, whose mass conversion preceded great responses from other tribes in the central highlands of Papua. The missionaries were told this about *hai.*

"Once our Damal people arrived at the place of *hai,*" Wolo (the father) continued, "but they lost it again. This is the story that my father told me, and you can tell your sons."

124

Two Damal men climbed up roots found hanging down from the sky. They climbed until they crawled through a hole in the sky and found the place of *hai*. Many little people lived in this place where no one died. The men had many wives, and the wives bore them many children. The men wore large pig tusks in their noses, and there was much dancing with chanting. Sweet potatoes and *mo* were so plentiful that they rotted for lack of someone to eat them. The pigs were huge—more than the people could eat. Every day the little people shared pork with the Damals. But the two Damals were greedy and decided to steal one of the pigs. They killed the pig, threw it down through the hole in the sky, and started down the tree root themselves. But the little people discovered that these earthly men had stolen a pig, so they cut the roots of the tree. Never again have earthly people been able to climb to the place of *hai*. (Gibbons 1981:77)

I don't know if other tribal groups in Papua knew this story. But I believe that the theme of this story, that heaven was once in our grasp but our ancestors lost it, was at one time present. I say this because when we turn to Australia, we again come across this theme. (It will also be obvious in the next chapter given to Africa.) In the chapter on Australia, more of a context will be given for this theme, the belief that *hai* is a place of eternal life. Please note that they believed that eternal life was associated with the sky and that mankind once had access to it.

In this chapter we have laid out the possibility that the Austronesian language speakers brought a new way of viewing the world to a rather significant portion of the globe. This worldview was summarized earlier in this manner: 1) each clan claims an ancestor who emerged from the earth or had some other singular origin; 2) these clans are often ordered in importance by the order of their emergence or some special competences (ritual knowledge) that they possessed; 3) the success of the society depended on the proper performance of the ritual used in expressing these competences. If the society became hierarchical in the classical sense of the word, the leader was accorded his high position and authority because of his ownership and his proper, that is, successful, use of these rituals.

Perhaps the Polynesians continued to use the separation of heaven and earth cosmology because of their elaborations about *po*, the word that indicated for them both the darkness before the separation and the place of the ancestors, the source of authority in their world. The rest of the area influenced by their worldview and social order did not follow them in this, preferring to overlook *po* and merely refer to the ancestors themselves as authority. The missionary stories from the highlands of Indonesian Papua suggest that the separation cosmology had been known and that *hai* may have been part of their earlier belief system. The relationship between these two concepts will be explored further in the next chapters.

Chapter Nine

Is Heaven Oppressive?

This chapter considers two tribes living side by side, each with one of the two worldviews of particular interest to us. One owns as its cosmology the separation of heaven and earth; the other believes that the creator provides for them. These tribes, the Dinka and Nuer, may be thought of as contemporary; they are found in Sudan on the upper Nile. Here we will be able, unmistakably, to view the immediate effect of separation cosmology. Perhaps not surprising, one tribe claims the creator is a just God, while the other holds that his nearness had been oppressive. An ancestor of one of the Dinka tribes affected the separation from the creator and established the office of "master of the fishing-spear." The person holding this office became the center of religious attention for the Dinka. This comparison then directly underscores the thesis of this book—namely that the separation of heaven and earth cosmology introduces the veneration of beings other than the celestial Creator.

Two of several tribes living on the upper Nile in southern Sudan were chosen for this comparison. This contrast is between groups living under similar economic circumstances with considerable cultural similarities, very similar languages, and frequent communication with each other. It is rare that two groups with substantial cultural similarities are structured socially in a significantly different manner from each other. But here they are. One has an institutionalized office of leadership with many rituals to support this institution. The other is egalitarian and recognizes no person with special abilities to control their environment. Further, we have the good fortune to have well-known and well-accepted ethnographies available for each group. Godfrey Lienhardt has written one for the Dinka, and E. E. Evans-Pritchard has written several ethnographies for the Nuer.

In Chapter Three, we highlighted that British anthropologists identified certain well-established social structures that characterized African hierarchy. While this is true, it is not at all clear just when many of these tribes of herders on the upper Nile first came to have social structures oriented around leaders thought to control the environment. Is there any clue from the distribution of African languages? The Egyptians spoke an Afro-Asiatic language along with the rest of the North Africans. The Nilotic tribes of the Sudan that we are considering spoke a Nilo-Saharan language. There are only two other principal language groupings in Africa—the Niger-Congo family in sub-Saharan Africa and the Khoisan family, the smallest group, which includes the Bushmen. There were some language movements within the Niger-Congo family (Bantu in sub-Saharan Africa) that probably reflected the movement of a specific hierarchy. But this tells us little about how or when a cosmology supporting social hierarchy may have come to the Dinka. The distribution of the Nilo-Saharan language group offers no evidence that the language was spoken in any other region. In short, the distribution of languages offers little clue as to the spread of this social hierarchy to the Dinka or to many of their neighboring tribes. This would not be surprising if this hierarchy and its justification were diffused rather than imposed.

In the third chapter, attention was also called to the presence of the separation of heaven and earth cosmology in both ancient Egypt and the contemporary peoples of the African continent. Along the west coast of Africa, people say that God went away from them. Along the east coast, they say that the sky was once close enough to touch but retreated. And indeed, when looking at the cosmologies as they are interpreted, there certainly seems to be equivalence between the symbols, God and sky or heaven. Therefore, a good starting point is to ask, what do God and/or heaven mean? In what way(s) are they similar?

Both tribes are from the Darfur region of the Sudan. Therefore, the tribes we are looking at are on the eastern side of the continent. Following the pattern indicated in the previous paragraph, heaven, rather than God, is the symbol of interest to us in the cosmology. And indeed, for Dinka the separation is from *nhialic*, a form of their noun meaning "sky," "up," or "above." However, for the other tribe, the Nuer, the name for God is *kwoth*, meaning "spirit." Interestingly, both tribes, in describing this being—yes, the Dinka do consider *nhialic* to be a person—offer us very similar attributes. All Dinka assert that *nhialic* is one. By this they mean that their *nhialic* is the same being as the one the Nuer call *kwoth*, the Muslims call Allah, and the Christians call God (Lienhardt 1961:56).

The Nuer would no doubt agree with the assessment that there is only one God. Their *kwoth* is addressed in more formal circumstances, as *kwoth nhial* or *kwoth a nhial*, Spirit of the sky, or Spirit who is in the sky. Over several pages, Evans-Pritchard delineates the attributes of the Nuer's God. He created the universe from nothing, and he made man—he did not beget him. He knows all things, he is everywhere present, he is ultimately responsible for all things, and nothing happens that he does not allow. Further, God is always right. He is called Father and is man's protector. He is favorably disposed to men but holds them morally responsible for their actions (Evans-Pritchard 1956:7–9). But to show further similarities and differences between Nuer and Old Testament teaching, consider the following:

> Therefore Nuer, who are unruly and quarrel-some people, avoid, in so far as they can restrain themselves, giving any gratuitous offence. Therefore also, a man who is at fault goes to the person he has offended, admits his fault, saying to him "*ca dwir*," "I was at fault," and he may also offer a gift to wipe away the offence. The wronged man then blesses him by spitting or blowing water on him and says that it is nothing and may the man be at peace. He thereby removes any resentment he may have in his heart. Nuer say that God sees these acts and frees the man from the consequences of his fault. Similarly, the consequences of faults which are more directly of a religious order, like the breach of an interdiction or the neglect of some spirit, may be avoided by a timely sacrifice, though Nuer say that sacrifice without contrition is of no use. (Evans-Pritchard 1956:18)

Although their principal religious concerns are with moral actions and personal relationships, Evans-Pritchard points out that the Nuer are an unruly and quarrelsome people. This seems surprising, but it must be remembered that Evans-Pritchard went to them during their quarrel with the British to find who among them could speak for the whole group. He found no one. And their quarrel was not only with the British; they also compete with their tribal neighbors and have been resistant to the Arab Muslims to the north. Another surprise, apparently typical for not just the Nuer but also the whole tribal area, is that the act of blessing often includes spitting. The blessing itself, "May you be at peace," includes peace with God as well as with man.

God may punish both religious and personal affronts. If the relationship is restored, then God may not punish. Notice that a possible religious fault is a "neglect of some spirit." This is, of course, foreign to our understanding of the Old Testament. But also notice that a sacrifice with contrition is required to bring about peace with God. If the offense is the neglect of some spirit (this would perhaps be occasioned by not showing proper respect for something representing a clan), it is not the offended spirit that punishes. The sacrifice is not to appease the clan spirit; it is to reestablish peace with God. This is one of the distinctions between the Nuer's and the Dinka's religious concerns. The Dinka may actually offend a clan or other spirit, not just God, and be punished by this spirit. The point that Evans-Pritchard was making with the above quotation was that, to the Nuer, a fault does not bring automatic consequences. It is God who brings consequences (Evans-Pritchard 1956:18).

Language similarities suggest that these two groups once shared a single language. Economically both groups are herders and attach a special, almost sacred, importance to their cattle. Since they live next to each other, we should expect good channels of communications for religious traditions between them. We ought therefore to expect many similarities in their religious teaching and practices, and indeed there are similarities.

Yet it is the sharp differences between the worldviews of the Nuer and the Dinka that are of interest to us. Within their worldview, the Nuer are in the providential care of the spirit being they call *kwoth*. They are also confronted as individuals with moral responsibilities to this spirit. But the central fact of the Dinka religious and social structure is the "master of the fishing-spear." For the Dinka, the master of the fishing-spear holds the life of his clan. He exercises civil and ritual authority over his clan during his life. It is said that this divine personage is buried alive "with his breath" since this breath symbolizes the life of his clan, which has been in his keeping (Lienhardt 1961:316). The Dinka's close identification with their master of the fishing-spear allows the rituals surrounding his death to become a celebration of their continued collective existence (Lienhardt 1961:316f).

At first glance, the Nuer do seem to have a similar office in the "leopard-skin priest." But the peripheral position held by the leopard-skin priest of the Nuer cannot really be compared to the civil and spiritual authority invested by the Dinka in their master of the fishing-spear. By contrast, the leopard-skin priest of the Nuer officiates at sacrifices and referees disputes. He does not even function as priest in his own clan. His authority to settle disputes is lent him by the disputing parties because they each acknowledge the need for help in this process. He has no special authority within his own clan, and he certainly does not hold the "breath," or the life, of another's clan (Evans-Pritchard 1956:292–293). Evans-Pritchard offers no mythical charter for leopard-skin priests.

One of the Dinka stories of the separation of heaven and earth describes the struggle of the first master of the fishing-spear in overcoming the constraints of heaven (heaven = *nhialic,* which Lienhardt translates as Divinity) and thereby gained his power, called in their language *jok.* In Lienhardt's book, *nhialic,* heaven (supreme being) of the Dinka is consistently identified as Divinity since Lienhardt feels that to translate his name either as "god" or "heaven" would lead to confusion.

> [In] the beginning the earth was already *created*, but there was no light, and hence it could not "appear." In this darkness Divinity created men, and he created one called Aruu Pabek. He pushed Aruu forwards, and then pushed him back, to what is called in the Dinka text "the opening in the fence, or dike," and the sense is here that Divinity made as though to let the man out, and then forced him back. Then Aruu twisted a rope, and Divinity gave him eyes so that he could see he was in the darkness. Aruu caught a game animal with his rope and gave the foreleg to the wife of Divinity, who suggested that Aruu should be rewarded. Divinity asked Aruu what gift he would like, and Aruu replied, "My father, if there is a little chink to see through, that is what I would like." Divinity refused the request, and offered him a spear, which he refused, and then an axe, which he accepted, then to quote a text:
>
> My grandfather Aruu Pabek took the axe, and he struck the earth, and said "Why do you not light up?" And part went above and a part below, and the earth lit up. And Divinity said to Aruu, "Why do you do so? I gave you a tiny little thing

before and why have you now done this? Now you are a prisoner." And Divinity pushed Aruu down to earth. And closed up the earth. And he gave people a path, one path, for them to walk in, and he stuck reeds (in the form of a fence made to catch fish) in the way. And when a man came along the way he struck him in the head with a fishing-spear, and said "Let man come out if he can!" He waited there, and he killed people.

And the people came to Aruu Pabek, and said "People are being finished - what shall we do?" My grandfather said, "Do not be anxious, I will see to it." And he took a stone and put it on his head and went to where Divinity was waiting with his fishing-spear. Divinity struck him on the head with the spear, and the stone deflected it and bent the point. He said "I shall have to have my spear straightened." He seized my grandfather by the neck and said "Why are you like a man?" (Lienhardt 1961: 34f)

This separation story is chosen because of its striking similarity to widespread separation stories. It is the only African one I have found that has these elements: the original darkness, the act and instrument used to bring about the separation, and the new conditions after the separation. By this I am referring to the new authority taken by Aruu Pabek, the one who brought about the separation with his axe. Lienhardt does not explain that this myth charters the office of master of the fishing-spear. Notice that Aruu in this cosmology was originally with Divinity but then becomes a go-between or protector of the people. In a section regarding the importance of cattle to the Dinka, Lienhardt says that the master of the fishing-spear has this responsibility: "Masters of the fishing-spear are required to pray nightly in the cattle-camps, and it is from their supposed ability to multiply and protect cattle by their prayers that they derive much of their importance" (1961:21).

These prayers are directed primarily to Divinity. Lienhardt says that the Dinka believed that at one time the only divinity (*yath*) that was addressed was Divinity (*nhialic*) (Lienhardt 1961:104, see also 169). Although it is true that such historical recollection is hardly proof, it is consistent with the proposition that the separation of heaven and earth described in the myth given above was the Dinka's earliest charter for special persons of power (*jok*). Without doubt, the myth describes an ambiguous relationship between the Dinka and their Divinity (*nhialic* = heaven or above). The first master of the fishing-spear confirmed his powers by outwitting the Creator himself. In Lienhardt's later chapter on myths of fishing-spear masters, the master of the fishing-spear of a new clan outwits the fishing-spear master of the group they are leaving. It is often by a ploy similar to the one used by Aruu Pabek. In these cases it is the former fishing-spear master rather than Divinity who is attempting to dispatch people by spearing them as they cross a river to establish a new clan.

But in other Dinka separation stories, it was all of mankind, not only the master of the fishing-spear, who was confined. After giving several illustrations of Dinka cosmologies, Lienhardt summarizes them as follows (note again Divinity = *nhialic*, "above" or "sky"): "Man is thus represented as having been originally confined and constricted by his closeness to Divinity. He might not eat more than a permitted grain of millet each day, and had to move carefully (this cautious movement is sometimes enacted by the Dinka when telling the story, and resembles in spirit the quiet and modest demeanor they adopt in situations in which they must customarily show formal respect); or he was enclosed in a fence or wall or pot, from which he eventually came out" (Lienhardt 1961:35f).

The Dinka's neighbors, the Nuer, either do not know or, at least, have not given importance to these stories about the separation of heaven and earth, nor do they allow that certain men have "power" over the environment. A moral universe and *kwoth*, their god, confront the Nuer as individuals. "Nuer take nature for granted and are passive and resigned toward it. They do not think that they can influence it to their own advantage, being merely ignorant folk. What happens there is the will of God, and that has to be accepted. Hence Nuer are little interested in ritual for bringing rain and even consider it presumptuous to think of asking God for rain before sowing.... Their sacrifices are concerned with moral and spiritual, not natural, crises" (Evans-Pritchard 1956: 200).

Before further comment on the contrasts between the Dinka and Nuer worldviews, I want to clarify the presence of Nuer separation stories mentioned in other books.

> God's separation and remoteness from men are accounted for in a myth reported by Father Crazzolara which relates that there was not always a complete separation of heaven and earth and that there might never have been but for an almost fortuitous event. I did not myself hear Father Crazzolara's version

of the myth, and I judge it to be of Dinka origin, partly because it occurs among the Dinka but more because I think
it is current only among Nuer to the west of the Nile which
would indicate recent introduction into Nuerland from Dinka
sources; but whether it is Dinka or not, it accords well Nuer
religious conceptions in general. (Evans-Pritchard 1956:10)

Then Evans-Pritchard recounts the myth itself. It is given later in this chapter.
However, there is an important comment to make here. Evans-Pritchard said it
accords well with Nuer religious conceptions because of God's greatness compared to man; he does not say that it is God's great distance from man. Surely
if the myth of the separation was an important part of the Nuer cosmology, as
it was with the Dinka, it would have been found by Evans-Pritchard. This is especially true since Father Crazzolara had alerted him to its presence. However,
if it was charter for the Dinka master of the fishing-spear, an office that most
emphatically does not exist among the Nuer, it should be no more than a tale
told by a neighboring tribe.

> *Both Evans-Pritchard and Lienhardt have missed this important
> point. And they are not alone. Much of Africa recognizes a sepa-
> ration myth. But it is usually interpreted as a paradise lost, not
> as a charter for the introduction of an office of leadership: a mas-
> ter of the fishing-spear, a rainmaker king, or other special office
> around which the society is oriented and structured. If they had
> caught this point, they would have to consider my proposition for
> at least these African tribes: The Supreme Being went (was sent)
> away to make room for ritual control of the environment.*

The worldviews of the Nuer and Dinka are not merely different; they oppose
each other. 1) In the Dinka view, a person with power can influence the environment; a just god controls the Nuer's environment. 2) The Dinka define
meaning in terms of community; the Nuer are responsible to their god as individuals. 3) The Dinka believe that their master of the fishing-spear holds the
life of the community; the Nuer are vigilantly egalitarian, rejecting that any
person could have such power. The Dinka worldview is certainly more typically
African. But was it always so?

Ancient Egypt's sacred personage was declared in a separation of heaven and
earth cosmology. In dynastic Sumer, men came from the earth at the very spot

where Enlil, the head of their pantheon, severed heaven from earth with a pickaxe, and at this place the king was recognized. True, cosmologies are subject to modification by later mythmakers, but the separation cosmology was clearly the cosmology both of ancient Near Eastern civilizations (ancient India and likely China as well) and many recent chiefdom societies.

Worldviews allowing individual access and responsibilities to a single, omnipotent being were negatively characterized in the separation cosmology as constraint and darkness caused by the nearness of heaven. Stories telling about this single and approachable being held sway among many hunters, herders, and even some early Neolithic settlements until the advent of the separation cosmology. I certainly agree with structuralists and functionalists that myth is held in a flexible manner, capable of reflecting social realities and attitudes. But I assert that new or changed mythology must accompany—likely even precede—major changes in society. Even so, dramatic changes in worldview cannot be expected often. Within a group numbering only a hundred adults participating in common rituals and the exchange of wealth and women, there is strong motivation for stability. After all, this is the worldview that defines the social roles for each of them. Certainly, the distribution of cosmologies with their subtle variations illustrates this conservatism. I do not deny that population pressures or other environmental circumstances affect social structures, yet the presence of very widespread cosmologies indicates the importance of available worldviews in the origin and growth of these structures.

Hopefully, after considering this chapter, my reader will understand that I have decisively illustrated my point with the ethnographic material from these two African tribes. Remember, that point is this:

> *The separation of heaven and earth cosmology replaced belief in a god similar to the God of the Old Testament. This was apparently done to establish a socially recognized office with ritual responsibilities to control the environment. The social structure became responsible for the providence previously ascribed to the Creator.*

Earlier, in Chapters One and Four, it was pointed out that at least historian of religion Mircea Eliade offered that "strong gods" replaced creator gods. He defined strong gods as gods who could be affected by ritual to control the environment. But if this myth can be so easily implicated in this process with these ethnographies, why haven't others made it? Anthropologists prefer a materialistic approach to this obviously idealistic one. But beyond that, recognition that a creator or Supreme Being preceded gods that could be affected by ritual would trouble much of secular academia.

Is it possible that the Nuer (and the Dinka) borrowed the concept of the Supreme Being from Jewish, Christian, or Arab peoples? The Dinka are properly included in this for their concept of *nhialic* can be described in somewhat similar terms. However, it can also be said of the Shilluk and Anuak, two close Nilotic neighbors. And further, it has been said that all of known traditional African belief systems have certain minimal beliefs about this Supreme Being. John S. Mbiti, born in Kenya and educated in Uganda, America, and England, writes about African religion using many African ethnographies and his personal perspective.

> In my larger work, *Concepts of God in Africa* (1959), I have collected all the information available to me concerning the traditional concepts of God. The study covers nearly 100 peoples from all over Africa outside the traditionally Christian and Muslim communities. In all those societies, without a single exception, people have a notion of God as the Supreme Being. This is the most minimal and foundational idea about God, found in all African societies. Obviously there are many who have much more to say about God than that, but apart from a few comparative studies, our written information about the concepts of God held by individual peoples is incomplete. (1969:29)

But if it is true that without a known exception Africans in their traditional religions have a recognizable concept of God as Supreme Being, then it is most unlikely that the source was Jewish, Muslim, or Christian. The Pygmy in the dense forest and the Bushman of the Kalahari Desert have beliefs about a Supreme Being. In fact, among these groups with egalitarian social structures, this Supreme Being is more important than among those with hierarchical social structures where he is said to be otiose, meaning disinclined to work.

The ethnographic material supports the statement that all traditional African societies knew of a supreme being. But along with this assertion, I am making another generalization about African societies. The more hierarchical the social structure of the African society is—that is, the more importance accorded to its sacred leader—the less importance is accorded this supreme being. I admit that there may be an exception to this rule, but generally it will stand. And it is logical that it should. The more the society depends on its sacred leader, who is thought to have control over the environment, the less it depends on the providence of the Supreme Being. In Africa the institution of the sacred leader is chartered by a separation cosmology. For Africans then, heaven certainly represented the Supreme Being himself.

But is there further meaning involved in the symbol "heaven"? Unfortunately, the African material only offers hints. But they are at hand, so let us explore them. It has been said that African traditional religions reject meaningful eternal life. Again to use Mbiti's book, "The soul of man does not long for spiritual redemption, or for closer contact with God in the next world.... Traditional (African) religions and philosophy are concerned with man in past and present time. There is no messianic hope or apocalyptic vision with God stepping in at some future moment to bring about a radical reversal of man's normal life. God is not pictured as in an ethical-spiritual relationship with man. Man's acts of worship and turning to God are pragmatic and utilitarian rather than spiritual or mystical" (1969:5).

The Nuer data clearly contradicts Mbiti's assertion that God is not pictured in an ethical-spiritual relationship with man. But there should be another qualification. The theme of restoration to youth and its rejection appears in conjunction with some of the separation of heaven and earth myths. Then the question becomes, did Africans accept this rejection of eternal life along with their acceptance of a pragmatic and utilitarian religion based on the separation myth? If it were a charter for special offices for control of the environment, those without these offices may not have rejected the notion of resurrection or eternal life. Let me illustrate my point through two myths. The first was recorded by Father Crazzolara and given by Evans-Pritchard. This is the myth mentioned earlier in this chapter that Evans-Pritchard thought was a Dinka myth rather than a Nuer one:

> The myth relates that there was once a rope from heaven to earth and how anyone who became old climbed up to God in heaven and after having been rejuvenated there returned to earth. One day a hyena—an appropriate figure in myth relating to origins of death—and what is known in the Sudan as a durra-bird, most likely a weaver-bird, entered heaven by this

means. God gave instructions that the two were to be well watched and not allowed to return to earth where they would certainly cause trouble. One night they escaped and climbed down the rope and when they were near the earth the hyena cut the rope. (Evans-Pritchard 1956: 10)

The second myth (Dinka) is from Lienhardt, and he credits it to Father Nebel's collection:

The creator created people in the East under a tamarind tree—or others say, on the bank of a great water. Their names were Abuk and Garang. He made them so small—only half a man's arm—of clay, and covered them with a pot which he then covered. When he uncovered it, the two stood up and were complete and fully-grown. In the morning, Garang was grown and carried the spear (the penis), and the breasts of Abuk were big, and they married. And they bore children. And the creator said "Your children will die, but after fifteen days he will return." Garang disagreed and said, "If people return again they will be too numerous. Where will they build their homes? There will not be enough land." (Lienhardt 1961:36)

Now there is something to note about these two myths. Evans-Pritchard did not hear these myths from the Nuer, and Lienhardt did not record them from his informants. Catholic priests working earlier among the people collected them. This is not to impugn their efforts, but it is to say that these myths talking about renewal or resurrection did not seem to be present for either Lienhardt or Evans-Pritchard to hear. However, from this lack of concern about the condition of the dead, we cannot conclude that eternal separation from God and the separation of heaven and earth are not linked. The separation myth, as summarized by Lienhardt (1961:37 brackets added) includes, "But freedom [from confinement by Divinity] then brought with it toil, suffering and death which he had not previously known."

It is true that the Nuer, who do not claim the myth, also know toil, suffering, and death. And it is true that our own traditions list these things as results of the sins of our ancestors. But, look past this. This is the human condition (sin), which the Nuer certainly acknowledge. However, in spite of awareness of their sinful condition, the Nuer continued to look to a just god. On the other hand, the Dinka considered that Divinity was unjust and that separation from him was necessary; they took man's side in the controversy. Further, they have institutionalized a leader to bridge their strained relations with Divinity. The Nuer have not followed them. But did the Nuer see the condition of the dead differently from the Dinka? Both respected their clans and their clan genealogy. But of the Dinka we are told, "Dinka greatly fear to die without issue, in whom the survival of their names—the only kind of immortality they know—will be assured" (Lienhardt 1961:26).

So for the Dinka, Mbiti's generalization apparently holds true. The ghost of a dead Dinka can trouble the living, especially those who have wronged him. Apparently, the troubled living person has recourse through making things right with the aggrieved ghost. This would include help by the master of the fishing-spear and the (dead) ancestors, so the dead are not merely gone. But what happens to them is not of concern if they do not bother anyone. Elaborate rituals are provided the dead to make sure they are pleased.

Mbiti certainly must have been somewhat acquainted with Nuer ethnographies. He should have known that at least the Nuer are in an ethical-spiritual relationship with God. True, no messianic hope or radical reversal of man's normal life has been expressed in Nuer ethnography, but Evans-Pritchard clearly states that the object of Nuer ritual was for a moral crisis, not a physical one. Still, have we ruled out closer contact with God after death?

With the Nuer, as with the Dinka, there was little that Evans-Pritchard discovered about the actual condition of the dead. The Nuer are certain that "life comes from God and to him returns" (Evans-Pritchard 1956: 154). They think of conception as the product of human and divine action (1956:156). Some of what Evans-Pritchard tells us suggests that the Nuer dead may also have issues with the living. But looking at the speeches given at their funerals, the greater concern seems to be that God may yet have issues with the living. They question whether this death was a punishment from God or merely the way of all flesh. But collective guilt is not the only issue; the souls of the dead who have returned to God have his attention to redress wrongs or to intercede for the living. Is this attention given to them in the sky? The Nuer do not appear to know. Evans-Pritchard offers this paragraph in an attempt to resolve the issue in his own mind even though the Nuer do not seem to be concerned.

> Is it possible that the apparent contradiction between being
> under the earth and being with God in the sky arises from
> the vagueness of the concept of *tie* and in particular from
> the absence of any dogma that it is *tie*, soul, which becomes
> a *joagh* (pl., *jook*), ghost? It is perhaps important that Nuer
> always speak of the *joagh* of the departed and never his *tie*
> when speaking of the survival as a person. They speak of the
> "ghosts" of the dead and not the "souls" of the dead. This
> distinction would seem to allow both for the idea of the dead
> leading some sort of existence in the Nuer sheol as shadowy
> replicas of the living and also at the same time for the idea
> that their souls are taken on high by God. They cannot say
> anything more definite about this question of what is con-
> ceived to survive, or how or where. (1956:160)

There may be actions taken in the name of the dead person (*joagh*). These actions are considered to be by him even though he is dead. The occasions for
these actions may include a collective sacrifice for funeral and mortuary ceremonies, settlements of blood feuds started on account of their violent deaths, and
the marriage of their children. They are sometimes remembered by sacrifice.
Generally, however, the Nuer are little interested in the conditions after life.

The symbol "heaven" in the separation of heaven and earth can definitely be
associated with God in the African experience. The Dinka dead apparently do
not return to God as the Nuer dead do. It is true that the Dinka consider death
the result of God's going away. And two myths tell that before the separation,
there was the chance of restoration of youth. But since existence after death
is of little concern to the Nuer, it is difficult to argue with conviction that the
symbol heaven means life with God (after earthly life) and not merely God
himself. However, in Australia, covered in the next chapter, this is not true.
There the argument can be clearly made that those who continued to believe in
a celestial creator had an expectation of continued life in his care.

This chapter is titled "Is Heaven Oppressive?" I would like to explore this
question further. Please excuse a short digression while I try to underscore
the importance of understanding my answer. Evans-Pritchard was very careful
to represent accurately the Nuer's religious thought. It clearly includes things
unfamiliar to us. Yet their *kwoth a nhial* can surely be said to be transcendent.
He is absolute, unqualified, ineffable, and transcendent of every phenomenon,

the one and only cause of all existence. All values are ultimately his. Now this rather philosophical definition is not mine; it is a description of the Hebrew concept of God as interpreted by Henri Frankfort (Frankfort 1978:343). This author and scholar of ancient Near Eastern religions contrasted Egyptian and Mesopotamian forms of kingship. But when he turned to the Hebrews in the epilogue, he denied that they were part of the ancient world. His reasoning was that it has no place in a study of ancient Near Eastern religion as an integration of society and nature (1978:344). The Hebrews did not ascribe to their king any power over nature. In my mind, though perhaps not in Frankfort's, to do so would have been idolatry for the Hebrews.

But this does not tell us why Frankfort did not consider the possibility that Mesopotamia and Egypt put aside a transcendent creator to gain control over nature. Eliade did believe this. Of course, Eliade did not suggest that it was to invest the social structure with power over nature, merely that the "strong gods" they came to worship were said to have power over nature. But as Frankfort tells it,

> In Hebrew thought nature appeared void of divinity, and it was worse than futile to seek harmony with created life when only obedience to the will of the Creator could bring peace and salvation. God was not in the moons and the stars, rain and wind; they were his creatures and served him (Deut. 4:19; Psalm 19). Every alleviation of the stern belief in God's transcendence was a corruption. In Hebrew religion—and in Hebrew religion alone—the ancient bond between man and nature was destroyed. Those who served Yahweh must forego the richness, the fulfillment, and the consolation of a life which moves in tune with the great rhythms of earth and sky ... never an actor in the perennial cosmic pageant in which the sun is made "to rise on the evil and the good" and the "rain on the just and the unjust." (1978:343)

The quotation is startling to me! Perhaps Frankfort does feel that the Judeo-Christian thought system was a great fall from the richness of a "consoling" nature. Yet it was, after all, that thought system that made possible the development of modern science in the seventeenth century. Would Frankfort have us return to control over nature through rituals performed by elites in our society? What Frankfort is certain of is that neither the god-king of the Egyptians nor the representative of the gods of the Mesopotamians could have survived within Hebrew thought. The institution of Israel's kingship "lacked sanctity" (1978: 41). And may I add that I hope they can no longer survive within Western thought systems.

The Nuer also could not obey a fully transcendent creator and accept a "sacred king." Hence, if the neighbors of the Nuer had originally recognized the Creator or Supreme Being as their benefactor, it became necessary for him to go away. The acceptance of the separation of heaven and earth cosmology as a charter for a position with ritual control of the environment requires the denial of God's providence.

A question remains: which came first—egalitarian social structures or hierarchical social structures? On this point there is a consensus that it was egalitarian social structures. But then the cosmological justification for equality must have come before the cosmological justification for inequality. Then Nuer (and Hebrew) thought systems must be more primitive. Please understand: this does not prove either that belief in God was primeval or that he revealed himself to man. But it certainly calls into question any argument that monotheism is the product of the great thinkers of the ancient civilized and hierarchical world. Looking at the situation more globally, it certainly appears that this cosmology, the separation of heaven and earth, ushered in an ancient world filled with divinities that could be moved by the rituals of a social elite.

Let us review some of the facts about African religions treated in this chapter. After listing the pertinent ones, then we can answer the question of whether heaven is oppressive. It is taken for granted that all of Africa at one time was egalitarian. It also appears that those who are still egalitarian accept the Supreme Being as their provider. All known African societies have some minimum concepts of this Supreme Being, even though most of them now depend on elites within their social structure to influence nature to their benefit. How can we account for these circumstances? The most direct way to explain these circumstances is to say that most tribes in Africa rejected the providence of the Supreme Being for dependence on sacred leaders.

On one hand, the Nuer remained vigilantly egalitarian; they would not have a sacred leader. The Dinka were quite content to rely on sacred leaders rather than on the Supreme Being. The Dinka followed the pattern of most of the African continent. Therefore, the simple answer is that most tribes of Africa thought heaven to be oppressive. But the simple answer can sometimes be deceiving.

Egalitarianism is a fragile system. The issue is not only that the members consider themselves to be equals. Since they recognize no human superior, their cooperation cannot be coerced. It would seem that without recognized leadership, such a society would be handicapped. However, as shown in Chapter Two, hunter-gatherers domesticated plants and animals and, as farmers, thrived for about four thousand years before the introduction of social hierarchy. During that time many important technologies came into being. The people of a huge area traded the products of their specialization in manufacturing, agriculture, and mining. This period was remarkably stable and without obvious ethnic divisions. Apparently, egalitarianism is a most efficient form of political and social structure. Yet when the loss of this egalitarian social structure came, it totally engulfed the area and spread to other areas as well.

Archaeological evidence shows a similar pattern for the several other places where it has demonstrated that independent plant and animal domestication took place. The only question raised in the book about this was, could all the social hierarchy in the Old World be traced back to events in the lower Mesopotamian valley? That is, while plant and animal domestication took place independently within egalitarian groups in a number of areas, was their hierarchy also a local invention?

Answering the question about the oppressiveness of heaven should be considered in the light of this information as well. Egalitarian social structure appears to be creative, inclusive, peaceful, and apt to include large areas. Hierarchical social structure tends to be unstable, limiting wealth to its elites, possessive of its own area, warlike, and engaging in long-distance trade primarily for the benefit of its elites. In view of these considerations, heaven is hardly oppressive. Yet the evidence is clear nearly all groups living in areas that were thought to be economically useful came under control of a hierarchical social structure.

It seems that once hierarchy is established, for whatever reason, it does not go away easily. How might we account for this apparent anomaly? Likely, within an egalitarian society, freedom is extended in regards to both thought and speech. Within a hierarchical social structure, this freedom is restrained both by the hierarchy and those who expect to benefit from it. Apparently, the identification of heaven as oppressive in the cosmology can be used as an argument both to introduce social hierarchy and to justify its presence once established. In short, hierarchy is easier to acquire than it is to lose.

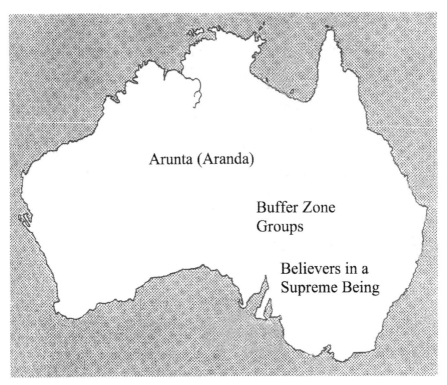

Arunta (Aranda)

Buffer Zone
Groups

Believers in a
Supreme Being

When missionaries and ethnographers investigated the beliefs of Aboriginal Australia they found that those in the southeast believed in a Supreme Being. The beliefs of the Arunta or Aranda) are contrasted with those of the southeast in this chapter. Between these two areas, the buffer zone, the tribes may acknowledge a Supreme Being while holding beliefs and practicing rituals similar to the Arunta in the central desert.

Chapter Ten

The Separation of Heaven and Earth in Australia

This chapter again compares tribal groups with and without the separation cosmology living under similar economic conditions. This time, however, they are hunter-gatherers. The point made in the previous chapter will be made again: the separation of heaven and earth cosmology charters a social system that is thought to have control over the environment. Again, similar to the African cosmologies of the withdrawal of the creator, the myth sets aside the creator by having him ascend into heaven after he created all things needed. Among the Australians, unlike the Africans, many tribes who accepted the cosmology either no longer claimed any contact with the creator or changed his attributes in such a way as to make him unrecognizable as the creator in their cosmology.

Much of the continent lived under a system that is often called Australian totemism. Totemism has to do with the name of a group, usually for purposes of identifying marriageable partners. An animal name is often chosen. There may be restrictions placed on the animal by whose name they are identified. Each of the Australian totemic ancestors have a particular place from which they emerged. But Australian totemism may be distinguished from other totemic groups by its particular increase ceremonies. Australian totemism includes ceremonies to increase the totem to which the group belongs. The rituals performed in these ceremonies are meant to guarantee the bounty of the totem for the whole tribe; the totem is usually a food item, either plant or animal. These same ceremonies are also meant to guarantee the continued presence of the human members of that totem.

Before moving on, recall that in Chapter Eight, several characteristics were identified that specified an Austronesian social structure. They were 1) the clans each claimed an ancestor who emerged from the earth or had some other singular origin; 2) these clans were often ordered in importance by the order of their emergence or some special competences (ritual knowledge) that they possessed; 3) the success of the whole society was thought to depend on the proper performance of the ritual used in expressing these competences. Substitute *totem* for *clan*—a totem represents each clan—and you see the Austronesian social structure is clearly demonstrated. One difference between the totemism as practiced by the Australian aborigines and that practiced by the Trobriand Islanders, definitely an Austronesian social structure, is that the Australians have their competence in making their own totem bountiful. In contrast, the Trobriand Islanders' competence had little to do with the animal that lent its name to their totem.

It is important to recognize that Australian totemism is an Austronesian system of hierarchical social order. The premise throughout the book has been that egalitarian access to a single creator was first limited by one cosmology scattered to number of areas and then spread from those areas. This differs significantly from the approach of many anthropologists. They work on the premise that hierarchy grew as the need for social controls grew. And only later the privileges of this hierarchy were justified by a cosmology that claimed ritual control of the environment. My premise infers that the cosmology first promised ritual control of the environment, not the control of society. Often the elite with the responsibilities for these rituals were then given social privileges. Specifically, the cosmology that first initiated these changes has been identified in this book as the separation of heaven and earth. That this was also the cosmology of the Austronesians is demonstrated by abundant Polynesian mythology. It has been shown that this same cosmology also chartered the polytheistic cultures around the Mediterranean, the sacred king or leader in Africa, likely the pantheistic system of the Indo-European subcontinent of India, and by inference the hierarchical system of ancient China.

In less than a quarter of the Australian continent, the extreme southeast section, the tribes believed in a creator. These tribes claimed to have communication with that creator and believed that at death he would meet them and care for them in the sky. These tribes did not practice circumcision or increase ceremonies, as did most of the tribes in the rest of the continent. Here it seems that the symbol "heaven" in the separation myth can be associated confidently both with the person of the creator or supreme being and the place of eternal life for those who accepted his gracious invitation.

In this chapter we will give the separation cosmology associated with a central desert tribe, specifically the cosmology of the Arunta. We have already seen that Australian totemism, thought by some to be uniquely Australian, fits the Austronesian model. More specifically, the Arunta had beliefs about conception and reincarnation that are quite similar to beliefs known to exist in and around the area of the Trobriand Islands. This suggests that this Austronesian type of organization may have come about later through communication with people groups from that area, rather than directly from the first wave of Austronesian speakers.

In Chapters One and Four, historian of religion Eliade was quoted as saying that the cosmology of the separation is not found among hunters. This statement is in error, however. At least two myths will be given that demonstrate the separation's presence in Australia among nonagricultural people. If it were not so, the hypothesis of this book would be undermined by Australian totemism since most of those living under Australian totemism have little use for the providence of a creator.

By considering the ethnographic material from Australia, we have in a sense come full circle. The principal ethnographies to be considered were written by anthropologists going to the field to gather data from the Australian Aborigines to demonstrate E. B. Tylor's evolutionary scheme at the end of the nineteenth century. Sir Baldwin Spencer and A. W. Howitt were two of these ethnographers. Spencer was a professor of biology at Melbourne and a friend of F. J. Gillen. Gillen had won the respect of the aborigines by ending the brutal treatment of them in Central Australia. Because of this respect, Gillen and Spencer became the first whites to witness the complete ceremonial cycle of the Arunta. Howitt was the ethnographer in the south and east, and he also had a previous history of contact with the natives. Both Spencer and Howitt approached the field expecting to demonstrate Tylor's theory.

The observations in the previous paragraph are a review of material already given in Chapter One. This review is pertinent for our purposes. It is important to remember that these ethnographies came before Malinowski formulated his concept of mythical charter. But few anthropologists have gone back to these ethnographies and applied this approach to them. In fairness to Howitt, he did attempt to understand how the tribes were structured, but he was working without the benefit of the structural theories that Durkheim and Radcliff-Brown later developed.

The ethnography that is of interest is from the Arunta, a tribe that covered a large part of Central Australia. This ethnography was not published until 1927, although the event described took place in 1896. As mentioned above, Gillen and Spencer witnessed these initiation ceremonies, and it was at these ceremonies that the complete cycle of the Arunta's origin stories was given. Our interest will be focused on the content of the information given at the initiation of young men in the final stage of a four-stage initiation series. In order to provide context for this information, it is necessary to give some of the preliminary information received at the earlier initiation stages. These stages were given in local (totem or clan) settings. The whole tribe was brought together for the final initiation; these fire ceremonies the Arunta called the *engwura*.

The Arunta young men who were ready for their final initiation rites had already been circumcised and subincised. At these earlier rites, they had learned about the "dreamtime"—in their language, the *alchera*. Since our concept of a dreamtime does not really represent the importance accorded to this time for the Arunta, their word, *alchera*, will be used to represent it. In native thought, this is the time when the totemic ancestors emerged from particular totem sites, produced children, and established certain traditions. The young men also learned of the link between pregnancy and the spirit essence (*kuruna*) of each person. These spirit essences were each represented by a piece of decorated wood as well as a stone (*churinga*) kept in the totemic storage site since the *alchera*. Each of these pairs of emblems represented an *alchera* ancestor. These stone or wood representations had since been the source of the spirit essences, the necessary life essence for all people and animals of that totem. At an earlier ceremony, a boy would be given the wooden emblem that represented his ancestor. He was told that the spirit essence associated with that emblem was the very essence of his own being. The stone one would stay in the storage site. You see, every person was a reincarnation of one of the *alchera* ancestors.

All the youth of the tribe who had gone through the first stages of their initiation were brought together for the final initiation ceremony. It went on for weeks with many performances celebrating activities of each of the clan *alchera* ancestors. Near the end of the time, the focus changed to certain ancestors of the wildcat totem (*achilpa*).

This is a summary of the cosmology given by Baldwin. This cosmology concerned a being the Arunta called *Numbakulla*. The word *Numbakulla* means "self-existent one"; he brought the landscape, including all the totemic sites, into being. He invented the emblems, rituals, and symbols. Perhaps most important from the natives' perspective, he was the source of all the spirit essences of mankind and of the animal world. He created the first man, the Great Chief (*inkata achilpa maraknirra*) of the wildcat totem. And he commissioned the first Great Chief of this totem to travel to the rest of the totemic sites to "activate" them. *Numbakulla* stayed at his camp while the Great Chief of the wildcat totem carried out his orders. When he returned from this mission, *Numbakulla* invited the Great Chief to visit him in his sky camp by climbing up his pole (the Kauwa-auwa). *Numbakulla* climbed up himself, but the Great Chief of the wildcat totem was unable to climb the slippery pole, and eventually the creator pulled up his pole after him into the sky. *Numbakulla* was never heard from again.

The Great Chief of the wildcat totem and his subordinates continued the program given by the creator, *Numbakulla*, teaching and initiating young men at each of the totemic sites throughout the land in the dreamtime. This cosmology was the verbal content of the final revelation of the Arunta male initiation ritual and served as charter for the preeminence of the wildcat totem, giving the most important position to the Great Chief. At each local site, the first totemic ancestor became a local chief. These original totemic ancestors started the Arunta society, and the reincarnations of them by way of the spirit beings have continued it (Baldwin & Spencer 1927:355–372). By reliving the lives of the ancestors, the Arunta participated in a fixed social hierarchy.

So for the Arunta tribe, the wildcat totem was the preeminent one. This is consistent within the Austronesian pattern. This totem also had a chief. In each generation, the senior men of the tribe identified him before he was born. His spirit had entered a woman from the proper totemic site at the proper time. She was not even aware that her offspring was the Great Chief of the Arunta. Of course, from their perspective he was not an offspring in our sense of the word. He was the pre-existent Great Chief. If the men chose to label a pregnancy the reincarnation of a Great Chief, and the one born of the pregnancy was a female, the girl would never learn her status. The man who took her as wife would act as the chief in her stead.

Viewed from the outside, this system greatly handicapped young men and all women. The young men were unable to have a wife until after their long and many staged initiation was complete. The girls, on the other hand, were awarded to an initiated (older) man even before they reached first menses. It apparently was the responsibility of each totemic group to bring about a bountiful supply of their totemic food source and to be sure that the spirit essences from their totems reached married women. Although marriage rules often regulated which totems could intermarry, the offspring from each marriage did not depend on the totems of the parents. Instead, it depended on the spirit essence that was said to have entered the mother from the totemic site nearest the location when she first felt the fetus move within her. The belief was that conception had little to do with sexual contact. This was not true of the Polynesians. However, as mentioned earlier, a very similar belief was found among the Trobriand Islanders. Among them, the spirit essence (*waiwaia*) was always placed in the correct woman by a spirit woman (*baloma*). This, too, was unrelated to sexual contact.

This story, the exit of *Numbakulla*, is similar to many African stories except that when the African High God went away, he did not go permanently beyond reach. In the Arunta tradition, he was only an originator; in the Dinka cosmology, he was both originator and sustainer since it was his power (*jok*) that empowered the "master of the fishing-spear." The exit of the Australian creator treats this originating god in a more radical manner, banishing him more completely. Even as we considered a neighboring tribe in Africa without the myth of the separation for context, we will next consider the beliefs of the southeast Australian tribes that did not practice Australian totemism.

As we look at the tribal customs of the southeast, we see they are obviously different. They did not practice circumcision, subincision, or other rituals requiring blood from the participants. Although they had totemic names, they did not claim separate origin sites for each clan. Their ceremonies did not include the decorated poles common to the rest of the continent. Their young men had only one stage of initiation, and their girls married only after first menses. I point out these differences without treating the difference in belief systems to show that if an ethnographer lived with tribes from this area as well as some that practiced typical Australian totemism, there would be obvious, unmistakable differences. When these ethnographers went to the field, Australia already had a well-established European settlement. That was especially true of the southeast since the climate there was similar to that in Europe. Therefore, most of the tribes in that area were already in some state of disarray. Nevertheless, Howitt, the ethnographer there, was able to give us a picture of their beliefs that has withstood most of the considerable criticism brought against it.

Recent ethnographies have been written to satisfy neoevolutionary thought on the development of complex social systems. All these theories start with egalitarian hunters as the first social order. Hence, Australia, with the largest remaining areas given to hunters left on the globe, became especially important. These ethnographers were not interested in the intellectual underpinning of the system, just its order. They soon realized that those remaining Australian hunters in the desert area of central Australia were not ordered in a typical egalitarian pattern. With this assessment I certainly agree. Other more recent material about the southeast has been rehashes of the early reports since these tribes no longer initiate their youth.

Further, unlike the ethnographies for the African continent, the primary ethnographies with material useful for our purpose were written from informants about events that happened before 1900. The ethnographers who wrote them had been sent out to verify Tylor's evolutionary theory of the origin of religion. This is why they did record myths and other intellectual information—Tylor's theory is an intellectualist theory. Although some British structuralists give this kind of information, it is of little importance to neoevolutionists.

Howitt is the ethnographer we will use for those tribes with a supreme being. Howitt called this being an All-Father. Howitt was in contact with Spencer, and they referred to each other in their reports. Howitt compared the beliefs of the natives of the extreme southeast and the Central Australians while drawing attention to some differences. He summarized one important difference in belief about the spirit world in the following quotations:

> Then *Daramulun* went up to the sky, where he lives and watches the actions of men. It was he who first made the *Kuringal* (initiation ceremony) and the bull-roarer, the sound of which represents his voice. He told the Yuin (tribe) what to do, and gave them laws which the old people have handed down from father to son until this time. He gives the *Gommeras* (medicine

> men) their power to use *Joias*, and other magic. When a man dies his *tulugal* (spirit) goes away, it is *Daramulun* who meets and takes care of it. (Howitt 1904:495)

And:

> This supernatural being, by whatever name he is known, is represented as having at one time dwelt on the earth, but afterwards to have ascended to a land beyond the sky, where he still remains, observing mankind.... [H]e is said to be able to go anywhere and do anything. (Howitt 1904:500)

Some of the names by which he was known in different groups include *Daramulun, Baiame, Bunjil*, or simply Our Father. When Andrew Lang pointed out that Howitt had identified a high god in southeast Australia, he started a controversy. Later Schmidt's elaboration of a theory of origins, which included Howitt's "All-Father," added to that controversy. But a comparison of Spencer's apparently acceptable *Numbakulla* of the Arunta with Howitt's controversial "All-Father" of the extreme southeast is instructive. *Numbakulla* was not associated with any totem, yet he was identified as a man. So was the All-Father. *Numbakulla* created all that the Arunta recognized as needing explanation. Howitt's All-Father was also given that honor. Both *Numbakulla* and the All-Father went to the sky without dying. Each established the tribal rituals. Each extended the invitation to join him in his sky land.

The basic difference viewed from this perspective between *Numbakulla* of the Arunta and the All-Father of the tribes of the southeast is that *Numbakulla* is said to have separated himself permanently from his earthly creatures, while the All-Father was said to care for them now and in his sky land after death. Perhaps this is the difference between the separation cosmology and the creator cosmology. If so, heaven represents not only the celestial creator but also eternal life with him.

But there were profound differences in the social structure and practices associated with the presence or absence of this being. In the southeast where the All-Father was revered, the people did not practice increase ceremonies and therefore had no inherited positions of ritual authority. Nor were there circumcisions or rituals requiring blood from the participants. When the Arunta died, they returned to a totemic site, ceased to exist, or both. When the Aborigines of the southeast died, they went to the sky to be cared for by the ever-living All-Father. Even as the story of *Numbakulla* was given only at the end of a young man's initiation, the secret name of the southeast All-Father was revealed to the initiates at the climax of their initiation. The women knew of this being but only as "Our Father." In some settings he was presented as a man by a drawing, a carving, or a star in the sky—sometimes along with the admonition, "You see him, he sees you."

The Aborigines of the Southeast were both responsible to and dependent on the All-Father. By contrast, a tall pole whose top was decorated as a man's head represented *Numbakulla* to the Arunta. The very nature of this representation drew attention to the fact that he did not see them. He was absent; their dependence on him was past. The Arunta viewed his pole as autonomous men within an unchanging social system fixed in no little part by *Numbakulla's* departure.

Before looking at other material of interest in our undertaking, let us make several observations. *Numbakulla* was part of the charter of the totemic system of the Arunta, an important part. But no logical reason required the creation of such a being as *Numbakulla*. To say that this being was the result of the philosophic speculation of the Aborigines does not help. Why would the totemic ancestors need to be first created by someone else? They could simply have emerged from the earth without further explanation (see endnote Chapter 10, note 1: Comparison of Arunta and Trobriand Islanders' beliefs about the separation of heaven and earth). Why invent such a problem as *Numbakulla*? When present, he had been the source of everything. Therefore his absence—not his presence—was required if their fixed social system was to be based on the performance of rituals to increase the bounty of the land. Even if such a being did fill a philosophic need, why send him away to heaven? Why not consign him permanently to earth at his own site as with the rest of the totemic ancestors?

My argument is simple. This part of the charter, the exit of *Numbakulla*, treated a once well-defined obstacle to the introduction of the new religious system. The Arunta totemic system could not coexist with an All-Father. This charter, as ideology, opposed an All-Father system that had been earlier known to the Arunta and was still known by others close enough to be a threat to their system.

It is difficult to see how nearby and interacting populations could hold worldviews as different as those of the extreme southeast with an All-Father and those of the central desert with the absent *Numbakulla*. Actually, there was a buffer zone between these opposed beliefs. Ronald Berndt is an anthropologist and respected author of works concerning traditional Australian belief systems. He identified this buffer area as the Mura-Mindari Complex (Berndt 1974:23). He also mapped the distribution of the male initiation rites that included subincision (Berndt 1964:139). This area included nearly the entire continent except the extreme east and the extreme southeast. Howitt was a major source of information about these Mura-Mindari Complex tribes as well as those of the extreme southeast and east. He clearly distinguished between the types of initiation rituals, identifying those with circumcision and subincision as western and those with an All-Father as eastern (Howitt 1904:638–642). While treating the beliefs of the tribes in this buffer area, Howitt mentions several separation of heaven and earth stories. In one he gives this bit of information: "At one time the sky rested on the earth and prevented the sun from moving" (1904:427). My summary of the details of one of the longer myths of these separation cosmologies follows:

Two beings, probably from the Milky Way (Roheim 1971:46f), presented themselves in time to save the boys from being initiated by a fire stick (see endnote Chapter 10, note 2: Fire sticks circumcision: another polemic against the Supreme Being?). While hunting between the circumcision and the subincision phases of the initiation, the youth killed a kangaroo. They lifted it above their heads, and the animal came to life again. From this episode it seems that we are to recognize one of the disadvantages of having heaven so near. In heaven there is life, not death. Nevertheless, they were able to kill another kangaroo, and this time its skin was stretched on a pole in order to separate heaven from earth. In a footnote, Howitt offers that the natives explained that this separation also gave men space to move about (Howitt 1904:646–649).

Notice that in this story, a pole is again the instrument of separation. *Numbakulla* climbed up a pole. The pole is one piece of paraphernalia present among the tribes practicing Australian totemism, but not those tribes with an All-Father. This story is also similar to the form of some separation of heaven and earth stories as encountered among the Polynesians, especially in that the sun and man were both prevented from moving about freely before the separation. It does not prove that the Australian totemic system was chartered by the diffusion of the same myth that served as charter for the hierarchy of the Polynesians. But it is very suggestive, especially since the resulting social structure is Austronesian in form. Notice also that there was a more polemic quality to the separation cosmology in this buffer area: the sun was prevented; men were restricted. In the exit of *Numbakulla* myth, his going is given in a simple statement; it does not portray him (or heaven) as a hindrance.

How is it that the most typical accounts of the separation of heaven and earth are from near the center of the continent, not where contact with outsiders would have taken place? This myth introduced a ritual hierarchy where none existed before. Once this hierarchy was well established and completely surrounded by others with now similar views and social structure, the separation story itself lost its context.

It is likely that the totemic system of the Arunta may have first been a "rank society," in Morton Fried's terminology (1967:109f, also see Chapter One). This ranking does not in Fried's order require a differentiation of access to resources. Within rank society, a hierarchy of ritual responsibilities exists, meaning there are inherited offices with responsibilities that include rituals to renew the environment. Anthropology has tended to allow only social and economic (real or materialistic) motivations for ranking. Ritual control over the environment in this scheme becomes merely an adjunct to justify an already present inequality.

Among the African Dinka, there is little reason to believe that "a need" for social controls or economic redistribution motivated the creation of the office of master of the fishing-spear. Neither is there reason to find these motivations important among the Australian Arunta. Granted, this ritual renewal of the environment is not real to our way of thinking. However, this does not rule out its critical importance as a motivation for the creation or acceptance of this religious system. Perhaps it is a problem to materialistic anthropology; it should not be a problem to Christians. The Creator was set aside for a form of idolatry. Social rituals to control the environment are certainly a form of collective idolatry.

In the case of the Australian Aborigines, one might reason that an emergence from the earth did define an individual's association with a particular plot of land. However, Australians, although associated ritually with a particular place, are not territorial in the sense that they lived near this plot of land or defended it from others. It is difficult to come up with a reason for this cosmology that a materialist would find compelling. In fact, the cosmology seems so random that it is easy to understand how Malinowski could explain such a system as merely an adjunct to justify inequality. The problem with his solution is that the cosmology is widespread.

> *This myth broke down resistance to the concept of ranking (inherited position of superiority) with a two-pronged approach: (1) by denying access to, or the constraints of, a single providential being (2) while offering a socially ordered system of ritual control of the environment. Or, perhaps more correctly, through this cosmology, believers substituted dependence on a moral sky being for dependence on a system of elites who claimed ritual control of the environment.*

The myth held its form(s) as long as there remained context(s) in which they had meaning. By using the plural forms, I acknowledge that the story of the Creator going away and/or heaven being lifted from earth to make room for man (and the sun) are to us, at least, two different stories. But these two stories do move together; they are both found in the Sudan as well as in Australia. They were apparently in some critical sense interchangeable. Symbolically they must have had similar meanings.

T.G.H. Strehlow grew up as a missionary's son among the Western Aranda (different spelling for the same tribe, the Arunta). He later took advantage of his considerable skills within that language to further our knowledge of these people. His father came to a mission station among the Aranda in 1894 and worked among them for 28 years. Of interest to us is one of his stories from among the Western Aranda:

> Throughout the Aranda-speaking area it was generally believed that both sky and earth were eternal, and that each of them had their own set of supernatural beings. The Western Aranda believed the sky to be inhabited by an emu-footed Great Father (*naritja*), who was also the eternal youth (*altijira nditja*). This Great Father had dog-footed wives, and many sons and daughters—all the males were emu-footed and all the females dog-footed. They lived on fruits and vegetables in an eternally green land, unaffected by droughts, through which the Milky Way flowed like a broad river; and the stars were their campfires. In this green land there was only trees,

fruits, flowers, and birds; no game animals existed, and no meat was eaten. All of the sky dwellers were as ageless as the stars themselves and death could not enter their home.

Although I have not recorded any traditions about emu-footed or dog-footed sky dwellers outside of the western Aranda territory, it is nevertheless true that everywhere in the Aranda-speaking area a firm belief was held that the power of death was limited to earth, and that men had to die only because all connections had been severed between the sky and earth. Traditions about broken "ladders" were found at many ceremonial sites. (Strehlow 1964:725)

At this point Strehlow goes on to record other similar beliefs found by his father and Gillen. He then adds, "It is clear that it would be impossible to regard the emu-footed Great Father in the sky of Western Aranda mythology as a Supreme Being in any sense of the word; for neither he nor his family ever exerted any influence beyond the limits of the sky" (1964:725).

Since the Aranda believed this about the Great Father, I can only agree that he is not the Supreme Being to them. However, the premise of this book is that the Supreme Being was dismissed to introduce control over the environment. Therefore, it is reasonable to expect that the Supreme Being among the Western Aranda may have been reduced to the emu-footed Great Father. Chapter Eight describes a similar belief about a sky being that was recorded among the Uhundunis of New Guinea (their beliefs about *hai* and the being who lived there). This was not only true among the Damal (same as Uhundunis), but the Ekari sages in the Yali Valley announced that the gospel was a fulfillment of *ayi*. Both of these Papuan tribes (and all their neighbors) probably at one time accepted a separation of heaven and earth cosmology so that man could emerge with ritual controls over the environment.

Ronald Berndt (1974:23) divided the Australian continent into cultural areas. He called the area in which Howitt identified the All-Father as the Magico-Religious Bora Complex. Berndt was not only critical of Howitt's treatment of this area but also seemed uncomfortable with the beliefs that he himself recognized in this area. He described the concerns of the rest of the continent in these sympathetic terms: "Man is seen as being part of nature, and in harmony with it. Without that recognized harmony, semi-nomadic existence would have been difficult indeed. It underlines the need for patience and an assurance that renewal is a basic factor of living" (1974:19).

But of the Southeast Bora Complex, he says,

> It was not without reason that some of the early writers saw Baiame as a dominant being, and a Sky God at that. One possible explanation here is that the religious ideology of this region expressed man's preoccupation with a Hereafter. In saying that, it would be necessary to admit that the rest of Aboriginal Australia is interested in the Hereafter as in the Here and Now. In the "Kuringal," "Burbung," and "Bora," the totemic dances do not seem to be, at least not directly, associated with fertility, not in the same sense as elsewhere. (1974:29)

Notice Berndt's characterization of the Southeast Bora Complex. He distinguishes its people from those in the rest of the continent by these traits: they were not as concerned with "renewal," and they were "preoccupied" with the "Hereafter." This is reminiscent of Frankfort's appraisal of the differences in perspective between Israel's religion and those of ancient Sumer and Egypt. Berndt should have noted that the Sky God providentially cared for the tribes of the Southeast. It could be said that preoccupation with rituals to renew the environment was not necessary for their here and now.

It seems strange that Berndt uses "Magico" in referring to the Southeast, which he did probably because of the shaman-like healers mentioned on page 151. Perhaps he does not see magic in the primary religious practice of the people of the rest of the continent, the ritual renewal of the environment. The healers, Howitt's *Gommera,* remove foreign substances from the sick usually by sucking. They also have the power to injure others by removing vital substance from a distance. These powers are said to be from the All-Father. The healers themselves are "called" to this office by him, and sometimes they are said to go into his presence in the process. Berndt, like Frankfort in the preceding chapter, is sympathetic to an animistic view of the world. But to Berndt, in a world controlled by a Supreme Being, life after death in his care was a "preoccupation."

Considering Australian materials, what might the symbolism of heaven in the cosmology of the separation of heaven and earth mean? From these materials it is easy to argue that "heaven" is symbolized by Berndt's "Hereafter." This meaning should be considered seriously; it is difficult to conceive of a system that could blend the Australian totemic identification with the landscape while holding that man's destiny is a hereafter in the sky. Earlier in the chapter when *Numbakulla* climbed his pole never to be seen again, the symbolism suggested both the absence of the creator and the loss of eternal life with him.

Interpreting the symbol heaven as eternal life with the creator did not seem appropriate in Chapter Nine. The Dinka assigned at least certain of their ancestors a place in "renewal" activities, while the Nuer did not. The Nuer wished to have their relationship with *kwoth* in good order now. Yet, according to Evans-Pritchard, they had little concern about existence after death. He did find, however, that when a Nuer died, without dispute that person became one of the *kwoth*'s people.

Berndt identifies the Arunta and similar totemic groups as the Segmentary Religious Complex. He offers that they occupy the greater part of the Central Australian desert.

The northern cultural areas have been influenced by even more recent exchanges with mainland New Guinea. Between the southeast and the central desert complex, Berndt identifies a transitional complex (Berndt 1974:23). It would be within this complex that Howitt collected mythology that strikes me as being "transitional."

Here stories have been preserved that indicate interaction between competing cosmologies. Howitt offers these myths that seem to be compromises between the religious cosmologies of the central desert and of the Southeast. One of these is a myth in which *Bunjil,* one of Howitt's All-Fathers, held out his hand to the sun and warmed it. This in turn caused the earth to open and men to come out (Howitt 1904:492). Generally, the All-Father was said to create men. To the north, men emerged from the earth (totemic sites) in the *alchera* and the sun was said to shine first when the totemic ancestors emerged. Not only were there transitional mythologies, but also Berndt identifies the areas in which they occurred as transitional cultures.

> *Australian totemism is not a pristine Paleolithic culture as some in the past have suggested. It is an Aboriginal interpretation of a religious ideology from nearby Neolithic cultures. I have no*

desire to speculate when this ideology came to Australia. But the cosmology that carried this form of totemism was the familiar separation of heaven and earth cosmology.

(Endnote Chapter 10, note 3, further supports this statement.)

Chapter Eleven

The Americas

What about the New World? Did some areas in the New World develop social hierarchy without Old World influence? The premise of the book does not require that all hierarchy can be traced back to the events in the Mesopotamian Valley. The premise of the book is that 1) social inequalities came about as a result of a change in worldview, not a social need for inherited positions of leadership; 2) within this worldview, certain members of the society were thought able to ritually control the environment; and 3) these positions were possible only as equal access to the providential care of the Supreme Being and his heaven became unimportant.

Further, the thesis holds that this worldview was advanced as an intellectual argument. This argument was given in the form of a cosmology, a cosmology competing with a Supreme Being cosmology. For certainly, when both man's origin and his providential care are attributed to the Supreme Being, we are talking about a cosmology. By offering that the environment could be controlled by ritual, this cosmology diminished the importance of the Supreme Being as provider. Many of these ritual positions came to have authority over the population and to control its output. When that happened, belief in the Supreme Being was usually further suppressed.

A consideration of the separation cosmology in the Old World suggests that it was not merely the hope that ritual control would prove more effective in providing abundance. The cosmology was expressed as a rejection of the conditions that prevailed when all were equally and morally responsible to the

Supreme Being. While its first importance may have been ritual control over the environment, the whole of the population was involved in this cosmology. The cosmology denies life with the Supreme Being after death. Most societies whose cosmology declared a separation from heaven claimed interest in this life only.

It seems obvious that the first inhabitants of the New World had neither a hierarchical social structure nor a cosmology that justified it. The New World inhabitants first domesticated plants not long after domestication took place in the Old World. Yet the first obvious hierarchy in the New World appeared 2,500 years after the first hierarchy in the Old World. If the separation cosmology came from the Old World, when did it come and who brought it? And there is a further problem. Most of the ethnographic material about the Americas came quite early. Europeans populated these continents earlier than some other areas with nonliterate people groups. When American anthropologists collected this data, they did not share the agenda of European anthropologists. I have found little ethnographic information that allows me to identify the relationship between the cosmologies and the rituals to control the environment. But with this caution, let us move into the American continents.

If the myth came to America early, it probably would have taken root in at most a few spots and spread out from those areas. This should show itself as a certain pattern of culture and ritual practices, even as was shown for Austronesian or African groups. This would be true, of course, whether the myth was transported or locally invented. If it were true that there was one origin of hierarchy in the New World, it would be reasonable to expect this to be reflected in the ethnographic reports. Does there seem to be a pattern of cultures that can be identified as distinctly American? Franz Boas, often referred to as the father of American anthropology, wrote this about American cultures from his observations.

> In a general survey of the ethnic conditions a peculiar uniformity of culture may be observed among the Indians living around the Gulf of Mexico and the Caribbean Sea, on the Great Plains, in the Eastern United States and in a considerable part of South America. All these tribes, notwithstanding far-reaching differences among themselves, have so much in common, that their culture appears to be specifically American. The extended use of Indian corn, of the bean and

the squash, the peculiar type of ritualistic development, their social institutions, their peculiar angular decorative art are among the most characteristic features common to this area. When we compare this culture with the culture of Polynesia, Australia, Africa, of Siberia, the similarities appear clearly by contrast with the non-American types of culture, and the common American traits stand out quite markedly.

There are, however, a number of American tribes that differ in their culture from that of the large area just mentioned. In South America many tribes of the extreme south and of the Atlantic coast, far into the interior of Brazil, exhibit differences from their northwestern neighbors. On the northern continent the tribes of the Arctic coast, of the Mackenzie basin, of the Western Plateaus, and of California do not participate in the type of culture referred to before. Looking at the distribution of phenomena from a wide geographical standpoint, it appears that those tribes inhabiting the extreme north and northwest and those inhabiting the extreme south and southeast, have ethnic characteristics of their own....

The isolation of the tribes of the extreme south-east and of the extreme north-west suggests that these districts may have preserved an older type of American culture that has not been exposed or at least not been deeply impressed by the influences that swept over the middle parts of the continents and left their impress everywhere. If our point of view is correct, we might expect to find a gradual decrease of the typical middle American elements as we go northward and southward: and we might expect that on the whole the tribes least affected were also the latest to come under the dominating influences of the middle American culture. (Boas 1940:332–333)

There are a number of things to notice about this survey. First, the mere attempt to demonstrate a distinctly American culture pattern flies in the face of contemporary approaches to anthropology. Neither contemporary European structuralists nor American neoevolutionists would have a place for such an observation. The observation, accurate though it may be, belongs to an earlier time in American anthropology. Second, the willingness to see an overlay of typical Middle American elements on an earlier single culture implies strongly that before the Middle American complex overlay, there was one American culture. If you recall from Chapter One, the areas of the extreme north and extreme south, much of what Boas describes as "with ethnic characteristics of their own," were those areas where tribes believed in a supreme being and had a simple social order. Their social structure was egalitarian.

It appears that under this simple social order the large assortment of American plants were domesticated. Of course, agriculture is difficult where weather conditions are limiting, and so these groups at the extremes rarely used domesticated plants. Third, Boas does not discuss cosmology in this quotation. But he does mention "the peculiar type of ritualistic development," and that development was certainly based on cosmology. Since the practices are characteristically Middle American, we can assume that there was at one time a characteristic cosmology that accompanied them. My argument is that that cosmology was a separation of heaven and earth cosmology.

If that cosmology came to the Americas, how would it get there? Of course, it may be that such a cosmology could have been created in the Americas. The separation cosmology found in America has unique elements. But it also has too many of the motifs found in the cosmology in the Old World to simply dismiss the possibility that it was transported from there. I suspect that if it came from the Old World, it came there from across the Pacific. There can be little doubt that the Polynesians could have made such a voyage when they settled Easter Island, more than halfway across the Pacific. And they settled the Hawaiian Islands even earlier. Would these ocean voyagers have been early enough to account for the origins of the Middle American complex of social complexity? Not likely.

However, these settlements in the open Pacific were made with ships or caravans of ships capable of carrying large numbers of people, provisions for weeks of travel, and the plants and animals that would be used on the islands they were to settle. Much earlier, not only the Polynesians but also those who settled Japan, Taiwan, the Philippines, and perhaps New Guinea sailed over open water. Such smaller groups of people were often simply a storm away from a much longer voyage than they had planned. If their vessels held together and they had enough provisions to last the journey, they would probably end up on a Mesoamerican or South American shore.

The first areas of hierarchy in the Americas, circa 2000 - 1500 B.C.

It is difficult to firmly establish the first sites that archaeology identifies as obviously hierarchical. In fact, in the Mesoamerican zone, the area generally including Mexico and Central America, the first obvious hierarchy appears to be represented by a large number of similar sites over a sizable area. Along the coastal areas of Ecuador and Peru, similar events happened just a little later. These first sites demonstrating social hierarchy are all dated after 2000 B.C. and before 1000 B.C. Before that time, large areas were described as homogeneous in their social structure. Many agricultural practices, in fact the very practices used by later hierarchical communities, were developed within these homogeneous social structures. There was widespread trade of agricultural products as well as raw materials of stone and shell. For practical purposes, all the plant cultigens that would be domesticated were domesticated during this time. Referring specifically to the archaeological finds concerning the culture conditions of Mesoamerica, a university course book offers the following: "The very diversity of the Mesoamerican environment, with its widely distributed food resources and raw materials, made everyone dependent on one's neighbors, communities living in very different surroundings. From the earliest times, barter networks linked village to village and lowland groups to those living on the semiarid highlands or in the basin of Mexico. The same exchange networks spread compelling ideologies, which were to form the symbolic foundation of the ancient Mesoamerican civilization" (Scarre & Fagan 1997:355).

This assessment of living conditions in Mesoamerica before the appearance of social hierarchy shows them to be similar to those conditions in Mesopotamia. There was also a long period of homogeneous social structure during the Ubaid period before the appearance of social hierarchy. In both places, many different skills were practiced under different environmental conditions and the benefits were bartered over considerable distances.

I have openly criticized any approach that assumes that all cultures are on a path necessarily leading from small egalitarian groups to hierarchical states. Does Fried's scheme of evolution for social organization fit the data here? His scheme involves the proposition that social structures evolve in this order: egalitarian, rank society, chiefdom, and state. This approach recognized that rituals thought necessary for the community were chartered before those traits that usually mark social hierarchy were in place. I have preferred this approach to others because it asserted that a person of inherited rank, no doubt justified by a cosmology, could be in place without other evidences for hierarchy. In this, Fried's approach contradicts both the assumptions of Malinowski and American

166

neoevolutionists such as Timothy Earle. Fried contradicted Malinowski in that Malinowski held that mythic charters were invented to justify already existing social inequalities, not that they preceded them. Fried contradicted Earle in that Earle argued that these charters embedded in cosmology were just so much talk without some form of military or economic sanction. The person awarded "rank" in Fried's "rank society" had no such power. Yet it is obvious that ethnologists have found social organizations that could be described in terms of Fried's rank society.

To refresh the reader's mind, rank society recognized an inherited position of ritual importance to the community. The person who held this position was awarded prestige but was not advantaged in status by gaining a greater share of the community's output or granted markedly more authority because of this position. Fried reasoned that this social ordering would accommodate a larger group than the egalitarian groupings he envisioned. Perhaps, if one is restricted to considering thinly populated hunter-gatherers who roam over a large area, the reasoning is sound. However, in the conditions described by archaeologists for this area and in the few other areas on the globe where domestication happened independently, this reasoning breaks down. The greatest flurry of human creativity for the domestication of plants and the development of agricultural practices to exploit those domesticated plants happened during the "egalitarian" period. Further, crafts including pottery, cloth, wood products, and occasionally metallurgy were also developed. And the products of these cultural boons were bartered without boundaries between the different communities, each benefiting from the skills and efforts of the rest.

Now, the criticism of Fried's evolutionary order is this: recognizing a ritual position that facilitates the community's output through the position holder's activities necessarily limits the size of the community on the basis of its activity. Assuming that in egalitarian societies the extended family was the primary social unit, Fried's rank society may have enlarged the primary social unit. However, it also established boundaries that probably limited the interaction the egalitarian groups had previously enjoyed. These boundaries come into view as the first markers of hierarchy in the Mesoamerican area.

Scarre and Fagan give this description of first hierarchy:

> The first signs of political and social complexity appear in
> many parts of highland and lowland Mesoamerica between

2000 and 1000 B.C. during the so-called Preclassic or
Formative era. In many regions there appeared small but often
powerful chiefdoms, headed by a chief and a small nobility....
In Mesoamerica, as elsewhere, the new social complexity can
be identified by differences in house designs, by the appearance of small shrines, and through prestigious trade goods
such as fish spines and seashells from the gulf coast that were
used in bloodletting and other religious ceremonies....

There was no one region where this emerging sociopolitical
complexity occurred first. Rather it was a development that
took hold more or less simultaneously in many regions of
Mesoamerica. (Scarre & Fagan 1997:355)

So how did hierarchy appear to arrive simultaneously throughout sizable areas
in Mesoamerica? I think that the last part of the first Scarre and Fagan quotation above (page 166) explains that very well. Without boundaries, not only did
bartering take place freely, but also "compelling ideologies" were allowed to
spread. I believe that social hierarchy is not advantageous; most of any population struggle under its weight. Yet it became prevalent throughout most of the
world. Why?

> *Social hierarchy should not be considered a step on the way to the
> pinnacle of social development. It is rather a condition that man-
> kind seems very apt to fall into. A population is willing to give up
> its independence for the belief that the elites of the social structure
> will provide for them.*

The people who occupied Mesoamerica were not without religious beliefs before
they happened into what Scarre and Fagen refer to as social complexity. This social complexity was introduced with new religious ideologies to justify it. Notice
that this pattern is not described in the same terms as in the Mesopotamian
Valley. There, the hierarchical social structure could be identified as intrusive.
Here, it appears to bloom suddenly in many contiguous areas. This suggests
that there was no intervention here as in the Mesopotamian Valley.

Between 1500 B.C. and A.D. 1500, many cultures and cities grew and then
disappeared in the Middle Americas. Olmec culture was early in Mexico, followed by cultures represented in sites such as San Lorenzo and La Venta. Later

still, Monte Alban and then, during the classic period starting about A.D. 650, Teotihuacan unified the area. In the sites of this period, there were pyramids with temples on them, planned cities with paved streets, and probably human sacrifice. When the Spaniards came, this empire had long ago been replaced by others and was then controlled by the Aztecs. In Guatemala, there were many centers from A.D. 150 to A.D. 900, including the sites of the Maya, El Mirador, and Tikal. Here, there is glyph writing and evidence for a calendar. Looking to South America about the same time, there were early sites such as El Paraiso and Chavin de Huantar. Later, Moche with enormous monuments, where the people worked raw copper and gold, manufactured cotton and wool textiles. By A.D. 200–1000, Tiwanaku had unified a considerable area. When the Spaniards came, the Inca ruled and had built the amazing Machu Picchu religious shrine high in the Andes.

From these sites, archaeologists have been able to learn many things about the physical culture and some of the ritual practices of these people. But the reports of their beliefs are largely from the conquering Spaniards. They tell us little about the original cosmologies of these cultures. In fact, the original cosmologies may have been replaced many times with the various regime changes. There is little reason to have confidence that the Aztecs or the Incas would have been able to furnish the information we are seeking. For that, we need to go away from the center of the introduction of social hierarchy to those groups who were more recently and less completely influenced by it.

Human sacrifice, usually of prisoners of war, was widely practiced in South America. In order to find the groups less influenced by the high cultures of the Middle American area, we have to find those groups that did not follow such practices. It is reasonable that in those areas the cosmologies that first chartered social inequalities would most likely occur. I have found only a few South American cosmologies recorded from these areas, but the two below caught my interest. They are from a volume by Hartley Burr Alexander, a professor of philosophy from the University of Nebraska. He contributed this volume on Latin American mythology in 1920 and an earlier one on North American mythology in 1916. These volumes were included in a thirteen-volume collection titled *The Mythology of All Races* by Louis Herbert Gray. In the quotation below, both groups mentioned are from Brazil.

> The uniting of heaven and earth by a tree or rock which grows
> from the lower to the upper world is found in many forms,

and is usually associated with cosmogonic myths (true creation stories are not common in Brazil). Such a story is the Mundurucu tale ... which begins with the chaotic darkness from which came two men, Karusakahiby, and his son Rairu. Rairu stumbled on a bowl shaped stone; and his father commanded him to carry it; he put it upon his head, and immediately it began to grow. It grew until it formed the heavens, wherein the sun appeared and begin to shine. Rairu, recognizing his father as the heaven maker, knelt before him; but Karu was angry because the son knew more than he did. Rairu was compelled to hide in the earth. The father found him and was about to strike him, but Rairu said: "Strike me not, for in the hollow of the earth I have found people who will labor for us." So the first people were allowed to issue forth, and were separated into their tribes and kinds according to color and beauty. The lazy ones were transformed into birds, bats, pigs, and butterflies. A somewhat similar Kaduveo genesis ... tells how the various tribes of men were led from the underground world and assigned their several possessions, last of all came the Kaduveo, but there were no more possessions to distribute; accordingly to them was assigned the right to war upon the other Indians and to steal their lands, wives, and children. (Alexander 1920:308–309)

It is difficult to understand specifically what these cosmologies may have chartered as far as social structure is concerned, but it is obvious that the mythic structure fits into a class of cosmologies that has been identified as separation cosmology. So that it will not be missed, please note this: in the cosmology above, heaven, the bowl-shaped stone the son put on his head, at first lay on the earth. The sun became visible only after it was separated from earth. Preexistent beings, people and animals, emerged from their original condition only after heaven had been lifted off them.

As we move to the southern tip of South America, we find several hunter-gatherer tribes without hierarchy. These are the tribes Darwin had lightly dismissed by claiming he would rather admit that he was related to a monkey than to them. They are also famous for the fires they kept in their canoes when hunting in the harsh climate there. They are the Alakaluf, the Ona, and the Yaghan. Father Gusinde visited and studied the Yaghans at four different times during the first quarter of the twentieth century. His book is written in German, so I have chosen to use his report as found in Carleton Coon's book *The Hunting Peoples.* This is the same book referred to in the first chapter.

> One of them concerns the high god Watauinewa. He is formless, invisible, and has no special home other than in the sky. He is called The One Up There, or Father, or sometimes The Murderer. He controls the weather. He also laid down all the rules of behavior the Yaghans have to follow, and in the case of a serious breach he brings death to the offender or to a close relative, or particularly to a baby. People do not like to mention his name because it may remind others of deaths in their families. People pray to Watauinewa before going out to hunt on the sea in a canoe, asking for good weather, and they thank him when they return. During funerals they call him a murderer, but they take it back later. (Coon 1971:298–299)

The Yaghans, Coon tells us, have five origin myths. I have given the one that seems rather philosophic. The other four might be considered as "just-so" stories because they tell of the time when men were able to wrest rulership from women, how the original inhabitants of the land became animals, how men finally became men, and the introduction of the skills the people presently have. These stories, as Coon explains, are unrelated to their thoughts about their high god. This does bring up a problem with the available mythology. I think that the Yaghans actually worshiped the Supreme Being. However, collectors of myth may be far more interested in finding and recording the very colorful just-so stories, which seem to be common among all American Indians. Both the Ona and the Alakaluf groups also had belief in a supreme being. These three tribes are some that Boas mentioned as part of preexisting culture.

Starting at the opposite end of the continents among the northern tribes of North American Indians, we find the Great Spirit. These Indians were first encountered by whites from northern Europe and later interviewed by many, especially clergy. The northern Algonquians called their Great Spirit *Gitche* (or *Kitshi*) *Manitou*, which happens to be the Indian name for the Supreme Being we are most likely to have heard. But many other tribes have names for this being in their own languages. From the same H. B. Alexander who wrote about the South American tribes, we have this report about the Algonquian's *Gitche*

Manitou: "It should not be inferred that a manlike personality is ascribed to the Great Spirit. He is invisible and immaterial; the author of life, but himself not created; he is the source of good to man, and is invoked with reverence; but he is not a definite personality about whom myths are told; he is aloof from the world of sense; and he is perhaps best named as some translators prefer, the Great Mystery of all things" (Alexander 1916:19–20).

Alexander shows a certain prejudice himself although he argues against those of his own time who doubted that belief in such a being as the Great Spirit could have been present before Christians arrived (Alexander 1916:82). Notice that since the natives have no mythology about the Great Spirit, he cannot be personal. Applying this standard to our own beliefs, we might have to assert that our God is not personal. This Great Spirit is described by the Algonquians in the north of North America in a way very similar to the way that the Yaghans' *Watauinewa* is described in the extreme south of South America. Neither attaches mythology to him although each has many myths concerning the nature they encounter. However, although they have few myths concerning the Great Spirit, the story of how the calumet (peace pipe) was given might qualify as one such myth. Alexander credits the recording of this story to Father De Smet, a Catholic missionary to the Indians.

> The peoples of the North had resolved a war of extermination against the Delaware [an Algonquian tribe], when, in the midst of their council, a dazzling white bird appeared among them and poised with outspread wings above the head of the only daughter of the head chief. The girl heard a voice speaking to her, which said, "Call all the warriors together; make known to them that the heart of the Great Spirit is sad, is covered with a dark and heavy cloud, because they seek to drink the blood of his first-born children, the Lenni-Lenapi, the eldest of all the tribes on earth. To appease the anger of the Master of Life, and to bring back happiness to his heart, all the warriors must wash their hands in the blood of a young fawn; then loaded with presents; and the Hobowakan [calumet] in their hands, they must go all together and present themselves to their eldest brothers; they must distribute their gifts, and smoke together the great calumet of peace and brotherhood, which is to make them one forever. (Alexander 1916:21 brackets added)

The Algonquian language group, like the Yaghan in Chile, has other tales that come near to being cosmology. Some of these stories describe the adventures of the Great Hare. They also appear as just-so stories. The Great Hare goes about performing tasks that bring about the present environment while extricating himself from what are usually self-inflicted troubles. He is generally considered a friend of mankind.

Let us next consider the tribes occupying the Great Plains, again using Alexander:

> As a matter of fact, there is hardly a tribe that does not possess its belief in what may very properly be called a Great Spirit, or Great Mystery, or Master of Life. Such a being is, no doubt, seldom or never conceived anthropomorphically, seldom if ever as a formal personality; but if these preconceptions of the white man be avoided, and the Great Spirit be judged by what he does and the manner in which he is approached, the difference from the Supreme Deity of the white man is not so apparent. (1916:82)

The Indians of the Great Plains worship the sun as first representative of the Great Spirit. Their most important ritual is the Sun Dance. It is observed once a year and is usually eight days long. It is during these dances that the warriors fasten themselves to a pole with skewers inserted into the muscles of their chests and dance until their lacerated bodies are freed. These tribes typically referred to the sun as their father and the Great Spirit as grandfather (Alexander 1920:89–90).

> Great Sun Power! I am praying for my people that they may be happy in the summer and that they live through the cold of winter. Many are sick and in want. Pity them and let them survive. Grant that they may live long and have abundance. May we go through these ceremonies correctly, as you taught our forefathers to do in the days that are past. If we make mistakes pity us. Help us, Mother Earth! for we depend on your goodness. Let there be rain to water the prairies that the grass may grow long and the berries be abundant. O Morning Star! when you look down upon us, give us peace and refreshing sleep. Great Spirit! Bless our children, friends, and visitors

through a happy life. May our trails lie straight and level before us. Let us live to be old. We are all your children and ask
these things with good hearts. (Alexander 1916:90)

Alexander does not give a cosmology explaining how this rather pantheistic cosmos came into existence. It does seem that the ritual itself, properly conducted,
should be effective in providing food for the next year and that it should also
show the proper respect to the powers that furnished the people sustenance in
the past. However, the beings supplicated were asked to show pity and must
have been given some respect as persons. We are not told what the purpose of
their sacrifices might be. Some Great Plains Indians offered human sacrifices.

But if we move to the regions farther south and west, we know from Chapter
Five that the Zuni had a separation cosmology. With two exceptions, the myth
is typical of Old World separation cosmology. Often in the Southwest, man's
emergence is through a number, usually four, of intermediate stages, and for
the Zuni, heaven was willingly separated from earth. The people came up from
under the earth's surface to view the sun for the first time. The Zuni, Hopi,
and other Pueblo Indians have an ancestry that is often traced back to the
high civilization of Mexico. The cosmology of the Zuni allows that following
death, man will return to his place in the earth. Among the northern tribes, the
expectation was that they would traverse the Milky Way to the place of those
who had lived earlier. Some Algonquian even mention that this life is with the
Great Spirit.

The Northwest Coast Indians, whose wealth depended on the salmon run,
were extremely hierarchical, even though they did not practice agriculture. This
is a summary of a cosmology as told by the Coast Salish. In the beginning, all
creatures behaved as human beings. Among these beings, Eagle, with his sharp
vision, showed Wren an arrow sticking in the sky. Wren then shot other arrows,
each in the notch of an earlier one. In this way a ladder was constructed that
reached the sky. The people climbed this ladder and camped by a river, where it
was very cold and dark, but they could see a fire. Mink went to get some coals
but was discovered before getting back. The inhabitants of heaven attacked
the people of earth. The earth people were being defeated and attempted to
retreat down the arrow ladder, but when only half of them had made it, the
ladder broke, crushing those still on it and leaving some still in the sky. After
this time, those who were unable to get back to earth became stars, some more
powerful than their neighbors: Big Elk and Little Elk (the dippers), Cougar,

Bear, the Smelt Dip Net, etc., including rainbow, which can be seen sometimes in the day (Bancroft-Hunt 1989:90-91). This cosmology likely chartered important aspects of this tribe's social structure, but they largely escape me. What does present itself is that man no longer hopes to ascend to heaven, that light has come, and that, along with these events, man has become fully man. In this cosmology there is no mention of a creator. The great houses, for which these tribes are known, may have been said to resemble a house seen by those who ascended to heaven.

Although the Iroquois are best known as a northern tribe, their cosmology has considerable affinity to the Gulf region cosmologies. I choose to use it because it is quite different from the others already mentioned. As with many North American stories, it has tidbits of other tribes' myths, which my summary that follows does not identify.

The first scene of the story begins in the heaven above the visible heavens. Here, there was only life and abundance. But a girl child was born, and shortly after her birth her father sickened and died. While conversing with her dead parent, the girl was instructed to go to the realm of Chief-He-Holds-the-Earth, beside whose lodge grew the great heaven tree, and marry him. On her way there, the maiden went through various ordeals, which she successfully endured. But when she returned to her husband, she was pregnant. He became ill with an unjust jealousy from the Fire-Dragon. The cause of the illness of the Chief of Heaven was divined. And after his spouse gave birth to a daughter named Gusts of Wind, he was told to uproot the tree of heaven. Through the hole left when this tree was uprooted, he cast his spouse and her daughter wrapped by the Fire-Dragon with a great ray of light. Thus, Heaven and Earth were separated, for the spouse of the Chief of Heaven was none other than the Earth. Notice again that heaven was the place of abundance and without death, except for the circumstance noted. Even in that instance, communication after this death was possible.

In later scenes of the Iroquois cosmology, Earth was recovered from the watery abyss. The sun was stolen and, through a complex story, the present conditions under which man lives are finally realized (Alexander 1916:35–37). Again, the elements seem in order. In this cosmology, Earth was violently separated from Heaven. The sun became visible only after this separation; finally, men came into being following a pattern somewhat similar to that in the stories of other northern tribes.

I do not claim to give any decisive evidence that the separation cosmology came from the Old World. However, Boas makes the point that the American culture seems to have spread from Middle America to embrace most of both continents. Cosmology that certainly would be classed as separation of heaven and earth cosmology was found in widespread areas. The mythology we have of Native Americans is rich in imagination. Further, it seems abundantly clear, in spite of critics, that some tribes worshiped the Supreme Being and attributed to him traits similar to our own beliefs about God. Among some of these with this belief was an expectation of life in the sky with the Supreme Being after death. This expectation is usually absent among those who espouse a separation cosmology. As in the Old World, traces of the Supreme Being are generally harder to find in what has been called high civilizations. It is not unreasonable to suggest that the culture Boas has described as distinctly American, the one that spread from the middle Americas, was based on the cosmology of the separation of heaven and earth.

Chapter Twelve

Conclusion

The introduction of the book pointed out that my approach to prehistory is different from that of most other books on this subject. My approach has used primarily the scholarship from two disciplines: history of religions and anthropology. Anthropology recognizes a relationship between the cosmology or origin story of a group and its social structure. For anthropologists, this story justifies existing social privileges. While anthropologists accept the importance of cosmology within the social structure, they do not find it important that the thematic material for many of these cosmologies can be found all around the globe. If they choose to recognize these similarities at all, they have explained them as archetypes, a demonstration of mental development, or psychological tendency. In short, rather than considering the possibility that ideas were important in the past even as they are today, most anthropologists insist on materialistic rather than idealistic approaches in their craft (Chapter Four).

However, some scholars in history of religions trace these similar cosmologies to discover the history of their development. Yet, while history of religions traces the history of mankind's ideas about the cosmos, that discipline avoids questions about the importance of these cosmologies in the social structure of a society. Historian of religions Mircea Eliade found that following the prevalence of a cosmos in which a single celestial creator was central, a cosmology with various titles, called in this book the separation of heaven and earth, became dominant. My approach offers an obvious connection. Mankind spread across the globe with an egalitarian social structure and later adopted hierarchical ones. The connection is that the change from a single celestial creator cosmology to the separation of heaven and earth cosmology was related to the change from egalitarian to hierarchical social structure.

We cannot know directly the beliefs of man as he spread across the globe. The first written material we have follows clear archaeological evidence for social hierarchy by most of a thousand years. The Egyptian cosmology as recorded in the pyramid texts is the earliest written cosmology known (Chapter Three). Later the Sumerians left us with literature containing cosmological material that we could interpret. Considerably later, using the Rig Veda for information, we can claim some insight into the first cosmology of the Indo-Europeans. All of these, along with early Hittite and Greek cosmologies, offer representatives of the myth of the separation of heaven and earth. When an attempt is made to reconstruct Chinese early cosmological thoughts, they too suggested the presence of this cosmology. From this material we can infer that a separation of heaven and earth cosmology was used as the charter to introduce the first social hierarchy.

This is an important inference. True, it is only an inference. However, it is the most probable from the material available. It complements Eliade's observations (Chapter Five) about the cosmologies held by significant numbers of societies, and it recognizes an anthropological interpretation of cosmology itself. What neither anthropology nor the history of religions even try to answer is, why this cosmology? Malinowski (Chapter One) moved anthropology in the direction of finding cosmology to be an important tool in understanding social structure, but he left cosmology itself in the superstructure. That is, Malinowski interpreted cosmology as justification for social privileges, implicitly denying that cosmology, serving as ideology, could have been motivation for these privileges. From a materialist's point of view, the elites performed a useful function in social organization. To the materialist, therefore, the functional benefit of fixed leadership accounts for the presence of hierarchy. From this perspective, the claim that elites controlled the environment for the benefit of the society was declared mere rationalization for the special privileges of the elites.

However, from an idealist's perspective, this data underscores a possible relationship between the cosmology on which hierarchical social structure was first built and the cosmology of egalitarian societies. Egalitarian societies believe that the Creator provides for them. The elites in the social structure in hierarchical societies ritually manipulated the environment to provide for their people. Therefore, it was necessary to discredit the providence of the Creator, symbolized by heaven, in order to invest elites with the ability to provide for the society. As long as a celestial creator made man equal and providentially cared for him, there was no opportunity for social hierarchy to come into being.

Highly structured civilizations left us magnificent ruins both demonstrating technological skills and representing the organization of a great many man-hours of labor. With this in mind, many anthropologists look to a hierarchical social order to solve most of man's organizational problems. In the Mesopotamian Valley, city-states emerged without the lengthy precursor steps that their model for the evolution of the state predicts. In seeking to remedy this apparent anomaly, some anthropologists find that chiefdom hierarchy existed there without the evidence normally required for identifying this social order. Neoevolutionary anthropologists sometimes seek to demonstrate hierarchy (especially chiefdom society) where the normal criteria that indicate this social order do not exist.

In spite of this, most anthropologists recognize that mankind spread across the globe without evidence for hierarchical social order. They not only fed and clothed themselves within an egalitarian social order, they also invented crafts to enrich their lives. Among the known recent hunter-gatherers, family was important. Most of these hunters were monogamous. And surprisingly, the belief in a celestial creator was widespread enough to make it reasonable to assume that mankind spread across the globe with such a belief. The alternative that they communicated this belief to each other after they spread out seems preposterous, and to suggest that these people independently came to this belief system would also require considerable explanation.

Not only did man spread across the globe without inherited positions of leadership, in a number of widespread places he domesticated plants and animals. Pottery, too, seems to be an independent invention in several different areas. Even before these innovations, egalitarian hunters traded over large areas. We know that shells for ornaments and stone for tools were traded because they can be found in the remains of ancient camps far from their sources. This trade was not diminished as man turned to agriculture and a more settled existence. New crafts, including pottery and cloth making, were added to the artifacts that show this widespread network of trade. We can assume that a great many other things that were traded have not stood the tests of time. An egalitarian social order apparently enabled mankind to live a peaceful and prosperous life.

Hierarchy did not nullify man's creative abilities. New architectural skills were necessary for the great structures hierarchies required. Without doubt, egalitarian populations committed adultery, murder, and other crimes, but their burial remains seldom showed evidence for violence. War, weapons, and defensive structures were all introduced with hierarchical social structure. Often there was social ranking as well as slavery. Trade became a way for the elites of the social structure to mark their wealth and authority. Burials marked the great wealth of a few; in a number of places, human servants were entombed, likely while still alive, with the dead elite.

In the early chapters of the book, two points were made: 1) Man did very well without social hierarchy; and 2) across the Old World, much of this hierarchy appeared to be linked to activities in the lower Mesopotamian Valley. Neither of these postulates fit comfortably within anthropology's basic assumptions.

Let us examine two of the differences between the assumptions that I hold and those of anthropology. As an evangelical Christian, I have little use for evolution. However, present anthropological theories would not claim that man's physical or mental evolution were factors in the data treated in this book. DNA from man all over the globe strongly infers that modern man spread out with his present physical and mental abilities. The distribution of family organization suggests that mankind also had a well-established family structure. Well-developed language and communication skills are in use everywhere. There is no evidence that mankind, within the time frame I have examined, was without this ability. It also appears that mankind spread out with a belief in a providential celestial creator (Chapter One).

Anthropology would prefer to believe that the notion of a single celestial creator was the result of a long evolutionary process. Earlier anthropologists who believed that their materialism was the result of more highly evolved minds have rightly been called racists. It is, or at least should be now, recognized that belief systems are chosen, not the result of mental evolution. Assumptions about physical or mental evolution within the time constraints I have used are unimportant in the conclusions I have reached.

My second assumption differs from materialistic anthropological approaches. I assume that man's social structure cannot be accounted for without consideration of his beliefs about the cosmos. This is true not only of hierarchical social structures but also of egalitarian ones. This argument for egalitarian social structure was made in Chapter Four on the basis of our own society. The claim for egalitarianism is useless unless some meaningful indication of that equality is recognized. Anthropologists distinguish between egalitarian and hierarchical societies by pointing out that in hierarchical societies, elites are awarded their position by birth, while in egalitarian societies positions of leadership are ascribed on the basis of recognized abilities. But from within a complex society such as our own, it is obvious that privileges do come with birth. As was pointed out in Chapter Four, the argument for egalitarianism in our own society breaks down without the cosmological reconciliation of apparent and unequal opportunities. As stated in the preamble to our Declaration of Independence, this reconciliation takes place with the recognition that we are equal before our Creator.

This difference in assumptions in the second case is not at all meaningless. It is the divide between the thinking of much of anthropology and my own. Neoevolutionist archaeologists expect regularities in social structures that can be accounted for by one or a combination of material causes. Therefore, diffusion—the movement of skills or ideas—is not considered a likely cause of change in social structure. To many anthropologists, allowing other than material causes would deny their discipline the right to be considered science. To these scholars, my insights about how ancient and preliterate societies came to hold their cosmologies could not be a scientific explanation. It is not because data for these insights is lacking; rather, it is because these insights allow for the willful efforts of at least some members of the societies involved—they were not determined by material causes.

The problem is in the reconciliation between material causes and free choice. One could say I am attempting to reconstruct history; but they are attempting to establish the laws by which social structures evolve. Perhaps some day there can be some reconciliation of these two very different perspectives. For now, this lack of reconciliation is part of the same conundrum that philosophers face when claiming that man's actions are completely determined while holding man responsible for those actions, or that the anthropologist faces when claiming to reason from the data he collects while a consistent materialist would deny that man is capable of such reasoning.

The argument can certainly be advanced, on the basis of the information presented in Chapter Two, that for a good period of time before the first hierarchy appeared in the Mesopotamian Valley, a complex civilization existed. This complexity could not be avoided as soon as there was craft specialization. These specialized occupations would include the potter, the weaver, the farmer, the herder, the tanner, the fisherman, the stoneworker, and others that have not been named. The products of these specialized occupations were traded along with those materials made of stone, timber, shells, and metal unavailable in many areas. My point is that in order to remain egalitarian in attitude, the people in this society needed to reconcile their obvious differences in skills, opportunities, even wealth (although here none appeared to be ostentatious), and pride of location. Likely, this reconciliation took place in a shared cosmology in which they all recognized not only their equality but also the providence promised through this cosmology.

The obvious lack of great disparities in wealth in the Mesopotamian Valley for the long period before the emergence of hierarchy requires explanation. Two points are to be made: 1) They apparently did not need elites, and 2) they did not look to elites to control the environment for their benefit. This second point is not unimportant. The few egalitarian groups for which we have information thanked the Creator for their provisions. If they were truly part of a much more inclusive population (argument from Chapter One), it is likely that most people recognized the Creator as provider before the introduction of social hierarchy. Then it is a reasonable inference that the egalitarian population of the lower Mesopotamian Valley, among whom the first clear evidence for hierarchy has been recognized, had previously considered the Creator as their provider.

The argument is strengthened when comparing the Nilotic tribes in Chapter Nine and the southeast and central tribes in Australia in Chapter Ten. From these comparisons, we can see that the Creator was made distant in each case with the introduction of hierarchy. And in each case the charter for the elites in these hierarchies was a cosmology that is easily recognizable as a separation of heaven and earth cosmology. This appears to be the same cosmology that chartered the hierarchy of the ancient world. In each of these more recent cases, the social structure through its elites replaced the Creator as the provider.

Materialistic anthropology has recognized that elites in a hierarchy are believed to provide for the population in preliterate societies. But they underscore the falsity of this belief, claiming that a cosmology embodying such a belief is merely rationalization for the recognition of special treatment for elites. Of course, materialistic anthropology would also say that the providence of the

Creator is merely a false belief based on a faulty cosmology. The problem with this reasoning is that it denies the reality of culture, for surely human ideals and beliefs are an essential part of culture. Anthropology offers that cosmology rationalizes special treatment for elites. However, it has yet to recognize that not only inequalities within a complex hierarchical society but also inequalities within a simple egalitarian society need to be reconciled within a cosmology.

But if egalitarianism is basically a culture pattern—a belief system shared by a society or community—can some individuals hold it within a greater community that does not? The answer is a qualified yes, qualified because an individual cannot exist as a community. But an individual can indeed believe that all individuals are equal and provided for by the Creator. How do such persons fare in nonegalitarian settings? By and large, it is fair to say that most evangelical Christians are committed to an egalitarian perspective as defined in the preceding sentence. Today, many are in nations where they are persecuted. Why are they persecuted? Their belief system requires that they should be honest, hardworking, and kind. It would seem that they should be good citizens anywhere. Yet they are apparently a threat to both religious and political systems. What is the nature of that threat? I suggest that it is because their Creator, rather than the social structure, provides for them.

One egalitarian culture within a larger society whose history is recorded is early Christianity. Here again, Christians were persecuted as a threat in spite of their attempt to be good citizens. They were charged as haters of mankind. The reason for this charge was that they did not participate in the sacrifices to the gods. Without these sacrifices, it was feared that the provision of the gods would be curtailed. This underscores the importance of the interaction between the hierarchy and the destiny of the society. When Christianity became the religion of the Roman Empire, the empire did not take on an egalitarian social structure. The emperor himself called councils and became effectively the head of the church. Certainly, many individuals remained egalitarian in perspective, but Christendom itself became a branch, or at least an arbiter, of political power. Over much of its history, Christianity has not been egalitarian.

With the sixteenth century Reformation, there was a new interest in separating the church from its traditional entanglements with the Mother Church, the Roman Empire, and the Greek philosophers. Again there was persecution and even wars. Early in the seventeenth century, the first English colonists settled in North America looking to escape religious strife while practicing their faith.

But back in Europe, others with this new freedom to reexamine the traditions about their faith and the natural world turned their interests to what has become modern science. It is simply not true that these men found their efforts frustrated by their religious faith. In fact, they undertook to think the thoughts of the Creator himself. They rejected Aristotelian teleology and made noteworthy discoveries, some of which have stood the test of time, others of which have become the basis for further investigations. Their argument that God created a functioning universe and equipped us to understand its working well enough to be stewards of it became the philosophic basis for modern science. While it is not considered in these terms, this is still the only metaphysical basis for modern science.

Early in the eighteenth century, philosophers were successful in claiming that since the created universe was completed and functioned as a machine, God was unnecessary in the present. First came Deism, and later, after Darwin, it became possible to be a fulfilled atheist. It might seem that the notion of providence had become unimportant. But alas, especially in the United States, evangelical Christians who acknowledge the providence of God are still considered a threat. Although it is easily discovered that our prestigious early colleges and universities were started as Christian institutions, the present day leaders of these institutions now run from their own history. Although many documents and stonework on buildings in our nation's capital still reflect their origin, publicly acknowledging a providential creator now brings threat of a lawsuit. Again, why should this be? It is true that evangelical Christians, as their name suggests, want to convince others of the truth of their cosmology. But it is inconsistent for a person who believes all are equal before God to attempt to coerce another to hold this belief. Hence, it can be argued that people with egalitarian beliefs are not welcome whether they evangelize or not. Why would this be? I offer again that they are a threat in that they insist the Creator, not the social structure, provides for them.

When an egalitarian social structure in the past was set aside, as far as can be ascertained, the cosmology of the separation of heaven and earth accomplished it. This cosmology redefined the cosmos in such a way as to allow for nonhuman but living agents that did not create but did control the environment. The most influential of these agents were accessible by ritual to a few in the society. These few, of course, were the elites of the society. By performing rituals, they provided for the whole of the social structure and were thus worthy of the honor and fear of the society. The people of the society became the elites' dependents; these dependents could then be identified as the masses. This is, of course, the positive side of the contributions of that cosmology. Generally, our concern has been with the negation of the conditions that were in place before this cosmology was introduced.

Presently the academic community is also offering a different cosmos from the one brought to this country from Northern Europe in the early seventeenth century. This cosmos is a totally material one that is controlled by laws that the elites of the academic and scientific community claim to exploit for the benefit of the masses. Within this cosmos, there is no longer a need for a creator. The grand evolutionary cosmology explains all after the Big Bang Theory (hypothesis for universe's origin) as the result of time, chance, and necessity. How has this new cosmos been introduced?

The Enlightenment period of Western philosophy has already been mentioned several times (pp xxv, 5, 67). The term *enlightenment* implies that the time before it was a time of darkness, obviously symbolizing ignorance, even as the darkness did before the separation of heaven and earth in that cosmology. The move from not being able to prove God's existence by "rational" argument to saying there is no knowable God was not as difficult as it might seem. Philosophers have merely insisted that all that can be known can be known through reason or by empirical means. Reason is, of course, not used as the Apostle Paul used it in Romans 1:20.

Since God could not be known through philosophers' arguments or scientists' experiments, God could not be known at all. Since God could not be known, the Bible contained no useful information about God. At the start of the Enlightenment, Christians and rationalists shared a zeal for truth. But as time went on, the chief concern of the enlightened became the defense of their enlightened perspective. Rationalists who had earlier believed in God had already rejected God's grace and questioned the reality of eternal life. Since Darwin, the enlightened have rejected God as well. In effect, once again, we have the separation of heaven and earth. This new cosmos is not animated by spirit beings in charge of aspects of the environment; now it has become an entirely material cosmos that works as a machine. In the ancient system, elites sought benefits from the animated universe by ritual. Now enlightened elites seek to gain benefits by moving the levers of causation. In each case, the benefits are overshadowed by the loss of freedom for its citizens.

Shortly after the British colonies in North America had their revolution, the French had a revolution based not on the principles laid out in the Preamble to the Declaration of Independence but rather on the principles of the Enlightenment. After killing the elites of the French monarchy, the revolutionaries killed their own leaders for they, in turn, had become elites. France was disabled for some time after their revolution. But the Enlightenment gained adherents in spite of the experience of the French, especially in Europe. Philosophers proceeded with great enthusiasm to offer an agenda that would bring all nature, including human nature, under control. This agenda promised that by what could be known through reason and the senses, mankind could build a utopian world. Below is a listing of the ideals of the radical enlightenment in the nineteenth century (Rex Ambler 1966:143).

(1) The self is identical with consciousness and is directly knowable through individual introspection.

(2) The world, as essentially matter, can be identified with everything that is given through the senses, so that it can be thoroughly known, in principle at least, by the combined use of sensuous experience and rational mediation. The mind is a mirror of nature.

(3) The ultimate truth of the world, and of ourselves, can be known by us: the ultimate truth is the sum total of all the true things we can say about the world on the basis of sense and reason.

(4) In the world, things change according to single, one-way causation, on the model of a machine.

(5) Given (1) and (4), it follows that in principle we know how to control the world, and if necessary how to change it completely. All we need is the technical power to move the material levers of causation.

(6) Finally, given an introspective knowledge of what we free individuals want, it is possible to transform the world so that it answers completely to our desires (alternatively, our sense of rightness).

Both man's physical and social problems would be solved by this liberated reason. After Darwin, the Enlightenment gained a cosmology that purported to explain the obvious design in living things, eliminating the need for an intelligent creator. Humans were also considered the product of this mechanism. Enlightenment, with this new cosmological basis, had its influence on both Marxist and fascist thought. The events of the early twentieth century dampened some of the optimism for what the Enlightenment agenda could accomplish.

186

The effects of this thought system did not make inroads as quickly in the United States, where conservative Christianity was still influential. Enlightened reason first gained ground in our academic institutions. Increasingly, mainline Christianity bought into this evolution cosmology, although its adherents offered a compromise with it by holding that God created and revealed himself through evolutionary processes. The utopian view expressed in the agenda of the enlightened, now held by liberals or progressives, has continued to motivate political action in our own nation. As evidence of these inroads, consider the teaching of origins in our public schools. At the start of the twentieth century, only creation was taught. Near the middle of the century, neither cosmology was taught as a compromise with those who believed in evolution. Now creation is no longer allowed and evolution is increasingly found in the curriculum. Even the nature of religious concerns of our founders are overlooked. Of course, it is not immediately obvious to us that the grand scheme of evolution is cosmology in the same sense that the word has been used throughout this book. It is taught as knowledge gained by science. But then, by definition, a society's cosmology is believed.

Science was not always as useful as it has become to political and academic elites. As explained above, men with an egalitarian perspective pioneered this method of gaining knowledge. When they made discoveries, they were careful to submit them to others along with the procedures they used to get their results. The information thus acquired could be verified, and new circumstances under which the discoveries might be applied broadened the base of knowledge. In this way a hypothesis would be found useful or discarded. Science itself was an egalitarian process. But there was always an amount of uncertainty about the understanding that was based on new discoveries.

Today's scientists still insist on this uncertainty in the method of science. But when the Louisiana state law requiring balanced treatment of evolution and creation was challenged in 1987 in the Supreme Court, *Edwards* v. *Aguillard*, the attorneys arguing against the law were successful in marginalizing creation by labeling it religious rather than scientific. In other words, what had been competing viewpoints—God is responsible for our existence vs. purposeless material causes brought us into existence—compete no longer. The one is scientific by definition; the other has been marginalized as religious. Science is no longer a quest for truth. It is the quest for the best answer assuming material causes. The evolutionary cosmology has become the unassailable cosmology of the elites of the society.

Actually, many in our society have not kept up with this aspect of science since evolution became an all-embracing cosmology. When Darwin advanced his hypothesis, it was generally believed by the enlightened that the material world was itself eternal. It is no longer believed that the material world—or material itself—is eternal. It is now believed that material had its origin in the Big Bang—or perhaps more accurately, events started with the Big Bang brought material into being. If this is not considered a blow to the philosophy of materialism, it should be. Further, astrophysicists have found that the universe as we know it depends on the precise relationship of several constants. These constants appear to be fine tuned in order for the universe to accommodate the complexity needed for our existence. The name that the physicists have given this fortuitous situation is anthropic—that is to say that these constants must be precisely as they are for *man* to exist. In the creation cosmology, these discoveries would both be comfortably accommodated without new vocabulary. In fact, they would be taken as firm evidence for creation cosmology.

Shortly after Darwin published his book, Pasteur demonstrated that life comes from life. Among other things, this principle has led to canning industries since one can be confident that if no bacteria survives the canning process and the container prevents any more from entering, the canned goods will not spoil. This is well established. Yet if evolution is to be preferred over a creation model, it must account for the origin of even the simplest form of life. Considerable research has been done with the purpose of offering a pathway for the highly unlikely event that lifeless material would organize itself into something alive and capable of reproducing itself. After the efforts of 150 years, the results have not been promising. May we suggest a creator?

Darwin admitted that the fossil record as then known did not support his hypothesis. But he believed that with future finds from paleontology, the fossils he predicted would be found. But now it is admitted that the fossil record has not supported Darwin's hypothesis any better than it did in his day. Other scientists are working with DNA, the code that transmits the genetic material within the cell. It has been increasingly difficult to understand the DNA code in any way but the information needed for the cells to form and organize. Information requires intelligence; it does not happen by chance. Darwin offered that present forms of life could be traced back to a common ancestor, but that statement has not been better supported than his illustration with pigeons in his *Origin of the Species,* published in 1859. It is obvious that breeders of domesticated plants and animals are able to produce new varieties. What is not obvious is that these varieties would over time become new species. Neither the fossil record nor DNA studies have yielded conclusive evidence to support the proposition that all life can be traced back to a common ancestor. Yet this proposition continues to be taught (and believed) as truth.

I have suggested a few of the questions about the grand scheme of evolution to point out that there are plenty of reasons to doubt the truth claims from the scientists that offer evolution as fact. Evolution has become an undisputed fact, not from the evidence but by the declaration of the elites of the scientific community. Those who do question this assertion are not less knowledgeable concerning the evidence; they are simply not invited into the community. This exclusion of rivals is the way elites over the ages have always behaved.

True, science has given us a technological environment that is beyond what most of us older adults even imagined during the earlier years of our life. But the theory of evolution has had nothing to do with the development of these technologies. The truth is that science would do nicely without the burden of rationalizing the cosmology of the elites. The name given for this exclusive approach to science is "consensus science." It is a contradiction in terms. Yet we have a great illustration of consensus science offered presently by the advocates of human caused global warming.

Our egalitarian heritage is under siege. We are increasingly marginalized as religious if we hold that the celestial Creator created us equal and endowed us with certain unalienable rights. Our nation has several cultures within it, yet only one now has control of public academic institutions to train our leaders, teachers, and journalists. Only one, through past propaganda, has been able to persuade even our court systems that materialism is science and any other metaphysical position is religion.

Some have offered that religion and science each function in its own magisterium. From the magisterium of science, we discover the factual character of nature; from the magisterium of religion, we find meaning in our lives and a moral basis for our actions. I have two problems with this. First, I live in one universe, and the Creator gave me a stewardship that included knowing and understanding his world. And, it is the magisterium of science that has offered this division. When there are differences of opinion, science's magisterium is said to define reality and must overrule any dissent from the religious magisterium.

I do not know if we have the political will to keep our equality before God and the liberty that we still claim is ours as citizens. Many seem willing to trade their liberty for care from the state. This has always been the promise of idolatry, and it has always been a threat. I hope that this book has opened your thinking to a new understanding about prehistory. We have been taught that our present perspectives have evolved from the base thinking of a primitive mankind. However, mankind with an egalitarian social order successfully spread over the world. It is likely that he did this with the same equality before the Creator and rights from him that we have recently enjoyed in our nation.

If this is true, it seems that we have another chance to enjoy this knowledge, freedom, and provision. It is difficult to imagine that a move from these beliefs and ideals would bring us any good that could possibly repay our loss if we again separate ourselves from God.

Bibliography

Abeles, Mark. "'Sacred kingship' and formation of the state." In *The Study of the State*, edited by H.J.M. Claessen and Peter Skalnik. New York Mouton, 1981.

Adams, Robert McC. "Patterns of Urbanization in Early Southern Mesopotamia." In *Urban Settlements: The Process of Urbanization in Archaeological Settlements*, edited by Ruth Tringham. Andover, Mass.: Warner Modular Publications, 1973.

———. *Heartland of Cities*. The University of Chicago, 1981.

——— "Mesopotamian Social Evolution: Old Outlooks, New Goals." In *On the Evolution of Complex Societies,* Essays in the Honor of Harry Hoijer, edited by William Sanders, Henry Wright, and Robert McC. Adams. Undena Publications, Malibu for UCLA Department of Anthropology, 1984.

Akkermans, Peter M.M.G. Villages in the Steppe: Later Neolithic Settlement and Subsistence in the Balikh Valley, International Monographs in Prehistory. Ann Arbor, MI: International Monographs in Prehistory, 1994.

Alexander, Harley Burr. *The Mythology of All Races in Thirteen Volumes, North American*. Boston: Marshall Jones Company, 1916.

———. *The Mythology of All Races in Thirteen Volumes, Latin American*. Boston: Marshall Jones Company, 1920.

Algaze, Guillermo. "The Uruk Expansion: Cross-Cultural Exchange in Early Mesopotamian Civilization." *Current Anthropology* 30:1 (December 1989): 571-608.

Alster, Bendt. "Earliest Sumerian Literary Tradition." *Journal of Cuneiform Studies* XXVIII (April1976): 109-126.

Ambler, Rex. "The Self and Postmodernity." In *Postmodernity, Sociology and Religion,* edited by Kieran Flanagan and Peter C. Jupp. pp. 134–151. New York: St Martin's Press, 1996.

Anthes, Rudolf. "Mythology in Ancient Egypt." In *Mythologies of the Ancient World,* edited by Samuel Noah Kramer. Garden City, NY: Anchor (Doubleday), 1961.

Bancroft-Hunt, Norman. *Indians of the North American Northwest Coast.* New York: Peter Bedrick Books, 1989.

Bard, Katheryn A. "Ideology in the Evolution of Society in Egypt." *Journal of Anthropological Archaeology* 11:1 (March 1992): 1–24.

———. "The Egypt Predynastic: A Review of the Evidence." *Journal of Field Archaeology* 21 (1994): 265–288.

Bellwood, Peter. "The Austronesians in History: Common Origins and Diverse Transformations." In *The Austronesians: Historical and Comparative Perspective.* Published by the Department of Anthropology as part of the Comparative Austronesian Project, Research School of Pacific and Asian Studies. Canberra: The Australian National University, 1995.

———. "Hierarchy, Founder Ideology, and Austronesian Expansion." In *Origins, Ancestry, and Alliance: Explorations in Austronesian Ethnography.* Published by the Department of Anthropology as part of the Comparative Austronesian Project, Research School of Pacific and Asian Studies. Canberra: The Australian National University, 1996.

Berndt, Catherine, and Ronald Berndt. *The First Australians.* London: Augus and Robertson, 1964.

Berndt, Ronald. *Australian Aboriginal Religions*. Leiden, Netherlands: E. J. Brill, 1974.

Best, Elsdon. *The Maori*. Wellington, New Zealand: Harry H. Tombs, limited, 1924.

Boas, Franz. *Race, Language and Culture*. New York: MacMillan Company, 1940.

Bodde, Dirk. "Myths of Ancient China." In *Mythologies of the Ancient World*, edited by Samuel Noah Kramer. Garden City: Anchor Books (Doubleday), 1961.

Brown, W. Norman. "Mythology of India." In *Mythologies of the Ancient World*, edited by Samuel Noah Kramer. Garden City: Anchor Books (Doubleday), 1961.

Cashdan, E. A. "Egalitarianism among Hunters and Gatherers." *American Anthropologist* 82 (1980): 116–120.

Claessen, Henri J. M. "Specific Features of the African Early State." In *The Study of the State*, edited by H.J.M. Claessen and Peter Skalnik. New York: Mouton, 1981.

Coon, Carleton. *The Hunting Peoples*. London: Lowe and Brydone, Jonathon Cape Ltd., 1971.

D'Altroy, Terence N., and Timothy K. Earle. "Staple Finance, Wealth Finance, and Storage in the Inca Political Economy." *Current Anthropology* 26:2 (1985).

Dumezil, Georges. *Mitra-Varuna: An Essay on Two Indo-European Representation of Sovereignty*. New York: Zone Books, 1988.

Earle, Timothy K. "Chiefdoms in Archaeological and Ethnographical Perspective." *Annual Review of Anthropology* 16 (1987): 279–308.

Earle, Timothy. "The Evolution of Chiefdoms." *Current Anthropology* 30:1 (1989).

Earle, T. K. "The Evolution of Chiefdoms." In *Chiefdoms: Power, Economy, and Ideology*, edited by T. Earle. University of California, Cambridge Press: 1991a: 84-88

————. "Property Rights and the Evolution of Chiefdoms." In *Chiefdoms: Power, Economy, and Ideology*, edited by T. Earle. University of California, Cambridge Press: 1991b.

Earle, Timothy. *How Chiefs Came to Power: The Political Economy in Prehistory*. Stanford Press, Stanford Junior University: 1997.

Eliade, Mircea. *Myths, Dreams, and Mysteries*. New York, Evanston, San Francisco, London: Harper Colophon, 1975.

Elwin, Verrier. *Myths of the Northeast Frontier of India*. Calcutta: Sree Saraswaty Press Limited, 1958.

Evans-Pritchard, E. E. *Nuer Religion*. New York, Oxford: Oxford University Press, 1956.

Falkenstein, Adam. "The Prehistory and Protohistory of Western Asia." In *Near East; the early civilizations*. New York: Delacorte: 1967.

Firth, Raymond. "Introduction: Malinowski as a Scientist and as a Man." In *Man and Culture,* First Harper Torchbook Edition, edited by Raymond Firth. New York: Harper and Row, 1964.

Flannery, Kent V., and Joyce Marcus. "What is Cognitive Archaeology?" *Cambridge Archaeological Journal* 3 (1993): 260–270.

Fox, James J. "Austronesian Societies and Their Transformations." In *The Austronesians: Historical and Comparative Perspective*. Published by the Department of Anthropology as part of the Comparative Austronesian Project, Research School of Pacific and Asian Studies. Canberra: The Australian National University, 1995.

Frankfort, Henri. *Kingship and the Gods*. University of Chicago Press, 1978.

Freund, Philip. *Myths of Creation*. New York: Washington Square Press, 1965.

Fried, Morton. *The Evolution of Political Society.* New York: Random House, 1967.

Gibbons, Alice. *The People Time Forgot.* Camp Hill, PA: Christian Publications, 1981.

Godelier, Maurice and Marilyn Strathern, eds. *Big Men and Great Men: Personifications of Power in Melanesia.* Cambridge (England) New York: Cambridge University Press Ltd., 1991.

Grey, Sir George. "The Children of Heaven and Earth." In *Polynesian Mythology and Ancient Traditional History.* Auchland: H. Brett, 1885.

Keeley, Lawrence, T. Douglas Price, and Anne Birgitte Gebauer, eds. *Last Hunters, First Farmers: New Perspectives on the Prehistoric Transition to Agriculture.* Santa Fe, NM: School of American Research Press, 1995.

Heidel, Alexander. *The Babylonian Genesis.* University of Chicago Press, 1951.

Heidel, Alexander. "The Meaning of Mummu in Akkadian Literature." *Journal of Near Eastern Studies* (1947): 98–105.

Hitt, Russel T. *Cannibal Valley.* New York: Harper and Row, 1962.

Howitt, A. W. *Native Tribes of Southeast Australia.* London: McMillan and Co. Ltd, 1904.

Jacobsen, Thorkeld. *Toward the Image of Tammuz and Other Essays on Mesopotamian History and Culture,* edited by William Moran. Cambridge: Harvard University Press, 1970.

Jacobsen, Thorkeld. "Notes on Nintur." *Orientalia NS* 42 (1973): 273-300.

Katz, Richard. *Boiling Energy: Community Healing Among the Kalahari Kung.* Cambridge, Mass: Harvard Press, 1982. (The quotation used is based on an article by L. Marshall, "!Kung religious beliefs." *Africa* 32 (1962): 221–252.

Kirch, Patrick Vinton. *The Evolution of Polynesian Chiefdoms.* Cambridge (England): Cambridge University Press, 1996.

Klass, Morton. *Ordered Universes: Approaches to the Anthropology of Religion.* Boulder, San Francisco, Oxford: Westview, 1995.

Kramer, Samuel Noah. *Sumerian Mythology.* Garden City NY: Harper Books, Harper & Brothers, 1961.

———. *History Begins at Sumer.* Garden City NY: Doubleday Anchor Books, 1959.

———. "Mythology of Sumer and Akkad." In *Mythologies of the Ancient World,* edited by Samuel Noah Kramer. Garden City NY: Anchor Books, Doubleday, 1961.

———. *The Sumerians.* The University of Chicago Press, 1963.

Lambert, W.G. "The Reign of Nebuchadnezzar I." In *The Seed of Wisdom.* University of Toronto, 1964.

Lambert, W. G., & A. R. Millard. *Atra-hasis: The Babylonian Flood Story.* Oxford: Clarendon Press, 1969.

Lang, Andrew. *The Making of Religion.* London: Longmans, Green, and Co. Paternoster Row, 1898.

Lessa, William A., and Evon Z. Vogt. *Reader in Comparative Religion: An Anthropological Approach,* Third Edition. New York: Harper & Roe Publisher, 1962.

Lessa, William A., and Evon Z. Vogt. *Reader in Comparative Religion: An Anthropological Approach,* Fourth Edition. New York: Harper & Roe Publisher, 1979.

Lienhardt, Godfrey. *Divinity and Experience: The Religion of the Dinka.* Oxford: Oxford University Press, 1970.

Lincoln, Bruce. The Indo-European Myth of Creation, *History of Religions.* 1972 121-145.

Long, Charles. *Alpha: The Myths of Creation.* Toronto, Ontario: Collier Books, 1969.

Malinowski, Bronislaw. *Magic, Science and Religion.* Garden City NY: Doubleday Anchor, 1954.

Mallory, J. P. In Search of the Indo-Europeans: Language, Archeology, and Myth. London: Thames and Hudson, 1994.

Mallowan, M.E.L. *Early Mesopotamia and Iran.* New York: McGraw-Hill, 1965.

Mbiti, John S. *African Religions and Philosophy.* New York: Frederick A. Prager, 1969.

Muller, Jean-Claude. "'Divine Kingship' in Chiefdoms and States: A Single Ideological Model." In *The Study of the State,* edited by H.J.M. Claessen and Peter Skalnik. The Hague, New York: Mouton, 1981.

Parrinder, Edward Geoffrey. *African Mythology.* London: Paul Hamlyn Publishers, 1967.

Price, T. Douglas, and Gary M. Feinman. *Images of the Past,* Second Edition. Mountain View, California: Mayfield Publishing, 1993.

Price, T. Douglas, and Gary M. Feinman, eds. *Foundations of Social Inequality.* New York: Plenum Publishing, 1995.

Price, T. Douglas, and Anne Birgitte Gebauer, eds. *Last Hunters, First Farmers.* Santa Fe, NM: School of American Research Press, 1995.

Radcliffe-Brown, A. R. *The Andaman Islanders.* New York: Free Press of Glencoe, 1964.

Renfrew, Colin. *Before Civilization.* Cambridge, London, New York, Melbourne: Cambridge University Press, 1979.

Richardson, Don. *Lords of the Earth.* Ventura California: Regal Books, 1983.

Roheim, Geza. *The Eternal Ones of the Dream.* New York: International University Press, 1971.

Sahlins, Marshall. *Stone Age Economics.* Chicago: Aldine Publishing, 1974.

Scarre, Christopher, and Brian Fagan. *Ancient Civilizations*. New York; Reading, Mass.; Menlo Park, Calif.; Harlow, England; Don Mills, Ontario; Sydney; Mexico City; Madrid; Amsterdam: The Longman Inc., 1997.

Schmidt, W. *Origin and Growth of Religion*. New York: Cooper Square 1931. Page references are to the 1972 edition.

Sharpe, Eric J. *Comparative Religion: A History*. London: Duckworth, 1975.

Shore, Bradd. *Mana and Tapu in Developments in Polynesian Ethnology*, edited by Alan Howard and Robert Borofsky. Honolulu: University of Hawaii Press, 1989.

Spencer, Sir Baldwin, and F. J. Gillen. *The Arunta: A Study of a Stone Age People*. London: McMillan and Co. Ltd, 1927.

Sproul, Barbara C. *Primal Myths: Creating the World*. New York; Hagerstown; San Francisco; London: Harper and Row, 1979.

Stein, Gil. "Economy, Ritual, and Power in Ubaid Mesopotamia." In *Chiefdoms and Early States in the Near East: The Organizational Dynamics of Complexity*, edited by Gil Stein and Mitchell S. Rothman. Madison, WI: Prehistory Press, 1994.

Stein, Gil. "Heterogeneity, Power, and Political Economy: Some Current Research Issues in the Archaeology of Old World Complex Societies." *Journal of Archaeological Research*, 6:1 (1998) 1-44.

Strehlow, T.G.H. "Personal Monototemism in a Polytotemic Community." In *Festschrift Fur*, edited by Ad. E. Jensen. Munchen, Germany: Klaus Renner Verlag, 1964.

Tyler, Stephen A. *India: An Anthropological Perspective*. Pacific Palisades, California: Goodyear Publishing, 1973.

Appendix

Concerning the confusion of languages

Many in my community with a high regard for the scripture insist that the genealogy of Shem in Genesis must be taken to mean that Shem lived to see Abraham's day. In fact, the genealogy actually has Noah still alive during Abraham's life. If your perspective is that any material that contradicts this genealogy, taken as chronology, cannot be considered, then you will be uncomfortable with much of the work of archaeology. This is true of the material concerning the dates archaeology establishes for the earliest farming and the earliest hierarchical social structures.

This book offers an interpretation of the data of anthropology, archaeology, and history of religions concerning the development of the world's religions. In it, two spectacular events chronicled in Genesis, Chapters 9–11, appear to be confirmed. The first of them is the widespread knowledge of God found among hunter-gatherers. The second is the apparent social unity of mankind until an event in the late Ubaid period (see Chapter Two), at which time this unity became permanently fractured. Archaeology offers no evidence that the city of Babylon was involved, but it does identify Erech (Uruk) as a city that became important at the time this unity was shattered. It also confirms that Nineveh was one of its first outposts. But these confirmations come at the price of reconsidering the traditional meaning of the "scattering" of mankind over the earth mentioned in Genesis 11:8–9. Before looking more closely at those verses, I want to consider separately each of these confirmations.

Chapter One gives evidence that until recently, there were groups of widespread hunter-gatherers that knew a god similar to the God of our traditions. This can most easily be explained as a worldview that was once shared by most, perhaps all, hunter-gatherers. Since it is commonly accepted that before the

Neolithic period (characterized by the introduction of farming and the making of pottery) all of mankind were hunter-gatherers, it follows that all could have believed in a god similar to the God of our traditions. For some, even that economic circumstance—hunting and gathering rather than farming—is problematic. The reason for that is that Genesis 4:2 tells us that Abel kept flocks and that Cain worked the soil. However, that problem is easily overcome by a thoughtful consideration of Genesis 9:1–3. After the flood, Noah and his sons were commanded to be fruitful, multiply, and occupy the earth. Along with that command, God provisioned man by giving them leave to eat the meat of all animals. It is obvious that if mankind's first prerogative was to fill the earth and all animals became food to him, he was not to stop to "farm" the land until this task had been accomplished.

Some have argued that man was reduced to this economic level—that is, hunting and gathering—only when "scattered" at the Tower of Babel. But this fits neither the mandate given in Genesis 9:1–2 nor the data of archaeology. This data has man widespread, even in the Americas, before the lower Mesopotamian Valley had a significant population. Remember, this book is not an attempt to refute the data from anthropology and archaeology. It is rather an attempt to portray and understand this data without imposing an interpretation forced by a materialistic worldview.

Archaeology denies that the lower Mesopotamian valley was occupied early. This may have been because conditions after the flood and ice age made this floodplain unattractive for some time. When people moved into the valley, many of them were already farmers who knew how to practice irrigation agriculture. The archaeological data from this area suggests that it was there the first social hierarchy came into being. But equally important, this hierarchy was preceded by a long period of peace over a large area covering all of modern Iraq, Syria, substantial parts of Turkey, and other areas extending into Iran and Arabia. This was the culture that was suddenly shattered, never to be put back together again.

This fits well with the confusion of languages as told in Genesis 11. When hierarchy first came into being, it was in a limited area, that area identified as Shinar in Genesis or the lower Mesopotamian valley. Even as Genesis identifies Erech as the first city after Babel, archaeology identifies Uruk as the first great city. In fact, archaeology gives Uruk's name to this period. Uruk and Erech are the same city. Notice that in Genesis 10:10, Nimrod's first centers were Babylon, Erech, Akkad, and Calneh, all in Shinar. Erech becomes a city of first importance in Genesis, and Uruk is identified as the first great city by archaeology. This does not contradict Genesis since we are told in 11:8 that the people stopped building the city that brought God's judgment. "And the city they stopped building was called Babel (Babylon) because there God confused the languages of the whole earth." Babylon does not become known as an important city until much later. Genesis also gives us information that archaeology has not yet been able to confirm—that is, in the lower valley's several cities, including Akkad and Calneh, made up Nimrod's home base.

Another amazing thing about the Genesis account is that we are told that Nineveh was a city that Nimrod built outside Shinar. At Nineveh, archaeologists have located evidence of early and intrusive Uruk influence. Nineveh was never part of historic Sumer. How could the author of Genesis know about an Uruk civilization that had an early outpost in Nineveh? If Shem lived to the time of Isaac, he was a witness to the Babel event in Genesis 11. However, if archaeology is right in its interpretation of events, Sumer became literate almost 1,000 years later. When Sumerians did record events, they neither awarded Uruk a place of preeminence nor claimed an outpost in Nineveh. Nippur, the city of their chief god, was the place given special honor; there was no acknowledgement that Nineveh had ever been attached politically or economically.

How does this differ from the interpretation of Genesis 9–11 that I learned? In it, all of mankind went to Shinar. There they attempted to build a tower to make a name for themselves. They were frustrated by the confusion of languages and scattered from there over the whole earth. The version as given by archaeology is that mankind, perhaps most of them, did follow God's mandate to populate the earth. Only after this process was largely accomplished did mankind settle down to agricultural pursuits. Then some in Shinar, in pride, did attempt to make a name for themselves. It was at that point that God confused the languages.

How could these two different scenarios be reconciled? First, Genesis, Chapter 10, when listing the table of nations, puts each group into its territory. After this listing, Genesis10: 32 offers that this is how the earth was peopled after the flood, not after they were scattered from Babylon. It makes the point clearly since 10:9–10 puts Nimrod, the apparent offender who brought God's judgment, in Shinar, while the rest are said to settle in their territories. Although this may be an argument for spreading out after the flood as God commanded, there is still the problem of the language in 11:8–9.

There, two statements are given, and I believe they are parallel statements. They say that, there, God confused the language of the whole earth and that God scattered the people over the whole earth. By "parallel statements" I mean that the statements have the same meaning. This is a typical form of Hebrew poetry. Perhaps the meaning of the word translated as *scattered* can be understood to mean "separated" in the sense that ethnic groups could no longer understand one another's language. It is clear that due to God's interruption, the city of Babylon was not completed. And this always has been interpreted to mean that the interruption God intended was that the builders would no longer understand one another's language, not that they were suddenly and mysteriously dispersed from the area. But there is also an archaeological context given for 11:4:

> Then they said, "Come let us build ourselves a city, with a tower that reaches the heavens, so that we may make a name for ourselves and not be scattered over the whole earth." (Genesis 11:4 NIV)

The archaeological context can be found in R. McC. Adams's quotation on page 24 where we learn that the sudden mobilization of small communities into a large walled city "could have been for expansion and aggrandizement" just as well as for defensive purposes. Genesis 11:4 assures us that it was not for defensive purposes. Even though this interpretation is new, gathering the small local communities into one large walled city (mobilization) for the purpose of aggrandizement does fit the context given in Genesis 11:4 rather well. Perhaps the comment in Genesis 11:6, "now nothing they plan to do will be impossible for them," is to be understood precisely in context of plans for expansion.

The tower during early literate times demonstrated the separation of heaven and earth cosmology. Heaven could now be reached only through the elites that controlled the towers. The name of the temple in Nippur, *Duranki*, meant "bond of heaven and earth," and as Jacobsen translated it (quotation given on page 86), it was to heal the gash made in the earth when heaven was separated from it. This is another reason to expect that a separation cosmology motivated the first hierarchy. The confusion of languages has always seemed to me an apt response for this heretical cosmology of the separation of heaven and earth. In fact, if I have interpreted Genesis 11:8–9 correctly, the same word there translated "scattered" might suffice. Even as men separated themselves from heaven, heaven separated them from each other.

If we are to understand that Nimrod was involved in this mischief, it is clear that his activity was curtailed by the confusion of language. However, this expansion was not stopped altogether since we are told in Genesis 10:11 that he went to Assyria and built several cities, including Nineveh outside of Shinar. These cities, these outposts, were then intrusive. The unity of the land had been interrupted.

According to archaeologists, Uruk (biblical Erech) gives its name to the period and is identified as the first great city. But it is much later that language is reduced to writing and expressed in cuneiform on clay tablets. With the advent of writing that we can decipher, it is obvious there are several languages in Sumer (Shinar). Among these several languages are Semitic languages and the Sumerian language. This is interesting because while Semitic is from a well-known family of languages, Sumerian does not fit into such a family. It is totally speculative, but not impossible, that the perpetrator of the mischief would end up speaking an isolated language.

Endnotes

Introduction, note 1: Ice age or Pleistocene fauna

The animals portrayed deep in some of the cave art in Lascaux, France, perhaps painted about 13,000 B.C., represented the animal population present there during the ice age period. These animals were not of unknown species, but many of them were not present there during historic times in Europe. The animals during the ice age tended to be large and found in places where, today, no such animals would be expected. For example, remains of species of rhinoceros and elephants are found in Siberia. In fact, ivory from the tusks of those now extinct Siberian elephants became a significant trade item. Elephants were also found in Alaska and in the rest of the American continents. Horses are thought to have come across the Bering Strait from North America into Asia and Europe during this time. There were no horses in America when whites came from Europe.

Not only were there ice-age animals where there were glaciers, but also Africa and Australia had animals that have not survived from the Pleistocene. Much attention is given to the demise of dinosaurs, but little attention has been given these recent extinctions. It seems to make little sense to say that today it is too warm for elephants in Siberia or Alaska. The most common explanation for these extinctions is that man, the hunter, was responsible for them. However, that explanation has its critics as well.

Introduction, note 2: Concerning the Supreme Being

The title "Supreme Being" is one often applied to our God. But this term has also come to be used with regard to other groups with a celestial creator, specifically, certain widespread nonagricultural people groups. More formally, this being is called the Supreme Being of the Primitives. It is a premise of this book that belief in this being can be traced back to the mandate given in Genesis 9:1–3. Yet it does not seem appropriate to apply the title God, as in the God of our traditions, to this Supreme Being. In my mind, this is not because God has changed; rather it is because he has had a long history of interaction, first with Israel and then with followers of Christ that these people groups have not shared. Further, there are other reasons that this identification of God with the Supreme Being would lead to ambiguity. It might give the impression that all the preliterate groups who recognize a supreme being would ascribe to him identical traits. Other reasons that give me pause include the ability of the person representing his group to the ethnographer and the prejudices of that ethnographer.

Therefore, you will note in this book that there are occasions when the title is capitalized and some when it is not. Here, too, my reasons may not always be obvious. Usually, if discussing a quotation in which the title is capitalized, I will also capitalize the title. However, when saying merely that this or that group had a supreme being, I often do not follow that practice, preferring to recognize that among these groups the being they describe may not have all the identical attributes. They too have had a long history since they first became separated from each other.

Introduction, note 3: Linguistics and the movement of ideas

The science of linguistics includes a number of projects, but the one that is of interest to us concerns the identification of different families of languages. The earliest formal work done in this area was with Indo-European languages. It had long been recognized that the structure of the Indo-European languages was different from the structure of languages of the Semitic family. However, it was not until the nineteenth century that students of languages began to formulate the notion of "sound shift" to describe how languages changed, diverging into other languages within the same family. This understanding led to a method of tracing the movement of Indo-European language family groups and was key to relating changes in other language family groups as well. While these sound shifts cannot be predicted, there is regularity in the shifts within any particular group. Because of this regularity in sound shift, proto-languages can be reconstructed if there are enough early written materials for the project. Although these regularities are useful in showing patterns in these changes, they are limited in giving dating information. They can offer an order of their separating from each other, but dating these separations requires other confirming archaeological data.

This approach to linguistics suggests that all the members of a language group derived from one small group of speakers that can be at least tentatively located in a specific geographical area. Some of this linguistic theory was already known when Malinowski formulated his concept of functionalism that nearly forbade the movement of ideas (see Chapter One). Of course, if language families are the result of this language family dispersion from a small original area, it is possible that they also spread their social structure and its justification with them.

During the first half of the twentieth century, American anthropologists were more interested in reconstructing the prehistory of North American Indians than in demonstrating their social evolution. Under the guidance of Franz Boas, they actually contributed to the field of linguistics and used these skills to trace the movement of North American Indians. An observation of Boas's is used in Chapter Eleven.

Chapter 6, note 1: Enlil and his attributes

Both Jacobsen and Kramer interpret Sumerian literature in terms of the physical cosmos, and I have not found a book or article that directly contradicts their interpretations. However, even their translations suggest other interpretations. They both use the title Enlil to fix his attributes, using *lil* to mean "air." It can also mean "spirit of a dead person, a ghost." Why not "lord of the dead"?

Others have contributed to such a reinterpretation. For instance, R. Caplace in *Orientalia NS 42*, E-Nun in Mesopotamian Literature page 299, compares the uses of the name of this temple likely in Eridu to Enlil's temple. In this comparison, he states that Enlil's temple, the *e-kur*, can refer to a temple in general, specifically Enlil's temple, or the underworld (netherworld). A common epitaph for Enlil is Kurgal. In "Paradoxical Proverbs" in the *Journal of Cuneiform Studies* (p. 222), Bendt Alster interprets this epitaph as "Great Underworld." It is apparently a companion term to *Ereshkigal*, "dame of the netherworld." In other titles, Enlil is paired with his wife, Ninlil. One of the ordering myths of Sumer explains that Ninlil had been Sud of the city Eresh, which might account for the title Ereshkigal. I have not noticed others who have picked up on this, but many have commented on the otherwise unexpected situation in which, when finding himself in the netherworld, Gilgamesh's friend Enkidu, came on the goddess of the netherworld, she was identified as the mother of Ninazu (Ninlil) and not by her netherworld title, Ereshkigal.

207

Chapter Seven treats the *Atra-hasis* epic. In that epic, the names of those gods associated with Enlil's temple, including his chamberlain, are given. His name is the name of the seventh and last gatekeeper of Ereshkigal's underworld in the story of Inanna's descent into the netherworld.

Kramer and Jacobsen have set the tone of the conversation in understanding the Sumerian religion. But they could have easily interpreted the separation cosmology by saying that Enlil sent heaven away and gave mankind to his spouse Ereshkigal. Remember, Jacobsen does offer the translation "after earth had been presented to Ereshkigal as dowry." This is the fifth line of his translation referred to in Chapter Six (page 84). This is the same Sumerian composition that has Enkidu finding the mother of Ninazu in the netherworld. There is general agreement among those who interpret Sumerian material that abundance does come from the netherworld through Enlil. I only point out that he could well have been considered the god of the netherworld.

Chapter 10, note 1: Comparison of Arunta and Trobriand Islanders' beliefs about the separation of heaven and earth

The Trobriand Islanders did not include a separation from heaven story along with the emergence from their totemic places in the landscape. Perhaps the reason is that this part of the cosmology no longer served a useful purpose. This is more likely than that it was never a part of their mythic system. However, the Trobriand Islanders do illustrate my contention that the separation of heaven or the creator is not a philosophic necessity. Incidentally, Spencer in *Native Tribes of the Northern Territory of Australia* gives material about the cosmology of two other tribes, each with originating beings. Neither of them appears as full-blown creator, nor do they ascend into heaven during or after the *alchera* period. They return to a totemic well. It is, however, required by a context in which the interference of heaven is a possibility. By this I mean that it is required if your neighbors believe that they ascend to heaven in the care of the creator when they die.

Chapter 10, note 2: Fire stick circumcision: another polemic against the Supreme Being?

The theme of fire stick circumcision is very widespread in central Australia. In the buffer (between the Arunta and the southeast All-Father area), it was said that boys initiated this way *all* died. Since this is supposed to have been the former practice, we are led to a logical contradiction. There hardly could have been a traditional initiation ritual that caused the death of all the initiates. I take this to mean that fire stick circumcision disparagingly symbolized another initiation ritual, possibly one that did not include circumcision at all. This interpretation requires that the tribes whose mythology had heroes who replaced fire stick circumcision with stone knife circumcision did not consider their own circumcision initiation ritual as a ritual death. Initiation among the Bora Complex tribes (southeast Australia) was definitely identified as a ritual death. It was said that the Supreme Being himself destroyed the boy being initiated only to restore him completely new and whole except for one tooth (born again?). At that time, a tooth was extracted from the initiate. In the *Numbakulla* myth summarized on page 154, the polemic nature of fire stick circumcision was not emphasized; it merely stated that the original beings that introduced this ritual (*Twanyirrika*) were unable to circumcise with a fire stick (Spencer and Gillen 1927:366).

Chapter 10, note 3: Support for the argument that Australian totemism is a Neolithic religious system

A quick comparison of Malinowski's report (*Magic, Science, and Religion,* pp. 111f, 171f, 215f) of the Trobriand Islanders will illustrate my point. The Arunta looked to the *alchera* as the ordering principle; the Trobriand Islanders looked to a previous existence underground. The Trobriand Islanders claimed that this order included villages, clans, districts, distinctions of rank, property ownership, and magic lore. The Arunta emergence from the earth fixed their social positions for all later generations. Both look to local sites where their ancestors emerged, and they identified these sites in the present landscape and claimed to belong to them (or vice versa). Each group was kept in that social structure by a "conception" theory that included the introduction of the "essence" of a preexistent person into a married woman. The magic that the Trobriand Islanders depended on was given before the emergence and passed to the rightful heir. Similarly, the ritual renewal of the totem was instituted in the *alchera* as the responsibility of the rightfully born among the Arunta. I have chosen the Trobriand Islanders for this comparison since Malinowski's ethnography is readily accessible.

I have not seen ethnography from tribal groups in Papua New Guinea or Indonesian Papua with similar ideas about reincarnation. Ignoring conception perspectives, Polynesian cosmologies of emergence are certainly similar in that they describe a fixed social system, including the competences and claim that these positions were fixed before the emergence from the earth. Speculatively, I propose that this thought system came to Australia from influence later than the original wave of Austronesian speakers.

Index of Authors